RENAISSANCE DRAMA

New Series XV ☙ 1984

Renaissance Drama

New Series **XV**

Modes, Motifs, and Genres

Edited by Leonard Barkan

Northwestern University Press

EVANSTON **1984**

The front-cover illustration is a detail from the title page of *The Workes of Benjamin Jonson* (London, 1640).

The back-cover illustration is a detail from the title page of Nicholo Macchiavelli, *The Florentine Historie,* trans. T. B. (London, 1595). Reproduction courtesy Special Collections, Northwestern University Library, with special thanks to Russell Maylone, Curator, and Sigrid Perry, Library Assistant.

Publication of this volume was made possible by a grant from the College of Arts and Sciences, Northwestern University.

195535

Editorial Note

RENAISSANCE DRAMA, an annual publication, provides a forum for scholars in various parts of the globe; wherever the drama of the Renaissance is studied. Coverage, so far as subject matter is concerned, is not restricted to any single national theater. The chronological limits of the Renaissance are interpreted liberally, and space is available for essays on precursors, as well as on the use of Renaissance themes by later writers. Editorial policy favors articles on some scope. Essays that are exploratory in nature, that are concerned with critical or scholarly methodology, that raise new questions or embody fresh approaches to perennial problems are particularly appropriate for a publication that originated from the proceedings of the Modern Language Association Conference on Research Opportunities in Renaissance Drama.

The Editor gratefully acknowledges his debt to the members of the Editorial Committee, and similar warm thanks are due to the editorial assistant, Cheri Peters, and to our administrative assistant, Marjorie Weiner. The efficient and expert help of the assistant editor, Janice Feldstein, has been absolutely indispensable.

Volume XVI of *Renaissance Drama* will be concerned with Renaissance Plays: Rereadings and New Readings.

Inquiries regarding future volumes should be addressed to Professor Leonard Barkan, *Renaissance Drama*, English Department, Northwestern University, Evanston, Illinois 60201.

Contents

RENAISSANCE DRAMA

New Series XV 〰 1984

Moral Conceptions of Sexual Love in Elizabethan Comedy

MARY BETH ROSE

I

CRITICS HAVE NOTED OFTEN that Elizabethan romantic comedy is a dramatic form which can be distinguished as a generic celebration of marriage. Contrasting the erotic teleology of romantic comedy (which she calls "pure comedy") with the moral corrective of satire and the tragicomic emphasis on plot, Helen Gardner has written that

The great symbol of pure comedy is marriage, by which the world is renewed, and its endings are always instinct with a sense of fresh beginnings. Its rhythm is the rhythm of the life of mankind, which goes on and renews itself as the life of nature does. . . . The young wed, so that they may become in turn the older generation, whose children will wed, and so on, as long as the world lasts. The end of comedy declares that life goes on.[1]

I would like to acknowledge my gratitude to the Monticello College Foundation and the Newberry Library, whose generous support made possible the research for this essay.

1. Helen Gardner, *"As You Like It,"* in *Modern Shakespearean Criticism,* ed. Alvin B. Kernan (New York, 1970), pp. 193–194.

1

In romantic comedy, then, the sexual love that leads to marriage symbolizes the ongoing life of society, which, in Elizabethan terms, in turn suggests a spiritually integrated cosmos. But this configuration, which Shakespeare discerned and exploited until it had been thoroughly imagined and expressed, was by no means always developed or even implicit in earlier Elizabethan comedies. John Lyly was the first Elizabethan playwright to clarify the aesthetic realization that the theme of erotic love could be used to organize the disparate materials of early romantic comedy into a coherent design; yet, unlike the comedies of Shakespeare, Lyly's plays never acclaim sexual love and rarely end in a festive celebration of marriage. This essay seeks to trace the ways in which Elizabethan comic form developed in plays by Lyly, Robert Greene, and Shakespeare in accordance with the precise erotic teleology Gardner describes by relating changes in the dramatic representation of love and marriage to similar patterns of change in conceptualizations of love and marriage in the nondramatic literature, particularly in Elizabethan courtesy and conduct books.

Two salient modes of conceptualizing erotic love and marriage emerge from the complex controversy over changing sexual values articulated in Elizabethan conduct literature: a dualistic sensibility, in which sexual love is idealized beyond physical existence on the one hand or derided as lust on the other, and which views marriage as a necessary evil; and a more realistic, multifaceted sensibility, which, while retaining much of the skepticism about erotic love contained in the first view, nevertheless begins to conceive of affectionate marriage with great respect as the basis of an ordered society. Taking into account the inevitable overlapping and intermingling of shifting values and attitudes, historians have shown that in late-sixteenth- and early-seventeenth-century England, the second sensibility was gaining ground over the first.[2] What I would like to suggest is a parallel development between this shift in *mentalité* and the changing representations of sexual love and marriage that characterize the growth of Elizabethan comedy: Lyly, whose comic structures embody the dualistic

2. This change in sensibility is particularly apparent in the upper and middle classes, to whom my remarks are limited. The most comprehensive treatment of this subject is Lawrence Stone, *The Family, Sex, and Marriage in England 1500–1800* (New York, 1977).

sensibility, was unable to develop romantic comedy beyond a certain point; while Greene developed the form to a limited extent and Shakespeare brought it to fruition with *As You Like It* and *Twelfth Night* by representing a more complex vision, in which sexual love and marriage have increased significantly in moral stature and prestige.

My purpose in comparing changing moral and sexual attitudes to altering dramatic representations of sexual love is not, therefore, to demonstrate causal connections between them, but to show that the same concepts and values which inform the one can be seen as informing the other; and that the shifts discernible in one form are similarly discernible in the other. As a result my method involves suggesting reciprocal influences among kinds of evidence often thought to have a different value: the imagination of the individual artist, the aesthetic requirements of the comic form, and contemporary moral and religious writings about love and marriage. By synthesizing some familiar interpretations of the plays with the richly suggestive discoveries of historians, the following essay attempts to formulate a new perspective on the cultural context and development of Elizabethan comedy.

II

Lawrence Stone and other historians of the relations between the sexes have demonstrated convincingly that the institution of marriage enjoyed a considerable rise in prestige in post-Reformation England.[3] The precise origins and chronology of this change in sensibility are as difficult to determine as is the actual sexual conduct of medieval and Renaissance men and women. In terms not of actual behavior, but of the moral prestige granted to sexual love and marriage, it is clear, however, that those medieval values governing sexual relations which were officially articulated by homilists, theologians, and poets were predominantly ascetic. Although H. A. Kelly argues in his book *Love and Marriage in the Age of Chaucer* that a commonsensical, concrete

---

3. See, for example, Stone, pp. 135–138. Also see Christopher Hill, "The Spiritualization of the Household," in *Society and Puritanism in Pre-Revolutionary England* (London, 1964), pp. 443–481, and C. L. Powell, *English Domestic Relations 1487–1653* (New York, 1917).

counterideal of married love existed among ordinary people in the
Middle Ages, he concedes that homilists praised only the abstract aspects of love and marriage and actively discouraged the as-yet unmar-
ried from ever marrying at all. Sexual love was, needless to say, considered out of the question as a basis for marriage, which was regarded by
the upper classes as an alliance for the enhancement of family property and as an outlet for the avoidance of fornication. Indeed sexual love
was virtually out of the question, period. It is true that St. Jerome, who
felt that love between men and women was at best "to be endured, not
enjoyed," and preferably "to be avoided if at all possible," represents
the extreme of medieval opinion; nevertheless carnal love, even for
purposes of procreation, was usually conceptualized as tainted with
some odor of sin and was, at best, conceived of as morally neutral.[4]
Celibacy was upheld as the ideal behavior to be emulated, not only by
priests and nuns, but by the whole community.[5] Even St. Paul, cited so
often later by sixteenth- and seventeenth-century Protestant preachers as the main scriptural authority in their vehement defenses of marriage, could be seen to consider marriage as merely a necessary evil:
"For I would that all men were even as I myself am . . . [i.e., celi-
bate]," he writes in 1 Corinthians, "It is good for them if they abide
even as I doe. But if they cannot absteine, let them marrie: for it is better to marrie then to burne" (vii.7–9).

During the Renaissance, conjugal loyalty and affection replaced
celibacy as the officially idealized pattern of sexual conduct.[6] Yet like
other forms of medieval thought, much of the consciousness of love,
marriage, and sexuality persisted into the Renaissance.[7] Stone reports
that "marriage among the property-owning classes in sixteenth-century England was . . . a collective decision of family and kin, not an in-

4. Henry Ansgar Kelly, *Love and Marriage in the Age of Chaucer* (Ithaca, N.Y.:
1975), pp. 247, 284–285, 300, 315.

5. Kelly, p. 315, and Stone, p. 135.

6. Stone, pp. 135–138, and Hill, pp. 443–481. Also see Louis B. Wright, *Middle-
Class Culture in Elizabethan England* (Chapel Hill, N.C., 1935), pp. 201–227; Ian Ma-
clean, *The Renaissance Notion of Woman* (Cambridge, Eng., 1980), p. 59; and Carroll
Camden, *The Elizabethan Woman* (New York, 1952), pp. 109–148.

7. Linda T. Fitz, "What Says the Married Woman: Marriage Theory and Feminism in
the English Renaissance," *Mosaic,* XIII (Winter 1980), 1–22; and Peter Laslett, *The World
We Have Lost* (New York, 1965), pp. 130–131.

dividual one . . . Property and power were the predominant issues which governed negotiations for marriage."[8] Individual, rather than parental choice of a spouse, let alone prior affection between potential mates, seemed foolish, undesirable. The eminent sixteenth-century humanist Vives, whose works were accessible in English, observes, for example, that "they that marry for love shall lead their life in sorrow."[9] Montaigne, whose translated essays were also available after 1603, is less hostile to erotic love than Vives; nevertheless he affirms what he construes to be the essential incompatibility of erotic love and marriage:

Love disdaineth a man should holde of other then himselfe, and dealeth but faintly with acquaintances begun and entertained under another title; as mariage is. Alliances, respects and meanes, by all reason, waigh as much or more, as the graces and beautie. A man doth not marie for himselfe, whatsoever he alledgeth; but as much or more for his posterity and familie. The use and interest of mariage concerneth our off-spring, a great way beyond us. Therefore doth this fashion please me, to guide it rather by a third hand, and by anothers sence, then our owne: All which, how much doth it dissent from amorous conventions? . . . *I see no mariages faile sooner, or more troubled, then such as are hudled up for amorous desires.* There are required more solide foundations, and more constant grounds . . . this earnest youthly heate serveth no purpose.[10]

Furthermore, while priestly celibacy no longer flourished as an idealized model of behavior after the Reformation, the distrust of sexual desire and the ideals of maidenly virtue—virginity—and wifely chastity continued to preoccupy the Renaissance imagination of the moral and spiritual life well into the seventeenth century.

It is worth dwelling briefly on the tremendous spiritual weight put on sexuality in the Renaissance. A good example is the emphasis placed on premarital female virginity. Many have argued that the perceived necessity for premarital female chastity, as well as the double standard of sexual morality, arose originally from the economic need

8. Stone, p. 87.
9. John Louis Vives, "Howe the mayde shall seeke an husbande," in *Instruction of a Christian Woman,* trans. Richard Hyrde (London, 1557), book I, chap. xvi.
10. Michel de Montaigne, *The Essayes,* trans. John Florio (London, 1603), p. 510.

to legitimize property for the purposes of inheritance;[11] however this may be, the ideal of virginity accrued moral and theological overtones and became for poets a useful means of dramatizing female social and spiritual life. One need only think of Britomart, Spenser's embattled knight of chastity, dueling her way through a world full of erotic peril. In a courtesy book entitled *Instruction of a Christian Woman* (1523) and dedicated to Catherine of Aragon, Vives elaborates powerfully the consequences that loss of virginity entails for a young woman:

Turn her which way she will, she shall find all things sorrowful and heavy, wailing and mourning, and angry and displeasureful. What sorrow will her kinfolks make, when every one shall think themselves dishonored by the shame of that maid? What mourning, what tears, what weeping of the father and mother and bringers up. Dost thou quite them with this pleasure for so much care and labor? Is this the reward of thy bringing up? What cursing will there be of her acquaintance. What mocking and babbling of those maids, that envied her before. What a loathing and abhorring of those that loved her. What flying of her company when every mother will keep not only their daughters but also their sons from the infection of such an unthrifty maid. And wooers also, if she had any, all flee away from her. . . . I rehearse the hate and anger of folks for I know that many fathers have cut the throats of their daughters, brethren of their sisters, and kinsmen of their kinswomen.[12]

Could any young woman possibly have endured such an onslaught of threatened damnation, social ostracism, personal guilt and despair, open ridicule, and family catastrophe? In a chapter about when a maid should leave the house (to which his answer is never, unless absolutely necessary and, in that case, certainly never alone), Vives evokes a world of sexual desire which, like the world of Spenser's Britomart, is fraught with spiritual dangers. "Howsoever she turneth herself from God unto men, whether she like or be liked of them, she forsaketh Christ, and of Christe's spouse suddenly becometh an adulterer."[13] This statement, striking in its lucidity, starkly conveys the perils of sexuality, the evils of it, and the human responsibility for it; Vives has here clarified the association of sexuality with sin. Female entrance into the

---

11. Stone, p. 637, and Keith Thomas, "The Double Standard," *Journal of the History of Ideas,* XX (1959), 195–216.

12. Vives, "Of the Kepying of virginitee and chastitee," book I, chap. xii.

13. Vives, "How the mayde shall behave hyr self forth abode," book I, chap. xii.

sexual world, whether through body or mind, by choice or unwittingly, whether by reciprocating male affections or merely remaining the passive object of them, is equivalent to sin, *is* sin. Even when sexual love is viewed with a less holy and foreboding gloom, it is often regarded instead as bitterly degrading, bestial, and absurd. Once again we can turn to Montaigne for the liveliest and most direct articulation of this attitude:

When all is done, I finde that *love is nothing els but an insatiate thirst of enjoying a greedily desired subject* . . . which becometh faulty by immoderation and defective by indiscretion. . . . Now considering oftentimes the ridiculous tickling, or titilation of this pleasure, the absurd, giddie and harebrained motions wherewith it . . . agitates . . . that unadvised rage, that furious and with cruelty enflamed visage in loves lustfull and sweetest effects: and then a grave, sterne, severe surly countenance in so fond-fond an action . . . I beleeve that which *Plato* sayes to be true, that *man was made by the Gods for them to toy and play withall.* . . . And that nature in mockery leaft us the most troublesome of our actions the most common: thereby to equal us, and without distinction to set the foolish and the wise, us and the beasts. . . . In all other things you may observe decorum, and maintaine some decencie: . . . this cannot only be imagined, but vicious or ridiculous.[14]

Moral bankruptcy and degeneracy, fear, humiliation, and a kind of ridiculous madness: what fools these mortals be! Such distressing associations are made over and over again in Renaissance discussions of the place of sexuality in social and moral life. But were there not more positive conceptions of erotic love, beyond, that is, such occasional, begrudging tributes as Robert Burton's parenthetical concession that love "by a perpetual generation makes and preserves mankind, propagates the Church"?[15] One answer, of course, is that just as classical writers had treated love both philosophically and sensually, so Christian writers recognized both a sacred and a profane love.[16] This dualistic, idealizing cast of thought granted love the highest respect and prestige when it was conceived of either as separate from, or having transcended, sexual desire. I cannot do justice here to the profound

14. Montaigne, p. 527.
15. Robert Burton, *The Anatomy of Melancholy,* in *Seventeenth-Century Prose and Poetry,* ed. Alexander M. Witherspoon and Frank J. Warnke (New York, 1963), p. 192.
16. John Charles Nelson, *The Renaissance Theory of Love* (New York, 1958), p. 67.

and complex legacy that the Renaissance inherited from this mode of conceptualizing love, which had been articulated systematically in Christian orthodoxy.[17] But of the many literary variations on the theme of this tradition which are of immediate relevance to English Renaissance drama, Neoplatonism and the related phenomenon of Petrarchism are salient.

The ideas of the Florentine Neoplatonist Marsilio Ficino are expanded and popularized in Castiglione's *The Courtier*, which was translated by Thomas Hoby in 1561. In the fourth book of *The Courtier* the favored figure of the ladder of love, inherited from Plato's *Symposium*, is set forth in eloquent detail. In this image the beauty of the female beloved inspires the male lover to ascend by stages a metaphorical ladder which will lead him to the beauty that "shall make a universal conceite, and bring the multitude of them to the unitie of one alone, that is generally spred over all the nature of man." Now able to ascend by contemplating its own beauty, the soul of the lover then transcends this stage, along with all earthly things, to gaze on "the maine sea of the pure heavenly beautie." Castiglione allows for the appropriateness of sensual love in the young; but the mature, civilized society has transcended sexuality. While the female beloved serves the crucial but limited function of original inspiration, the true Neoplatonic lover will keep "alwaies fast in minde, that the bodie is a most diverse thing from beautie, and not onely not encreaseth, but diminisheth the perfection of it." The speech in which the ladder of love is described includes many of the characteristically idealistic love themes: sacrifice (in this case of the soul to God through burning or consuming of the body); liberation from the self; transcendence; transformation; the ideals of contemplation and union with God.[18]

Se urs Jayne points out that Platonism became permanently associated in the English mind with Petrarchism.[19] The Neoplatonic ideas of love both as "a cosmic phenomenon informing the universe and ap-

17. See, for example, Irving Singer, *The Nature of Love* (New York, 1965); Maurice Valency, *In Praise of Love* (New York, 1975); and Denis de Rougemont, *Love in the Western World,* trans. Montgomery Belgion (New York, 1956).

18. Baldesar Castiglione, *The Courtier,* trans. Thomas Hoby (London, 1588). See book 4, which Hoby describes as telling "of honest love."

19. Cited in Neal L. Goldstein, *"Love's Labor's Lost* and the Renaissance Vision of Love," *SQ,* XXV (Summer 1974), 339.

parent in nature," and as an independent force transcending nature and creating its own world directly influenced the Petrarchan tradition through Castiglione and Pietro Bembo.[20] As in Castiglione, the beloved in Petrarch's poetry remains an idealized, unattainable icon. Although in Petrarch the lover oscillates "between restrained wooing and distant adoration," actual union is nevertheless envisaged only in dreams. Leonard Forster stresses the central importance of the lover's experience of love as dual, as "interpenetration of pleasure and pain. . . . The elaboration and exploitation of antitheses is the essence of Petrarchism."[21] The Petrarchan style and diction, which reached England via Wyatt and Surrey in the first half of the sixteenth century, was most notably exploited in the latter half by Sidney, Spenser, and Shakespeare and their followers in the numerous, fashionable sonnet sequences of that period, sequences which created an image of a courtly, melancholy, obsessive lover, doomed to frustration and rejection, a little foolish for putting so much hope and faith in the desire of a woman.

According to the mentality being described, sexual desire, even when conceived as leading to a consciousness of the divine, was never considered beneficial or good in itself. Loved women were better left exalted, remote, and untouched. It is therefore not surprising to discover that where idealization of women occurred, misogyny was rarely far behind. With significant exceptions, English Petrarchism and its corollary, anti-Petrarchism, tend to articulate that consciousness which simultaneously exalts and idealizes the image of Woman while regarding actual women with neglect or contempt.[22] Notwithstanding the persistence of this mode of thought in our culture, what is both new and significant in the English Renaissance is that this dualizing, polarizing consciousness begins to break down, to lose its authority as the predominant, or at least as the only, articulated view of women and sexuality. A burgeoning awareness of a more complex, problematic moral and emotional reality ensues; and it is in this changing moral

20. Leonard Forster, *The Icy Fire: Five Studies in European Petrarchism* (Cambridge, Eng., 1969), p. 21.

21. *Ibid.,* pp. 1–60.

22. Regarding exceptions, see, for example, C. S. Lewis's discussion of Spenser as the poet of married love in *The Allegory of Love* (Oxford, 1958), pp. 297–360.

atmosphere that romantic comedy, with its celebration of married love, comes into its own as a dramatic form.

In the development under discussion, the work of John Lyly represents an encounter between the dualistic, idealizing Petrarchan sensibility to which he was heir and the more realistic, multifaceted view of married love which was beginning to announce its presence both in the drama and in the moral and religious outpourings of the surrounding society.[23] Lyly was the first great Elizabethan playwright to recognize the importance of the erotic love theme to the coherence and design of his plays; consequently he was the first to organize early romantic comedy by subordinating the disruptive medley of spectacle, song, ritual, pageant, magic, folklore, slapstick, and farce which comprised it to a central love story. Lyly emerged from the tradition of aristocratic early-sixteenth-century humanism in which literature existed in service to the prince and the state, not as an independent profession. As G. K. Hunter has demonstrated, Lyly's values and beliefs, his apparent disdain of writing for the increasingly powerful, popular public theater, doomed him to outlive his early success and to die in disappointed poverty, having hopelessly depended on favors from Queen Elizabeth that never were forthcoming.[24] But the anachronistic humanist idealism which tied Lyly to an outmoded literary tradition caused him to conceive of his plays as select entertainments, dramatizations of the elegant, refined manners of a stately court; as a result, while Lyly retained many of the native traditions that gave Elizabethan comedies their vitality, he also imposed on them a new sense of integration, balance, and grace. Nevertheless, the lack of flexibility in his conception of sexual love prevented Lyly from developing romantic comedy in accordance with the changing sensibility around him.

---

23. Cf. Robert Weimann, *Shakespeare and the Popular Tradition in the Theater,* ed. Robert Schwartz (Baltimore, 1978), p. 197: "It is a new sense of the interdependence of character and society, and a fully responsive interplay between dramatic speech and dramatic action in the process of reproducing the cause and effect of human behavior that defines 'realism' in the Renaissance theater." Weimann also makes the point (p. 173) that Lyly stood "at the very threshold" of such a complex apprehension, remaining "too bewildered to realize that the contradictions (which he points out) are about to yield a new and superior unity."

24. G. K. Hunter, *John Lyly: The Humanist as Courtier* (London, 1962).

In his early success, *Euphues* (1578), and its successor, *Euphues and his England* (1580), Lyly creates an image of love and sexuality which he develops throughout his plays, and which is recognizable as emanating from that polarizing consciousness which posits idealization of women or misogyny, chaste worship or lust, as the only possibilities for love. In these two tracts, Lyly establishes a prose style which, with its witty similitudes, puns, antitheses, and parallelisms, mirrors his ideal of a learned, courtly, graceful, and sophisticated society. As a means of recommending manners and morals to their readers, both of these courtesy books wittily relate the adventures of two elegant young men, Euphues and Philautus, whose coming of age Lyly depicts as an ongoing encounter with temptation in the form of love and desire. In the indiscriminate, capricious fickleness of most of the female characters and the continually wrongheaded, hopelessly infatuated state of Philautus, Lyly depicts sexual desire as a compulsive, impersonal, and ridiculous passion, which can be understood only in direct contrast to reason and wisdom. "What new skirmishes dost thou now feele between reason and appetite, love and wisdom, danger and desire?" Philautus asks, rhetorically echoing conventional Petrarchan sentiments and antitheses.[25] All in all we are expected to perceive that "the disease of love . . . is impatient, the desire extreame, whose assaultes neyther the wise can resist by pollicie nor the valiant by strength."[26] One wants to protest that the sensible could ignore this self-indulgence by intelligence, so utterly self-centered, obsessive, and infantile an experience does love become when Lyly presents it. As might be expected, Euphues' heroism consists in his transcending sexual desire, his realization that "the effect of love is faith, not lust, delightful conference, not detestable concupiscence, which beginneth with folly and endeth with repentance."[27] At the end of *Euphues and his England* we find this polarized perspective figured forth concretely. In a concluding diatribe Euphues, who has returned to Italy from a visit to England determined to devote the remainder of his life to soli-

25. John Lyly, *Euphues and his England,* in *The Complete Works of John Lyly* (Oxford, 1902), II, 89.

26. *Ibid.,* p. 112.

27. *Ibid.,* p. 158.

tary idealization of the Virgin Queen, exhorts the Italian women, whom he misogynistically maligns, to be like the English women, whom he sentimentally idealizes. Philautus ends up in a second-best, rebound marriage that pointedly does not ensue from any of his perpetual courtships.

This configuration, in which love remains a marginal experience, finding fulfillment either in the dream life or in an unsatisfactory lowering of expectations, becomes a structural principle in Lyly's plays. *Sapho and Phao* (1584) concludes with the image of an idolized female monarch, victorious over desire and remaining an object of the chaste, constant adoration of a solitary admirer and subject. Although *Endymion* (1588) ends with several happy couplings, the hero of the play conceives an impossible, idealizing love for the Moon who, descending to the action in the form of a chaste and benevolent queen, rewards the hero for his solitary devotion by restoring his youth and granting him permission to worship her from afar for the rest of his life with celibate, contemplative, Neoplatonic joy.

Lyly's preference, clearly, is for sublimation; and his habitual tendency is to dissociate sexual love, which he distrusts, from social order, which he idealizes. In Lyly's earliest play, *Campaspe* (1584), a distracted Alexander the Great at last magnanimously transcends his love for a lower-class woman who does not return it. The potential threat to the orderly, efficient running of society implicit in Alexander's sexual desire is domesticated to a harmless, frivolous interlude, a digression in the career of his greatness. Lyly replicates this situation in *Sapho and Phao*: the virtuous monarch, Sapho, overcomes her unseemly attraction for a lower-class boatman, Phao, and usurps the capricious authority of Venus by capturing Cupid, in an elegant victory over desire.

In Lyly, then, sexual desire, while powerful and unavoidable, cannot be incorporated in a civil, humane society. Instead it must be conquered, overcome. Lyly accounts mythically for the inevitable association of chaos and sexuality in one of his most absurd, charming, and misogynistic plays, *The Woman in the Moon* (1593). Here his conception of female weakness and duplicity is allegorized in Pandora, a drastic parody of the remote, idealized Petrarchan lady. Pandora, a sort of ur-woman, is created by Nature and then abandoned to the whimsical mercy of the envious planets. In a mad, obsessive, and uncivil chase, several shepherds pursue the helplessly victimized, indiscriminate, perpetually inconstant and deceptive Pandora through a series of comically futile attempts to possess her. In one of Lyly's repeated images of sexual desire, Pandora, like the heroine of *Euphues,* ends by being attracted to a clown.

In spite of Pandora's outrageous behavior, the real cause of these ridiculous effects is actually desire itself. The play begins with an image of the longing shepherds kneeling to Nature, begging and praying for the creation of a female. The three reasons which the shepherds give for desiring a woman turn out to be the very reasons cited in the Elizabethan *Book of Common Prayer* as the justifications for marriage: the procreation of children; the avoidance of fornication; and the need for companionship.[28] Nevertheless, marriage, if and when it enters the scene at all, is not granted much prestige in a Lyly play. The shepherds in *The Woman in the Moon* end by praising a single life, while Pandora is assigned to permanent residence in the moon—remote and heavenly, but also wayward, fickle, and false.

It should be emphasized that, although erotic love which, with one exception, is always Lyly's subject, is continually presented by him as a threat to the brilliant, graceful society patterned in Euphuistic prose, the tone of his comedies is invariably delicate, witty, and light. This refinement of mood is partially achieved by the ordered introduction of that mixture of musical, magical, folkloric, allegorical, and mythological material which Elizabethan comic playwrights loved: singing and dancing; magic fountains and wells; Ovidian transformations; gods and goddesses; fairies and monsters; ugly, wise old hags who speak with the cynical clairvoyance of desire. All of these characters and motifs, woven together with witty repartee, constitute not a narrative of rising intensity with which we are asked to identify, but a series of static tableaux, balanced against one another, which we are asked to admire.[29]

Lyly's allegorical characters and static, balanced scenes serve as emotional distancing devices. M. C. Bradbrook has noted aptly that in

---

28. *The First and Second Prayer Books of Edward VI* (1549; rpt. London, 1949), pp. 252–258.

29. Cf. Hunter, p. 103.

Lyly's comedies passion is merely a postulate;[30] the evocation of felt emotion is not part of the playwright's courtly representation of love as a wooing game, a witty lark which provides an amusing, if occasionally dangerous, diversion from the serious activities of society. When erotic love is first appropriated from the Petrarchan lyric and begins to be dramatized, it is seen as abstract, magical, playful.

Along with the fact that erotic love is dramatized abstractly as a frivolous game, I believe there is also another reason that Lyly's basically negative and skeptical portrayal of love and sexuality never violates the brittle gaiety of his comedies. Although sexual desire, whether or not it leads to marriage, is viewed by Lyly and many others as dangerous, humiliating, anarchic, and absurd, still the consequences of indulging it appear determined beforehand. There is no need to take a complicated, certainly not a suspenseful view of the matter; the moral position of sexuality is fixed and predictable: "All this the world knows . . . well." What I am suggesting is that the consciousness that polarizes love is inherently undramatic.[31] As has been noted, this dichotomizing perspective, in which love becomes either degrading lust or spiritual idealization, traditionally took poetic form in the lyric, a genre designed to explore individual emotion, not to represent situational conflicts that drive toward resolution among various characters. Lyly's sense of dramatic conflict is epitomized in *Campaspe,* in which, in a story of unrequited love, there is never once dramatized a scene alone between the frustrated, powerful lover Alexander the Great and his unresponsive, captive beloved Campaspe. As a result love is depicted as an isolating, self-absorbed experience; the meaningful conflict is clarified not as an emotional struggle between Alexander and Campaspe, but as an abstract debate taking place in Alexander's mind, an intellectual exercise. Furthermore, in an imaginative vision that, like Lyly's, idealizes the superiority of the elegant, contem-

---

30. M. C. Bradbrook, *The Growth and Structure of Elizabethan Comedy* (Cambridge, Eng., 1979), p. 65.

31. Cf. Robert J. Meyer, "'Pleasure Reconciled to Virtue': The Mystery of Love in Lyly's *Gallathea,*" *SEL,* XXI (1981), 193–208, in which the author correctly warns us not to assess Lyly's "masque-like" and "non-developing" drama in terms other than its own. My purpose is not to judge Lyly's dramaturgy as inferior, but to point out why, given his moral perspective on sexual love and his structural techniques, Lyly could develop romantic comedy only to a limited extent.

plative soul, which has managed to remove itself from the muddy contingencies of physical existence, we must recognize a level of perception that is profoundly anticomic, particularly insofar as comedy is associated morally, emotionally, psychologically, and symbolically with birth, rebirth, the cycle of the seasons, with ongoing, natural life.[32]

Northrop Frye has clarified the necessary structural relationship between fulfilled sexual love and the form of romantic comedy as Shakespeare discerned and perfected it. Frye shows that the sense of vitality underlying comedy often takes the form of a drive toward identity which, in romantic comedy, is always erotic. The harsh and irrational laws which impede the fulfillment of the sexual drive of the hero and heroine must be overcome in order to bring about the freedom and self-knowledge which will form the basis of the new society symbolized in the festive conclusion. Romantic comedy, then, dramatizes that longing for a happy ending which is a wish-fulfillment fantasy of attaining all of one's desires with neither social, emotional, nor moral cost: "Jack shall have Jill / Nought shall go ill." It should be mentioned that by wish-fulfillment Frye does not mean escapism, although romantic comedy can serve that purpose. But Frye stresses instead what he calls "an imaginative model of desire." In his comedies Shakespeare pits the world of individual imagination and sexual desire against the more tangible world of social and historical fact, causing the spectator to question the reality of both worlds and then reconciling the claims of both in a final, inclusive vision of the social and spiritual harmony symbolized in marriage.[33]

Interestingly, in a later play, *Mother Bombie* (1589), Lyly moves toward a comic plot in which wit and vitality *are* joined to sexual desire. But the emphasis in this play remains with the servants' intriguing, not with the inherent drama of erotic love that gives shape to romantic comedy. Love still is not represented as a felt emotion. Lyly consequently fails to unite love with marriage. G. K. Hunter believes, not

---

32. See Susanne K. Langer, *Feeling and Form* (New York, 1953), pp. 326–350.

33. Northrop Frye, "The Argument of Comedy," in *Modern Shakespearean Criticism,* ed. Kernan, pp. 165–173; *A Natural Perspective* (New York, 1965), pp. 118–126; and *Anatomy of Criticism* (Princeton, N.J., 1957), p. 184.

without justice, that what Lyly gains in narrative and integrative power in this play, he sacrifices in delicacy and grace.[34]

Yet the fact that Lyly moves in *Mother Bombie* toward an uncharac-
teristically festive conclusion celebrating marriage, no matter how unsuccessful the attempt, indicates that he is beginning to detect a more
profound pattern at the heart of the comic form. Although Lyly could
discern this possibility, though, his polarized conception of love and
sexuality prevents him from either fully imagining its ramifications or
realizing them artistically. These achievements instead can be found to
coexist in the drama with a different set of articulated beliefs which,
while retaining much of the Renaissance sense of the wicked bestiality
and folly of sexual desire, nevertheless included these skeptical elements in a larger configuration that unites love with marriage and conceives of the combination as the foundation of an ordered society. I am
not, of course, arguing that polarized conceptions of love and sexuality expressed in Neoplatonic and Petrarchan patterns and images disappeared from post-Lylyan Elizabethan comedy, but that these conceptions became part of an expanded vision that incorporates the
dualistic sensibility but is not limited to it. The fact that romantic comedy, a dramatic form which celebrates erotic love and marriage, flourished in the environment of a new sensibility which embraced marriage both as the spiritual foundation of society and as the repository
of hope for personal happiness strongly suggests a parallel development between the increasingly complex, optimistic comic representations of eros that followed Lyly's plays and the more positive moral
conceptions of sexual love and marriage that were beginning to be articulated in Protestant conduct literature.

III

Whether or not it originated with the Protestant theologians of the
sixteenth and early seventeenth centuries, this optimistic vision of
marriage was articulated explicitly by them. As Lawrence Stone points
out, "sanctification of marriage—'holy matrimony'—was a constant
theme of Protestant sermons . . . which were directed to all classes in

34. Hunter, pp. 227–228, 243.

British society."[35] Forty years ago, in a seminal article entitled "The Puritan Art of Love," William and Malleville Haller showed how "it was the Puritan preachers who set forth an ideal pattern of love and marriage based upon traditional Christian morality, vitalized for the popular imagination in terms of the English Bible, and adapted to the new conditions in which men were having to live."[36]

Reiterating the holiness of the married state, the Puritan preachers went about idealizing marriage and the family with all the fervid determination that their Catholic forefathers had lavished upon celibacy and virginity. The Puritans no longer felt the need to attack the prestige of celibacy: "There is no man now so dull as to think it is a sin to marry," Heinrich Bullinger announces confidently in the important *Golden Book of Christian Matrimony,* translated by Miles Coverdale in 1543.[37] In the Puritan outpourings of sermons, conduct books, and spiritual autobiographies, marriage becomes "the type and source of all human relations, the seminary and model of all polities, the church and the state in little, the image and reflection of Christ's union with his elect." [38] John Dod and Robert Cleaver's influential courtesy book, *A Godlie Form of Household Government* (1598), makes it plain that the proper running of one's household has become, like the preservation of virginity, a matter of the greatest spiritual importance, of salvation and damnation.[39]

Several salient themes mark those Puritan tracts which idealize marriage as the basis of an ordered society. First, rather than stressing the avoidance of fornication or even the procreation of children, these documents instead emphasize a third motive for marriage, which was added by Archbishop Thomas Cranmer to the *Book of Common Pray-*

---

35. Stone, pp. 135–136.

36. William and Malleville Haller, "The Puritan Art of Love," *HLQ,* V (1941–1942), 242.

37. Heinrich Bullinger, *The Golden Book of Christian Matrimony,* trans. Miles Coverdale (London, 1543). Cf. William Perkins, *Christian Oeconomie or Houshold Government* (London, 1631), III, 683. Perkins sees celibacy as a kind of punishment for those isolated and marginal figures who are unable to participate in normal social life.

38. William and Malleville Haller, p. 270.

39. John Dod and Robert Cleaver, *A Godlie Forme of Householde Government* (London, 1598). See, for example, "Epistle Dedicatorie."

er in 1549:[40] namely, companionship, or the relief of what Milton was later to call "that . . . God forbidden loneliness."[41] This new emphasis on the spiritual, rather than the physical quality of the marriage relation, along with the Puritan stress on the unique relationship between each individual and God, accompanied a recognition of the value of individual, rather than parental, choice of a marriage partner; the importance of the woman as helpmate and companion; the need for love in marriage; and, finally, the desire for personal happiness.

The Puritans linked happiness inseparably by hope to their ideal of love and marriage. When the Hallers remark drily that "it was a nice and subtle happiness these men conceived for themselves when they abandoned celibacy and embraced matrimony," they are referring to the latent contradictions in Puritan thought on this subject.[42] While insisting on the obedience and subordination of women, for example, the Puritans simultaneously stressed woman's importance, both as a companion to her husband and as supervisor of the newly exalted household.[43] Furthermore, the fact that Puritan doctrine gives woman's soul full equality with man's in the sight of God grants woman an undeniable dignity. Similarly, the Puritans continue to express a wholehearted distrust of sexual desire, dwelling—often with obsessive relish—on "abominable adulterers, stinking whoremongers, unclean fornicators, and detestable sodomites";[44] yet their perception that sex in the context of marriage—when practiced with moderation, of course, and as a solemn religious duty—is a "holy and undefiled action"[45] does grant consummated erotic love a distinct prestige. Further, while the Puritans strongly emphasize the importance of individual choice of a mate, deriding "the buying and selling of children among parents and the forced marriages,"[46] they nevertheless insist

---

40. See Stone, p. 136.

41. John Milton, *The Doctrine and Discipline of Divorce,* in *John Milton: Complete Poems and Prose,* ed. Merritt Y. Hughes (Indianapolis, 1957), p. 707.

42. William and Malleville Haller, p. 250.

43. Hill, pp. 443–481.

44. Thomas Becon, "Preface," in Bullinger, *The Golden Book Of Christian Matrimony.*

45. Perkins, p. 689.

46. Samuel Hieron, "The Marriage Blessing," in *The Sermons of Master Samuel Hieron* (London, 1635), p. 405.

on parental consent to a match. Finally, while the preachers reiterate that adultery, which should be punished with death, is the only reason to dissolve a marriage, the logical extension of their arguments about the absolute necessity of companionship results eventually in Milton's divorce tracts where, in arguments that surely would have horrified the preachers, Milton declares that incompatibility alone is sufficient cause to declare a marriage void.

The Puritan tracts therefore comprise a complex expression of double-mindedness: women must be totally subordinate while also being fully capable and equal; freedom of choice in marriage must be pursued, while absolute obedience to parents is maintained; individual personality and desire must be asserted and fulfilled, but spiritual authority and social stability must never be violated. The preachers did not acknowledge these potential contradictions, however much their unforeseen consequences may have revealed the strains inherent in them. It is one of the striking features of post-Lylyan romantic comedy that a similarly complex, apparently inconsistent or paradoxical awareness of the moral ambivalence of sexual desire, freedom of choice in marriage, and the social and spiritual position of women is both evoked and resolved; and that the reconciliation of these erotic tensions itself becomes the subject of the drama.

Robert Greene's popular comedy, *Friar Bacon and Friar Bungay,* written in 1589–1590 for the public theater, provides an excellent example of the reciprocal relation between this complex moral and sexual awareness and the development of romantic comedy. *Friar Bacon* is a characteristically chaotic medley, but, as in a Lyly comedy, a dominant love story gives the play its shape. Unlike Lyly, however, Greene develops the love story as a conflict which first arises from the diverse social, emotional, and sexual needs of three individuals and then moves through a suspenseful confrontation to a resolution in which all protagonists are married and happy.[47] A brief review of the plot will recall how this works.

---

47. See Norman Sanders, "The Comedy of Greene and Shakespeare," in *Stratford-Upon-Avon Studies,* III (1961), 40. Sanders observes that Greene realized the dramatic possibilities of love, "the surprises, psychological quirks and inconsistencies of human love which constitute its logic in art as in life."

Edward, the Prince of Wales, amusing himself by hunting in the
country, has become infatuated with Margaret, a farmer's daughter,
whom he has been attempting to seduce while disguised as a farmer.
But Margaret is not interested and, his ploy failing, Edward sends his
friend Lord Lacy to plead his case for him. Lacy and Margaret fall genuinely in love. The germane point about this material is that Greene
works through the ensuing erotic complications to a wish-fulfillment
conclusion in which "nought shall go ill" by dramatizing love and sexuality as variable, complex components in the moral and social lives of
his characters. Edward, the future king of England, cannot possibly
marry a commoner and is merely trifling with Margaret; unlike Lyly's
Alexander, who overcomes his inappropriate infatuation in isolation
and goes off alone to heroic martial exploits, Edward relents in a fully
dramatized confrontation with Margaret and Lacy, from which he exits happily and honorably to marry the princess of his father's choice.
Lacy, an earl, in turn proves *his* worthiness by ignoring conventional
class barriers and marrying the farmer's daughter, Margaret of Fressingfield, the woman of his own personal choice. Interestingly, all of
Edward's wooing is rhetorical, allegorical, and cast in the conventional antitheses of the Petrarchan lover: "Her bashful white mixed with
the morning's red / Luna doth boast upon her love cheeks" (i.56–57),
he recites, recalling the Renaissance sense of the abstract impersonality of sexual desire.[48] In contrast Lacy speaks of his love with a
straightforward passion full of concrete references to his immediate,
individual situation: addressing Edward he says, "Love taught me that
your honor did but jest / That princes were in fancy but as men, / How
that the lovely maid of Fressingfield / Was fitter to be Lacy's wedded
wife / Than concubine unto the Prince of Wales" (viii.19–23).

Finally, it is Margaret's character—her wit, vitality, gratitude, and
chastity—which gives love its felicity and dignity, therefore making
possible the harmonious and stable society of the conclusion, in which
the two marriages simultaneously take place. At one juncture Margaret, wrongly thinking Lacy has betrayed her, decides to become a nun.
"And now I hate myself for that I loved / And doted more on him than

48. All citations are from Robert Greene, *Friar Bacon and Friar Bungay, Drama of
the English Renaissance,* ed. Russell A. Fraser and Norman Rabkin (New York, 1976),
pp. 359–382.

on my God . . . / All love is but lust, but love of heavens" (xiv.13–14, 18), she says, despairingly polarizing the position of love in the moral life. But the point is that Margaret *is* in despair when she makes this speech. The scene in which Lacy confronts her in her nun's habit and persuades her to marry him reads like a final farewell to medieval ideals of love and sexuality: "Either a solemn nunnery or the court; / God or Lord Lacy. Which contents you best. / To be a nun, or else Lord Lacy's wife?" (xiv.82–84). She replies, "The flesh is frail . . . / Off goes the habit of a maiden's heart; / And, seeing Fortune will . . . / All the shroud of holy nuns, farewell. / Lacy for me, if he will be my Lord" (xiv.86, 89–92).

Thus does *Friar Bacon* provide a fledgling example of the way in which Elizabethan comedy, like the Puritan marriage tracts, manages to have things both ways. In the courtship of Lacy and Margaret, individual choice and healthy sexual desire leading to marriage are conjoined and affirmed. But Greene also suggests the anarchy and folly of sexual desire by having two of Margaret's suitors destroy each other, as well as having Edward change costumes for a time with the Fool. Similarly, the Margaret-Lacy union recommends the harmonious breakdown of traditional class and rank barriers. But Edward's happy acceptance of an arranged marriage assures us that the courtly, aristocratic hierarchy, despite the welcome intrusion of the pastoral world, has remained intact. And, while it is the heroine's sexual powers—both of resistance and surrender—that have brought about these congenial conditions, she nevertheless acknowledges her subordination at the end of the play in a speech of joyfully grateful obedience. The private claims of individual personality and desire have been asserted, recognized, and assimilated into a public vision of social harmony.

Northrop Frye has remarked that "The presiding genius of comedy is Eros, and Eros has to adapt to the moral facts of society."[49] As we have seen, Lyly's polarized attitude toward eros as either deviant or ideal makes such an adjustment impossible. Greene takes romantic comedy a step further by working both with Lyly's perspective and with a different set of moral terms, one in which sexual love gains legitimacy as the true source of a coherent society. Although many elements in *Friar Bacon* remain chaotic and virtually unassimilable, the

---

49. Frye, *Anatomy of Criticism,* p. 181.

love story does give the play a distinct shape; consequently it moves significantly toward the vision of inclusiveness symbolized in marriage that is the crowning achievement of Elizabethan comedy. The movement from Lyly to Greene therefore comprises a development from a view of sexual love as abstract and impersonal, polarized, static, emotionally simple, and morally predictable to another vision which, while retaining much of the skepticism of the first perspective, incorporates it into a view of eros as more concrete, individualized, dynamic and suspenseful, essentially creative, and morally and emotionally complex.

It was by his unique ability both to discern and express this movement that Shakespeare brought romantic comedy to fruition. The early comedy *Love's Labor's Lost* (1594–1595) can be read in this light as a self-conscious comment on what Shakespeare perceived to be the structurally inevitable relationship between sexual values and the comic form. *Love's Labor's Lost* begins with the youthful King of Navarre and three lords swearing to retire from social life for three years, declaring war against their "own affections / And the huge army of the world's desires" (I.i.9–10).[50] The absurdity of this oath, which is broken immediately when four eligible young ladies appear, is in part a revelation of the absurdity of sexual desire itself, with its imperious, mechanical urgency. But more important than the silliness of the vow of celibacy is its unnaturalness and futility. "The sea will ebb and flow, heaven show his face: / Young blood doth not obey an old decree" (IV.iii.211–212), states Berowne, the wittiest of the young lords, at the moment of the play when self-knowledge begins. The rejection of celibacy, however, is not enough; the King, Berowne, and company also must learn the meaning of eros as itself a civilizing force, as well as a force that must be civilized. Shakespeare conveys their sophomoric callowness as an infatuation with verbal wit, an enchantment with their own cleverness. Upon deciding to pursue his heart's desire, Berowne immediately begins to posture and attitudinize in the conventional courtly manner of a Petrarchan lover, the manner which Edward assumes in *Friar Bacon*. The wit and charm engendered by this pose recall Lyly; as in Lyly, these qualities make up the substance of the

---

50. All citations are from William Shakespeare, *Love's Labor's Lost,* ed. Alfred Harbage (Baltimore, 1973).

play. But *Love's Labor's Lost* eventually rejects the courtly-love syndrome as sterile, shallow, and static. Love conceived as a frivolous game is simply inadequate: when the men approach the women in ridiculous disguises, the women see through them at once. Sensing that the men are not quite ready for grown-up reality which, in Elizabethan comedy means married love, the women, true to romance tradition, demand a year of separation complete with appointed tasks for their lovers before marriage can take place. The play therefore ends with the promise of marriage and not the actuality; the exchange of overblown rhetoric and narcissistic posturing for a plain style and shared experience has not yet come to pass. Consequently, the profound emotional and psychological demands of the comic form have not been completely met, a fact which is acknowledged directly in a brief conversation between Berowne and the King. Berowne grumbles,

> Our wooing doth not end like an old play;
> Jack hath not Jill. These ladies' courtesy
> Might well have made our sport a comedy.
> KING
> Come, sir, it wants a twelvemonth and a day
> And then 'twill end.
> BEROWNE
> That's too long for a play.
>
> (V.ii.864–868)

Shakespeare is announcing clearly here the structural secret of romantic comedy. This clarification of the relationship between fulfilled sexual desire and the comic form releases his ability to represent love as the complex spiritual, emotional, and psychic force that guarantees the perpetuation of society. What is stated so boldly in *Love's Labor's Lost* is fully dramatized in the great comedies that follow: for example, *Love's Labor's Lost* concludes with a song celebrating summer and winter and suggesting the alliance among fruitful sexual love, the predictably recurring cycle of the seasons, and the ongoing life of society; in ensuing comedies like *A Midsummer Night's Dream* (1595) and *As You Like It* (1599), this seasonal imagery becomes fully integrated into the action and poetry, clarifying the inevitable association between human sexuality and great creating nature.

The King of Castile, a character in *Friar Bacon,* remarks at one point that "Men must have wives and women will be wed" (xiii.20). "The world must be peopled" (II.iii.237)," says Benedick in *Much Ado About Nothing* (1598),[51] and there are no facts of life to which romantic comedy assigns greater value than these. As we have seen, this dramatic celebration of generative sexuality would not have been possible without a significant increase in the prestige of marriage, which historians have shown took place in the Renaissance. The movement out of the forest and back into court that dramatizes the harmonious alliance between sexual and social life which characterizes Shakespeare's pastoral comedies and which is also evident in *Friar Bacon* is never completed in a Lyly play. Shakespeare manages to develop Greene's optimism about sexual love and social life while eliminating his crude awkwardness, just as he refines Lyly's skepticism while retaining his grace and sense of design.

When viewed in terms of chronological development, Shakespeare's romantic comedies, like the Puritan marriage tracts, reveal an increasing sense of confidence that sexuality as individual assertion can be organized for society's good. At the same time—and the difference from modern conceptions of romantic love is crucial—sexual desire is never idealized for its own sake, never seen as by itself leading to personal happiness, never conceived as a positive value—as love—apart from marriage or procreation. The sexual anxiety that haunts and humiliates the Renaissance mind is always present in Shakespearean comedy, mocking the hope of unique or ideal love with its distrustful sense of the mechanical impersonality of sex. It is the imperative, arbitrary quality of sexual desire that makes it seem bestial and foolish to the Elizabethans; but in Shakespearean comedy submission to this imperative also joins humanity to nature in fruitful union. Sexuality therefore presents itself as a paradox: the human need for sexual relationships could lead to the mindless disruption of society; but without fulfillment of this need, there would be no ordered society at all.

Shakespeare's rendering of Berowne in *Love's Labor's Lost* as commenting with freely conscious knowingness on the absurdity of his

---

51. All citations are from William Shakespeare, *Much Ado About Nothing,* ed. Louis B. Wright and Virginia A. La Mar (New York, 1968).

own desires reveals an early effort to encompass the paradoxes of sex; but the abstract choreography of the play makes full dramatization of this issue impossible. The dramatic conflict of *A Midsummer Night's Dream* is, of course, set in motion by the issue of individual choice of a mate versus forced marriage. Although the young lovers triumph over irrational parental opposition to their desires, their victory is suffused with irony. While the lovers imagine they are defiantly asserting their individuality, the lack of differentiation among them and the mix-up in the forest clarify both their lack of uniqueness and the arbitrary quality of their choices. Demetrius never does know what hit him when he returns to Helena, any more than he ever did when he loved and rejected her in the first place. The arrogance and complacence of both Theseus and the young lovers are further qualified by the final assertion of the irrational, imaginative authority of the fairies; and the absurd, arbitrary, and mysterious nature of sexual desire is distilled in the joyful parody of Bottom's dream. While the tensions inherent in achieving erotic identity are never resolved, the suggestion in *A Midsummer Night's Dream* is that harmony is attained by the intervention of a benevolent, reconciliatory providence, which manifests itself on the social level in the final wedding feast.

As Arthur Kirsch has shown in his masterful analysis of *Much Ado About Nothing,* the tensions between freedom of choice and submission to authority are not necessarily imposed from without, but are rooted psychologically in sexuality itself.[52] Claudio and Hero never acknowledge these internal tensions between the immediate demands of their appetites and their deeper fears of surrender and rejection in love. They become engaged thoughtlessly, following the conventional clichés of society while never imagining the complex, mixed nature of sexual love; as a result of their psychological and emotional oblivion, they remain completely vulnerable to doubt and fear. Claudio and Hero are contrasted to the witty Beatrice and Benedick who, more thoughtful and consequently more wary of love's complications and paradoxes, pride themselves on their independence. But this brilliant couple needs the manipulative, busybody society of *Much Ado* to liberate them from the lonely trap of their uniqueness. Released from their

---

52. Arthur Kirsch, *Shakespeare and the Experience of Love* (Cambridge, Eng., 1981), pp. 40–70.

fears, they are free to join society by loving one another. Benedick and Beatrice are one of the first outstanding pairs of lovers in Shakespeare, the first to command complete sympathy because of their individuality. "Man is a giddy thing and this is my conclusion" (V.iv.120–121), Benedick announces at the end of *Much Ado,* revealing that the paradoxical awareness of sexual desire, enjoyed by the audience of *A Midsummer Night's Dream* with a kind of superior irony, is appropriated in *Much Ado* by Benedick and Beatrice themselves, who are humbly aware that in seeming to lose their individuality, they have in fact gained self-knowledge. In the sense of gratitude for life which is consequently released in them, Shakespeare exhibits the same awareness of the joyful mysteries of sexual love that he has always portrayed. But I believe that in individualizing Benedick and Beatrice to the extent that he has and in allowing them to achieve self-knowledge, he reveals an enhanced respect for the human dignity of sexual life as well.[53]

As I have tried to show in discussing the Puritan marriage tracts, the increasing moral prestige of love and marriage in the Renaissance was accompanied by a wider acknowledgment of the social, emotional, and spiritual dignity of women, whose freedoms of action and influence were nevertheless explicitly and severely limited. Developing an insight latent in Greene, Shakespeare seems to have assimilated these paradoxical facts imaginatively by giving women the heroic roles in many of his major comedies; their heroism consists, however, in choosing to preserve the status quo by wisely and lovingly assimilating themselves to it. Rosalind in *As You Like It* is the supreme romantic comic heroine.[54] With her realism, openness, and depth, she seems blessed with self-knowledge from the beginning, superbly adapted to exploit successfully the ironies of experience and desire. The mastery of her erotic quest is epitomized in her education of Orlando, in whom she instills a knowledge of the demands of love for a real woman in ac-

53. Cf. R. A. Foakes, "The Owl and the Cuckoo: Voices of Maturity in Shakespeare's Comedies," *Stratford-Upon-Avon Studies,* XIV (1972), 132; and B. K. Lewalski, "Love, Appearance and Reality: Much Ado About Something," *SEL,* VIII (1968), 243. For an opposite view of Beatrice and Benedick, see A. P. Rossiter, *"Much Ado About Nothing,"* in *Shakespeare: The Comedies,* ed. Kenneth Muir (Englewood Cliffs, N.J., 1965), p. 51.

54. Cf. Clara Claiborne Park, "As We Like It: How a Girl Can Be Smart and Still Popular," in *The Woman's Part,* ed. Carolyn Ruth Swift Lenz, Gayle Greene, and Carol Thomas Neely (Champaign, Ill., 1980), pp. 100–116.

tual life that allows him to grow beyond the shallow, remote conventionalities of the Petrarchan lover.[55] The extent to which Rosalind's individuality remains in complete spiritual harmony with nature becomes apparent in the way she controls the timely release of erotic energy embodied in the array of marriages at the end of the play. Just as the negative components of sexual desire are largely displaced onto Claudio and Hero in *Much Ado,* so the other couples in the procession at the end of *As You Like It* suggest the less attractive aspects of sexuality, leaving the Rosalind-Orlando union relatively free of ironic qualification. The fact that Rosalind finds the freedom to accomplish all that she does while disguised as a boy and then sheds this disguise at the end of the play again brings to mind the insoluble contradictions of the female condition, much as these contradictions present themselves in the Puritan marriage tracts. But Shakespeare emphasizes reconciliation, not contradiction; nothing like the sentimental, didactic surrender of Margaret in *Friar Bacon* exists to mar the feeling of harmony at the end of *As You Like It.* If any paradox about the loving surrender of individual identity to society comes to mind, it is the Christian one of losing in order to gain, dying in order to live.

That the potentially contradictory functions of Rosalind's disguise should be reconciled symbolically in marriage clarifies the idea that the erotic teleology of Elizabethan comedy demands an "imaginative model of desire" which is based upon the harmonious resolution of sexual conflict. Given his skeptical, polarized view of sexual love, Lyly could not make the desired reconciliation demanded by the wish-fulfillment pattern at the heart of the comic form. Greene discerned the need to harmonize both the anarchic and the civilizing components of sexual desire into a vision of social and spiritual harmony. But it was Shakespeare who perfected this vision, drawing out all its implications with neither awkwardness nor sentimentality. I have implied that the witty vitality with which Shakespeare endows the lovers in *Much Ado* and *As You Like It* contributes to an enhanced sense of their individuality and self-knowledge; since the imperative, urgent impersonality of sexual desire was what made it seem both dangerous and ridiculous to the Elizabethans, these more individualized characterizations consequently suggest a greater respect for the human dignity of sexual ex-

55. Cf. Kent Talbot Van Den Berg, "Theatrical Fiction and the Reality of Love in *As You Like It," PMLA* (October 1975), pp. 885–893.

perience. But comedy cannot accommodate too much individuality, any more than it can lose its sense of the ridiculous. As is well-known, comedy focuses not on the destiny of the individual, which ends in death, but on the destiny of human society as a whole, which is perpetual.[56] Interestingly, in his last romantic comedy, *Twelfth Night* (1600), the play in which Shakespeare completely masters and exhausts the possibilities of this form of drama, he focuses less on the self-knowledge of the characters and more on the intervention of a benevolent providence in sorting out human affairs satisfactorily.[57] On the one hand, the idea of a benevolent providence assisting human destiny illuminates all of his romantic comedies; and, on the other, the lovers in *Twelfth Night* are distinctly more individualized than those in *Love's Labor's Lost* or *A Midsummer Night's Dream*. But it is a question of emphasis and degree.

Elizabethan romantic comedy was able to achieve its aim—the representation of a harmonious, spiritually integrated society symbolized in marriage—in a cultural environment in which love and marriage were gaining moral prestige and, as a corollary, personal happiness and freedom began to be considered goals worth pursuing. Currently a debate has arisen about whether Puritan marriage ideology, which, like Rosalind's disguise in *As You Like It,* enhanced female dignity and autonomy while at the same time explicitly reinforcing the double standard, had positive or negative effects for women.[58] The important point here is that a clear correspondence exists between the potentially contradictory view of sexual values presented in the Puritan tracts and the representation of sexual tensions in Elizabethan comedy. In both forms we can see certain conceptual antitheses beginning to take

56. Gardner, p. 193.

57. Cf. Salingar, pp. 240–242. Salingar believes that "*Twelfth Night* is the summing-up of a major phase of Shakespeare's writing, the last romantic play at the end of a decade, because it deals with the psychological value of revelry and its limits as well; it is a comedy about comedy . . . As the play advances, psychological mistakes dissolve into 'errors' of identity; Time and Nature, assuming the guise of Fortune, are stronger than characters' 'reason,' their conscious will. Although the actors have been given some of the depth and self-awareness of individuals in real life, they are caught up in a situation that evidently belongs less and less to real life and increasingly to the stage."

58. See Fitz, "What Says the Married Woman," and Juliet Dusinberre, *Shakespeare and the Nature of Women* (London, 1975).

shape: personal freedom and social convention; happiness and stability; civilization and its discontents. But neither the theologians nor the playwrights drew final attention to the conflicts implicit in their conceptions of erotic love and marriage. The Puritan preachers simply did not perceive the inherent contradictions in their sexual values. Although the playwrights discerned the outlines of comic structure in the drama of sexual desire seeking and finding satisfaction, they represented potentially conflicting erotic forces mainly in order to reconcile them. In Shakespearean comedy happiness and stability are the same.

Keith Thomas has linked the preponderance of sexual humor in Tudor and Stuart England to a pervasive anxiety about changing sexual relationships. As Thomas recognizes, among its many functions, comedy can perform the conservative one of introducing potentially disruptive elements only to represent them as harmoniously assimilated within the existing social structure.[59] As the implications of the idealization of marriage and the claims of the individual self became more pressing, conflicts which were evoked but contained in one form of drama became grist for the mill of other forms. In Jacobean England love and sexuality began to be subjected to the savage scrutiny of satire and tragedy.

Tracing the growth of romantic comedy in Elizabethan England provides insight into the ways in which people conceived of their emotional experience and represented it not only to the world, but to themselves. When the most intimate emotions are given popular, public expression in dramatic forms, we can perceive the paradoxes and contradictions that comprised the mental formulations of sexual love as England moved into the modern age. The drama not only illuminates the inner life of the surrounding culture, but plays a significant part in creating it. An awareness of this reciprocal relation between sexual values and their symbolic representation in dramatic forms should become increasingly germane as scholars move more deeply into unearthing the history of the private life.

---

59. Keith Thomas, "The Place of Laughter in Tudor and Stuart England," *TLS* (21 January 1977), pp. 77–81. Also see Mary Douglas, "The Social Control of Cognition: Some Factors in Joke Perception," *Man,* III (September 1968), 361–376.

A Shrew Yet Honest:
Manliness in Jonson

RONALD HUEBERT

IN CONVERSATION with Drummond of Hawthornden, Jonson is by turns belligerently scornful, ironically dismissive, intemperately vain, lucidly perceptive, and (on rare and moving occasions) clairvoyantly honest about himself. In one of these moments of deep self-knowledge he reports that, while visiting Sir Robert Cotton's country estate, "he saw in a vision his eldest sone," who appeared to him with the mark of the cross on his forehead, "of a Manlie shape," and full-grown, as Jonson believes "he shall be at the resurrection."[1] Meanwhile, a letter arrived from Jonson's wife to confirm that the boy had died. The sincerity of this account is beyond question, even without the support of Epigram 45, "On My First Son." And it reveals, aside from Jonson's emotional integrity, his belief that the shape of the immortal soul is the perfection of manliness. This idea, though not the striking metaphysical context of the occasion, is always near the center of Jonson's thinking about life and art. It motivates his choice of a

1. *Ben Jonson,* ed. C. H. Herford and Percy and Evelyn Simpson (Oxford, 1925–1952), I, 139–140, hereafter cited as *H & S.* Whenever I quote from old-spelling texts, usage of *i/j, u/v,* and long *s* is silently modernized, and a few archaic abbreviations are expanded without comment.

31

name—Eustace Manly—for the only moral survivor of the social wreckage he dramatizes in *The Devil is an Ass*. It stands behind his public image as the master of a literary circle known as the sons of Ben. It colors his language when, as "Judge & Professor of *Poesie*," he praises the work of a younger poet "with some passion" by declaring, *"My Son Cartwright writes all like a Man."* [2] What Cartwright made of this compliment, and whether he deserved it, are questions that no longer matter. What Johnson meant by it continues to count for anyone sufficiently dazzled by *Volpone,* annoyed by *Epicoene,* or bewildered by *Bartholomew Fair* to care about meeting Jonson on his own terms.

To care about meeting Jonson at all, I could have said, because unless you're willing to take him on the terms he prescribes, Jonson will always be somewhere else: not at home, out to lunch, otherwise engaged. So it's best to begin by catching Jonson in his various prescriptive moods: reeling off pronouncements, however spiced with irony or sack, to the recording angel of Hawthornden; jotting down the wit of other men or the products of his own invention, however unsystematically, in a compilation of *Discoveries;* affirming where he stands, however indirectly, in the poems.

"Looke upon an effeminate person," Jonson writes in *Discoveries;* "his very gate confesseth him. If a man be fiery, his motion is so: if angry, 'tis troubled, and violent. So that wee may conclude: Wheresoever, manners, and fashions are corrupted, Language is. It imitates the publicke riot. The excesse of Feasts, and apparell, are the notes of a sick State; and the wantonnesse of language, of a sick mind." [3] To dismiss the effeminate person with a scornful shrug is authentic Jonson; it's a gesture he animates pointedly at the expense of Inigo Jones, ironically at the expense of Sejanus. But there's more to Jonson's manliness than contempt for men who don't measure up. In the passage just quoted I think Jonson is attacking three separate kinds of effeminate

2. This judgment is recorded by Humphrey Moseley in his preface to the first collected edition of Cartwright (1651); see Appendix A in *The Plays and Poems of William Cartwright,* ed. G. Blakemore Evans (Madison, Wis., 1951), p. 831.

3. *H & S,* VIII, 592–593. This passage, like many others in *Discoveries,* is a free translation from Seneca the elder (see *H & S,* XI, 244). But here and elsewhere I'm assuming that an idea didn't matter less to Jonson just because he found it in an author he admired.

behavior as if to define, by opposition, three kinds of manliness. First, the manners and fashions of an effeminate man—and his way of walking—are qualities which belong to his public image. In opposition to the courtly gait of his effete antagonist, Jonson imagines the actions of real men to be fiery, angry, even violent. Secondly, where the health of the state and the individual is at stake, manliness is a moral concern: foppery is a sign of moral sickness, manliness a mark of social and personal sanity. Finally, in relation to language, manliness is a question of style: effeminate language is a form of corruption to be opposed by speaking and writing in the genuine idiom of men.

Since each of the territories I've just named—public image, morality, and style—amounts to a Jonsonian obsession, I've chosen them as the basis for the map of Jonson's mental geography which follows. The distortions in my map will be obvious to anyone who has lived in Jonson's world: poems and prose comments are noticed only selectively, and the comedies—though set aside for special scrutiny—are deliberately marked with a view to making the larger pattern visible. I think such distortions are endemic to mapmaking, and preferable to the myopic adjustment that occurs when you look at Jonson's art one compartment at a time. The idea of manliness doesn't nestle into any of the compartments; it's ingrained in Jonson whether he's serious or flippant, drunk or sober, walking to Scotland or entertaining the court, celebrating solidity in his poems or scourging chaos in his plays. Manliness turns out to be an idea you need if you want to encounter Jonson whole.

The public self Jonson created, both for his contemporaries and for posterity, is typically engaged in the manly art of competition.[4] In the grandest and pettiest senses of the word, he was a fighter. The motivation for his literary program—from the *Epigrams* to *The English Grammar*—includes a determination to rival the ancients. In his treatment of John Marston, to take a less elevated example, the same com-

---

4. For a brief and witty account of Jonson's invention of his public self, see Edward Partridge, "Jonson's Large and Unique View of Life," *The Elizabethan Theatre,* IV (1972), 145–150. My discussion draws on suggestions made by Robert M. Adams in "The Games of the Illusionist," *TLS,* 11 Feb. 1977, pp. 142–143 (a review of George Parfitt's *Ben Jonson: Public Poet and Private Man* [London, 1976]), and by Jennifer Brady, both in conversation and in " 'Beware the Poet': Authority and Judgment in Jonson's *Epigrammes,*" *SEL,* XXIII (1983), 95–112.

petitive urgency expresses itself as a snarl of antagonism. It's a public war of words when Jonson parodies Marston as Hedon (in *Cynthia's Revels*) or as Crispinus (in *Poetaster*), if that indeed is what he's doing. It's still a war of words when he claims that Marston wrote his father-in-law's sermons, and that his father-in-law wrote Marston's plays. This is funny because it's outrageous, and it remains funny even if you realize that Marston deserved better after having dedicated *The Malcontent* to his unappreciative mentor. But competition for Jonson is also a matter of muscular self-assertion. In his late forties he can't resist boasting to Drummond of his "many quarrells with Marston," in one of which he "beat him & took his Pistol from him."[5] Playfulness? Maybe. The same kind of fun he had in the quarrel with his fellow actor, Gabriel Spencer, whom Jonson (by his own account) was able to kill in self-defense despite a handicap of ten inches in the length of his weapon.

It's easy to grant the high-mindedness of Jonson's desire to compete with Aristophanes, Horace, Juvenal, and Tacitus. It's easy to understand why a writer born into the same generation as Shakespeare and Donne would wish to disarm comparative judgments, or at least exercise a fair bit of control over them by recording his own evaluations. It's easy to tolerate a satiric writer's need to deface the sacred monuments of the recent past, as in his remark that "Sidney was no pleasant man in countenance, his face being spoilled with Pimples."[6] But as you move down the scale, discovering along the way that Jonson's literary enemies included Thomas Middleton, Michael Drayton, Sir John Harington, Edward Sharpham, Abraham Fraunce, Gervase Markham, John Taylor the Water Poet, and somebody called John Owen (epigrammatist), you begin to suspect that forming disinterested judgments isn't the point. Competition seems to have been a compulsive joy for Jonson. He didn't have to look back over his shoulder to see how far he had outstripped the Gervase Markhams of the world, but look back he did.

Jonson's most celebrated quarrel was his protracted assault on Inigo Jones. There were good artistic and ideological reasons for this antagonism; in declaring poetry and picture to be sister arts, "both . . . busie about imitation," Jonson appears eager to add the crucial

5. See the Conversations with Drummond, in *H & S*, I, 138, 140, 136.
6. *H & S*, I, 138–139.

qualification: "Yet of the two, the Pen is more noble, then the Pencill." [7] The court masque required intimate collaboration between pen and pencil, and if the pen was convinced of its own superior calling, it's not hard to imagine why the pencil might rebel. But I think Jonson's attacks on Jones are colored with something darker than artistic rivalry. "An Expostulation with Inigo Jones" gets most of its energy from Jonson's ability to make an insult stick:

> What makes your wretchedness to bray so loud
> In town and court; are you grown rich and proud?
> Your trappings will not change you: change your mind.
> No velvet sheath you wear will alter kind;
> A wooden dagger is a dagger of wood,
> Though gold or ivory hafts would make it good.

Clearly, Jonson hated Jones. He reduces his rival, rhetorically, to a dandified poseur who fails every test of real manhood. Elsewhere, "Sir Inigo" is caricatured as a butterfly. And if Epigram 115 ("On the Town's Honest Man") is indeed a veiled attack on Jones, then it shows Jonson at his belligerent best: the object of contempt is denied a name, deprived of a sexual identity (by having the neuter pronoun thrust upon "it"), and stripped of all values, even primary decencies: "'Twill see its sister naked, ere a sword.'" [8]

A fair assessment of the rights and wrongs of this quarrel would have to include other arguments and further evidence. It would have to make allowance for Jonson's natural advantages, where the weapon of combat is the pen. It would have to include Jones's one verbal response where he argues, in admittedly pedestrian verse, that Jonson has written "of good and badd things," though "not with equall witt," because "the good's translation, butt the ill's thyne owne." [9] What interests me, however, is not a fair assessment of a long-dead quarrel, but rather Jonson's attitude in what must have been the fight of his life.

7. *H & S,* VIII, 609–610.

8. Ben Jonson, *Poems,* ed. Ian Donaldson (London, 1975), pp. 321, 326, 67. Further citations from the nondramatic verse refer to this edition.

9. *H & S,* XI, 385. Readers who want a full account may consult D. J. Gordon, "Poet and Architect: The Intellectual Setting of the Quarrel Between Ben Jonson and Inigo Jones," *JWCI,* XII (1949), 152–178.

Whatever his shortcomings, Inigo Jones was a formidable opponent. And there were persuasive reasons—excellent professional reasons—which might have induced many a distinguished writer to make his peace with the rising virtuoso of the visual arts. What did Jonson do? He fought with bitter tenacity, convinced he could settle the score if only the world would listen.

The battle with Inigo Jones was part of a larger Jonsonian campaign—the one described by Jonas A. Barish in "Jonson and the Loathèd Stage." [10] Though he spent much of his life writing for the theater, Jonson was never stagestruck. His repertoire of antitheatrical stances included the willingness to berate his paying customers for their shallowness or to hector them into submission; an active distaste for most of what the London theaters had to offer, especially if the scenic effects were spectacular; a persistent mistrust of shape-shifting in a broad philosophical sense and of the acting profession in particular; and a lifelong suspicion of the seductions of ornament. Not, on balance, the portrait of a natural playwright. To these observations, all of them drawn from Barish's essay, I would add only a speculative question. I wonder how Jonson felt in a world where Celia and Lady Politic Wouldbe and Dol Common and Grace Wellborn weren't "real" women in any sense of the word, but young men in drag? I think the answer to this question is implied in *Epicoene,* and perhaps that's a sufficient answer in itself. I suspect that Jonson felt far more comfortable when he left the tiring-house at Blackfriars and entered the Apollo Room in the Devil Tavern, where his would be the only show in town, and where men could be trusted to be men.

As soon as you begin thinking about Jonson's cherished moral positions—generosity in friendship, loyalty to king and country, pleasure in moderation, fidelity to truth—you find yourself in the company of someone radically unlike the contentious ruffian who seems to have been asserting himself up to this point. And that's as it should be. Jonson's moral positions were not the casual inferences he drew without effort from a tranquil life; they were, like everything of value in Jonson, won with great labor from the mess of experience. Moderate en-

10. In *A Celebration of Ben Jonson,* ed. William Blissett et al. (Toronto, 1973), pp. 27–53. The essay reappears, slightly modified, in Barish's *The Antitheatrical Prejudice* (Berkeley, Calif., 1981), pp. 132–154.

joyment of liquor can be a major virtue only for someone who fears the chaos of being endlessly drunk.

It's difficult to catch Jonson the moralist in the act of struggling with experience, because of his habit of stating truth only after he's sure; but when you do catch him, the results can be rewarding. Epigram 65, "To My Muse," is the record of one such remarkable moment. It contains the astonishing admission (for Jonson) that he's made a mistake:

> Away, and leave me, thou thing most abhorred,
>   That hast betrayed me to a worthless lord,
> Made me commit most fierce idolatry
>   To a great image through thy luxury.
> Be thy next master's more unlucky muse,
>   And, as thou hast mine, his hours and youth abuse.
> Get him the time's long grudge, the court's ill-will;
>   And, reconciled, keep him suspected still.
> Make him lose all his friends; and, which is worse,
>   Almost all ways to any better course.
> With me thou leav'st an happier muse than thee,
>   And which thou brought'st me, welcome poverty;
> She shall instruct my after-thoughts to write
>   Things manly, and not smelling parasite.
> But I repent me: stay. Whoe'er is raised
>   For worth he has not, he is taxed, not praised.[11]

I don't think the final couplet works: the spectacular inversion can be carried off with agility by Donne or Herbert, but with Jonson there's too much bulk in the first fourteen lines to allow for a sudden pirouette. Still, the poem as a whole wins a special place in the *Epigrams* with its dignity of tone, its painful honesty, and its powerful imitation of the effort whereby Jonson extracts moral truth from baser stuff. He has fallen for a "great image," and he knows that to do so is to commit "idolatry." Worship of external greatness is false worship, and hence insincere (even if only in retrospect). So, although Jonson's error doesn't amount to simple hypocrisy, it still *smells* parasite, and that's enough to taint the experience. The honest way out is to admit the mistake, to renounce the art of the parasite, and to insist that the objects of worship live up to an exacting standard of "manly" integrity.

11. *Poems*, p. 35.

In its simplest terms, the principle Jonson invokes in "To My Muse" is a hatred of flattery. It's the same position he holds when, in conversation with Drummond, he claims that "he never esteemed of a man for the name of a Lord" and imagines himself (having incongruously taken holy orders) preaching a sermon to the king, in which "he would not flatter though he saw Death." [12] If you're wondering whether Jonson himself lived up to this demanding code, the answer is clear: of course he didn't. But from the experience of failing—of living imperfectly among members of a flawed and fallen race—he was able to earn an active sense of the value of his manly ideal.

The close bond between manliness and virtue in Jonson's thinking has some of its oddest results when he writes about women. One of these is an awkward and revealing touch in the portrait of the ideal woman he draws in Epigram 76 ("On Lucy, Countess of Bedford"):

> I meant she should be courteous, facile, sweet,
>   Hating that solemn vice of greatness, pride;
> I meant each softest virtue there should meet,
>   Fit in that softer bosom to reside.
> Only a learned and a manly soul
>   I purposed her. . . . [13]

Jonson's resistance to characterizing the feminine ideal by alluding to beauties of body or face borders on the spectacular; there's only one word in this poem (the ubiquitous and uninformative "fair") which could have the slightest reference to anybody's appearance. What interests Jonson is moral worth in what for him is its female form: the virtues of courtesy and sweetness which become the "softer bosom" of woman. But, arriving at the soul of his ideal creation, he finds himself in a rhetorical *cul de sac.* Can he give her a softer soul without endangering his portrait? Not if he wants his ideal to be more durable than the "easy wax" of antifeminist tradition. So he does the inconsistent thing, and gives her a "manly" soul instead.

The Jonson who offered this dubious compliment to the Countess of Bedford is the same man who got into trouble with the Countess of Pembroke by backing her husband's dismissive assertion that "Woe-

12. *H & S,* I, 141.
13. *Poems,* p. 41.

men were mens shadowes." According to Drummond's account, the Countess gave Jonson "a pennance to prove it in Verse,"[14] and he responded by composing a Song, "That Women Are but Men's Shadows" (*The Forest,* 7). Jonson deserves credit for discharging this obligation with more wit than he showed in contracting it. His poem is—and is meant to be— a trifle, but it still confirms the judgments he offers more soberly elsewhere:

> At morn and even shades are longest;
>   At noon they are or short or none:
> So men at weakest, they are strongest,
>   But grant us perfect, they're not known.
> Say, are not women truly then
>   Styled but the shadows of us men?[15]

Like Milton and many lesser men, Jonson simply can't confer the same moral independence on women as on men. And men become genuinely independent ("perfect") only by escaping the weakening influence of women entirely. Manliness is in part a code of renunciation. Resist flattery. Resist beauty. Resist women. It's worth remembering that two of Jonson's major sexual achievements, as reported to Drummond, were adventures in renunciation. His marriage included a period of "5 yeers" during which he had "not bedded with" his wife. And among the "accidents" of his sex life is the account of how he "lay diverse tymes with a woman, who shew him all that he wished except the last act, which she would never agree unto." [16] There's nothing preposterous about either of these events, nor anything inherently damaging (either way) to Jonson's sexual reputation. He may have had excellent reasons for deciding to live apart from a woman he described as "a shrew yet honest." As for the coy mistress of the anecdote, her thoughts may have ranged anywhere from fear of pregnancy to optimistic support for the view that pleasure can be reconciled to virtue. Whatever they were, they don't seem to have interested Jonson. And although the events themselves are understandable, what remains surprising is Jonson's eagerness to recount them for the benefit of a host as dull as Drummond of Hawthornden.

14. *H & S,* I, 142.
15. *Poems,* p. 99.
16. *H & S,* I, 139, 140.

The moral virtue of manliness, in Jonson, seems to require a defensive posture in relation to the blandishments of the world and the flesh. To give in to temptation is to become less than a "perfect" man. Thomas M. Greene has found a way of describing what I think is the same Jonsonian pattern in "Ben Jonson and the Centered Self." [17] The image of a justly drawn circle with a fixed center is, for Jonson, an emblem of positive moral achievement. Centrifugal pressures threaten the stability of the centered self, but these can and should be resisted by exercising the right centripetal forces. Sufficient moral "firmness," to adopt the famous language of Donne's "A Valediction: Forbidding Mourning," will make the human circle "just."

The traditional attributes of the circle include a concept which did almost the same work as manliness for Jonson and his contemporaries—namely, the concept of completeness. I'm thinking of the term in the sense in which it's used by Peacham in *The Compleat Gentleman* (1634), by Walton in *The Compleat Angler* (1653), or even by Charles Cotton in *The Compleat Gamester* (1674). Completeness in this sense is the condition of being amply endowed by nature and fully equipped by training to engage in manly action. Shakespeare's Ulysses gives the word exactly this weight when he addresses Achilles (though insincerely, of course) as "thou great and complete man." [18] To be a man in this sense is to be a virtuoso. But completeness shouldn't be a mere technical achievement, like the splendid physique of the body-builder who refuses to endanger the poise of his muscular development with anything so mundane as digging ditches. The complete man is willing to test his manliness by confronting experience. The nature of the test is implied, rather complacently, by the Duke's confident assertion in *Measure for Measure:* "Believe not that the dribbling dart of love / Can pierce a complete bosom" (I.iii.2–3). These are words which would fit more easily into Jonson's scheme of things than Shakespeare's. They confer value on the clearheaded self-reliance which ought to be the result of the moral exercise of manliness.

To watch Jonson putting manliness to the test of experience, I want to take a preliminary glance at two of his dramatic works: *Sejanus*

---

17. *SEL*, X (1970), 325–348.
18. *Troilus and Cressida*, III.iii.181. Shakespeare quotations are taken from *The Riverside Shakespeare,* ed. G. Blakemore Evans et al. (Boston, 1974).

(1603) and the masque entitled *Lovers Made Men* (1619). In terms of Jonson's career, these two works stand as prologue and epilogue to the period of the great comedies: *Volpone* (1606), *Epicoene* (1609), *The Alchemist* (1610), and *Bartholomew Fair* (1614). What interests me about the tragedy and the masque is the sense in which they show Jonson's mind at work just before and just after his period of greatest creativity.

In *Sejanus* the paragon of manliness is "the lofty cedar of the world, / Germanicus" (V.242–243).[19] He doesn't appear on stage (having been killed before the action begins), but his influence is never absent. He's the human standard by which all of the Germanicans judge their own behavior, and he seems to have left something of his manly soul to his widow, the "male-spirited dame" Agrippina (II.211). At the other end of the scale is Tiberius, the emperor who seldom appears on stage because he can't be lured away from the Island of Capri where he lives with his "stale catamite" (IV.404) and various other groupies of both sexes, acting out "strange and new commented lusts, / For which wise nature hath not left a name" (IV.400–401).

The action forces most of the characters to choose one of the two models: either the complete manliness of Germanicus, or its degenerate parody, Tiberius. Rome is thus sharply divided into "things manly" and those "smelling parasite." Sejanus himself, for all his apparent power, fails every major test of manliness. He began his career as "the noted pathic of the time" (I.216); that is, he got his start by sleeping with the right men. Subsequently he's been married and divorced. He decides he'll seduce Livia, not because he finds her attractive—"Venus hath the smallest share in it," he coldly admits (I.374)—but because she's a political stepping-stone. When Drusus openly challenges him with a blow to the face, Sejanus isn't man enough to strike back. His power is exclusively the kind you borrow from other powerful people, and his weapons are limited to subterfuge. That's why, when Tiberius withdraws his support and decides to back Macro, Sejanus crum-

19. Citations from Jonson's plays and masques refer to the relevant volumes in the Yale Ben Jonson, namely: *Sejanus*, ed. Jonas A. Barish (New Haven, Conn., 1965); *Every Man in his Humor*, ed. Gabriele Bernhard Jackson (1969); *Volpone*, ed. Alvin B. Kernan (1962); *Epicoene*, ed. Edward Partridge (1971); *The Alchemist*, ed. Alvin B. Kernan (1974); *Bartholomew Fair*, ed. Eugene M. Waith (1963); and *The Complete Masques*, ed. Stephen Orgel (1969).

bles. He's verbally impotent in the final Senate scene, and once offstage he's literally annihilated by the mob. Sejanus has never been a complete man, in the sense that his masquerade of manliness has always relied on secondhand attributes, never on anything integral to himself.[20]

In *Lovers Made Men* Jonson works out a symbolic ritual that reverses the action of *Sejanus.* This masque as a whole is an allegorical lesson in how to retain manliness in love. It begins with a parade of *"certain imagined ghosts"* (l. 11): these are lovers who, having taken the conceits of the Petrarchan tradition literally, suppose themselves to be dead. They are ferried over to Hades, but refused admission: only persons showing real death certificates may proceed. On the advice of the Fates, they drink from the waters of Lethe and enter a grove where they're miraculously *"changed"* (l. 68). "Yes, now they're substances and men," says one of the Fates as they emerge from the grove (l. 70). The action of the masque has moved from imperiled manliness to manliness restored. The men had been reduced to "Shadows for Love" (l. 86), but having been rescued and given substance, they are now free to *"take forth the ladies"* (l. 114) without losing their hold on reality. Love is possible for complete men, provided that they learn to "love with wit" (l. 142).

Just how this difficult feat can be accomplished Jonson demonstrates in *A Celebration of Charis* (*The Underwood,* 2), where the simpering Petrarchan courtier is replaced with a man of large substance who refers elsewhere to "My mountain belly, and my rocky face."[21] As an exercise in the art of loving with wit, the Charis poems illustrate the style which the manly lover ought to use:

> Have you seen but a bright lily grow,
> Before rude hands have touched it?
> Have you marked but the fall o' the snow,
> Before the soil hath smutched it?[22]

20. Alexander Leggatt, in *Ben Jonson: His Vision and His Art* (London, 1981), pp. 1–5, takes *Sejanus* as his point of departure in a chapter on "False Creations." This is one passage among several in Leggatt's book (such as the discussion of *Lovers Made Men,* pp. 165–167) that I've found suggestive.

21. See "My Picture Left in Scotland" (*The Underwood,* 9), in *Poems,* p. 145.

22. *Poems,* p. 133. There is a closely argued and entertaining discussion of these lines in S. P. Zitner's "The Revenge on Charis," *The Elizabethan Theatre,* IV (1972), 134–135.

These lines are splendid in themselves, even before you realize the genius of compression whereby Jonson was able to fill them with unexpected thoughts and sounds. Instead of a lily which defaces the lady's complexion by, say, striving for mastery of her cheek with the rose, Jonson gives you an independently growing flower. Instead of the paradise of eternal spring, he gives you the rudeness of human hands, the whiteness of winter, and the pun on "soil." Not for him the florid yet neutral praise which almost any lover could glibly offer to almost any mistress.

To explain what Jonson understood by manliness of style looks like a simple matter. He left plenty of clues in *Discoveries,* like the handy definition: "Too much pickednesse is not manly."[23] Easy money. All you do is find out what "pickedness" means, find out how much is "too much," and take the opposite. On "pickedness" the *Oxford English Dictionary* gives a useful list of synonyms—"adornment, elegance, trimness, spruceness"—and a string of examples including the sentence from *Discoveries.* If this isn't enough, you can look up the passage in Seneca which Jonson is translating: "Non est ornamentum virile concinnitas."[24] So "pickedness" in style amounts to ornamental elegance. Just to make sure, you can return to Jonson's text in *Discoveries* only to learn that the context isn't explicitly about language at all, but about manners: "*There* is nothing valiant, or solid to bee hop'd for from such, as are alwayes kemp't, and perfum'd; and every day smell of the Taylor: the exceedingly curious, that are wholly in mending such an imperfection in the face, in taking away the Morphew in the neck; or bleaching their hands at Mid-night, gumming, and bridling their beards; or making the waste small, binding it with hoopes, while the mind runs at waste: Too much pickednesse is not manly."

So Jonson himself gives you a rich contextual definition of "pickedness" and a secure feeling for how much would be "too much." And if he's talking about fopperies of character rather than vanities of speech, that shouldn't cancel out the value of the statement. In Jonson, manners and language always go together.

Jonson's contempt for what he considered effeminate language comes out more openly in the following attack on the degeneracy of

23. *H & S,* VIII, 607.
24. Quoted in *H & S,* XI, 255.

the times: "But now nothing is good that is naturall: Right and naturall language seemes to have least of the wit in it; that which is writh'd and tortur'd, is counted the more exquisite. . . . Nothing is fashionable, till it bee deform'd; and this is to write like a *Gentleman*. All must bee as affected, and preposterous as our Gallants cloathes, sweet bags, and night-dressings: in which you would thinke our men lay in, like *Ladies:* it is so curious." [25] Here the connection between punctilious grooming and affected language is explicit. And what's more, Jonson comes close to making a positive statement in support of "natural" language. But even this is a tricky proposition, since one man's nature is another man's artifice, and since Jonson obviously knew that without art man would be inarticulate.

What Jonson doesn't want is loutishness parading as manliness. There are some wits, he remarks, "that in composition are nothing, but what is rough, and broken." When a sentence threatens to come out smoothly, "they trouble it of purpose. They would not have it run without rubs, as if that stile were more strong and manly, that stroke the eare with a kind of unevennesse. These men erre not by chance, but knowingly, and willingly; they are like men that affect a fashion by themselves, have some singularity in a Ruffe, Cloake, or Hat-band; or their beards, specially cut to provoke beholders, and set a marke upon themselves." [26] Like effeminate language, the rough and broken style is an affectation, though at the opposite end of the scale. It's another way of making nature afraid, to borrow an appropriate phrase from the Induction to *Bartholomew Fair* (l. 115).

"The true Artificer will not run away from nature, as hee were afraid of her; or depart from life, and the likenesse of Truth." With these words Jonson begins a passage in *Discoveries* which sounds more like a manifesto than any other. An honest writer must be willing to resist going after flashy effects, Jonson believes, even if this means he'll be called "barren, dull, leane." Never mind. Posterity will recognize genuine merit: "his wisdome, in dividing: his subtilty, in arguing: with what strength hee doth inspire his Readers; with what sweetnesse hee strokes them." The "sharpenesse" of his satire and the "urbanity" of his wit will be admired; his ability to "invade" the minds of his audi-

25. *H & S*, VIII, 581.
26. *H & S*, VIII, 585.

ence will become legendary. As for "Elocution," he'll be praised for deciding "what word is proper: which hath ornament: which height: what is beautifully translated: where figures are fit: which gentle, which strong to shew the composition *Manly.* And how he hath avoyded faint, obscure, obscene, sordid, humble, improper, or effeminate *Phrase.*"[27]

There's considerable flexibility in Jonson's program for the ideal writer—more, I think, than the partisans of the plain style will allow him.[28] Sweetness and gentleness are not excluded, nor is ornament; used without restraint, these softer qualities could signal an effeminate style, but in themselves they are virtues. The mark of manliness, however, is strength of composition. This I take to be the "harmonious fitting of parts in a sentence," which can have almost the "force of knitting, and connexion: As in stones well squar'd, which will rise strong a great way without mortar."[29] Manly discourse has a strength which comes from the secure integration of well-fitting parts.

The qualities of manly writing as Jonson defines them are consistent, I believe, with most of his more famous pronouncements about style. When he says that "the chiefe vertue of a style is perspicuitie,"[30] he's defining further the naturalness of the manly style, especially in opposition to the vice of obscurity. When he says, "Pure and neat Language I love, yet plaine and customary,"[31] he's working out an agreement between the true artificer and the order of nature. Language won't be plain unless the excrescences of jargon and bombast are chis-

27. *H & S*, VIII, 587–588.

28. I'm thinking in particular of Wesley Trimpi's *Ben Jonson's Poems: A Study of the Plain Style* (Stanford, Calif., 1962), a book I find it exasperating to read, no doubt because my prejudices are in general the very ones Trimpi can't abide. For example, the fact that Jonson earned his living writing plays and acting in them is an embarrassing detail that Trimpi very nearly suppresses, and when he does mention it, you can feel the discomfort: "his admiration of Bacon and Selden shows a breadth of interest, intellectual adroitness, and learning that is astounding for a professional dramatist" (p. 149). The Jonson who emerges from Trimpi's pages seems to have avoided all those awkward years of apprenticeship (both in bricklaying and in the theater) in favor of moving directly from the tutelage of his early mentor, Camden, into the circle of Yvor Winters and the reverence for the plain style which he preached.

29. *H & S*, VIII, 623.

30. *H & S*, VIII, 622.

31. *H & S*, VIII, 620.

eled away by art; yet it won't be pure unless the artist is willing to accept what nature supplies. Somewhere near the center of this paradox stands the manly speaker and writer of the language: as natural as God made him, yet equipped with the tools he needs to make each stone fit square and strong.

The terms in which Jonson gives praise always tell us at least as much about himself as about the person he's celebrating. This holds true in spades for his "Epistle to Master John Selden" (*The Underwood,* 14). Jonson claims he's "lost" in admiration when he sees:

> the excellent seasoning of your style,
> And manly elocution, not one while
> With horror rough, then rioting with wit:
> But to the subject still the colours fit
> In sharpness of all search, wisdom of choice,
> Newness of sense, antiquity of voice![32]

This is high praise, which Selden merits rather for being Jonson's friend than for being the author of *Titles of Honor* (1614). I'm not saying that the praise is insincere: only that it's generous, and that it's Jonsonian. The warmest way Jonson can praise a friend is to single out the marks of manliness for which he wants to be admired himself.

For Jonson the poet and Jonson the critic, "manly elocution" is the model of excellence. For Jonson the playwright, the norm remains the same but the terms of reference alter drastically. The first great pronouncement he makes to his audience at the Globe is to tell them, in the Prologue to *Every Man in his Humor,* that he won't provide romance or spectacle, "But deeds and language such as men do use" (l. 21). Not the language men *ought* to use, but the language they *do* use. The comic dramatist has a special commitment to the idiom of human folly: that is, to all of the "faint, obscure, obscene, sordid, humble, improper, or effeminate" registers of speech which the manly stylist makes it his business to condemn and avoid. As a writer of comedy, Jonson repeatedly puts himself into the position of choosing between this commitment to folly and the requirements of his own cherished system of norms. The greatness of his art can be measured by the honesty of the choices he makes.

32. *Poems,* p. 154.

Even after the sexual revolution, North American society remains prudish as ever on at least one question: affectionate physical contact between heterosexual males. Just when you think you can violate this prohibition—with a hand on the shoulder, or something equally inno-cent—you find yourself shocked into asking the predictable series of questions (Does he think that I think that he thinks I'm gay?) and wish-ing you'd been satisfied with the unambiguous chastity of a hand-shake. I know of only one circumstance in which the prohibition doesn't apply: the moment after the decisive goal (or home run or touchdown) in team-sport competition. For a few sublime seconds the rules are suspended, and the men who have just become heroes are al-lowed to embrace like lovers before millions of approving eyes. It's as if Wayne Gretzky and Mark Messier can be permitted to leap into one another's arms after collaborating on the record-setting goal because nobody, not even the most hardened TV cynic, will be able to call them queer. They are exempt from the code—for a moment—by vir-tue of their status as models of manliness.

This paradigm is a helpful way of getting at one of the special (and otherwise troublesome) qualities in the relationship between Mosca and Volpone. After the duping of the first gull, Voltore, Volpone is wild with excitement: "Excellent Mosca!" he says, "Come hither, let me kiss thee" (I.iii.78–79). He repeats this demonstrative wish after the fleecing of Corbaccio in the following scene, and when they've hoodwinked the entire judicial establishment, Volpone has nothing but praise for his "Exquisite Mosca" (V.ii.4) who has managed things so deliciously that "The pleasure of all womankind's not like it" (V.ii.11). This looks like an invitation to see the bond between master and para-site in erotic terms, but that's precisely what it is not. The affection and the praise are part of a ritual of high spirits; in each case they fol-low a major scoring play in the competition between Volpone with his team of dependents and the established order of Venice. Under such conditions, an embrace in which the team captain celebrates his vir-tuoso performer is a demonstration (not a denial) of manliness.

This is not to say that Volpone is in any sense normal, but only that manliness is a key to the way in which he likes to display himself. True, Jonson qualifies his comic hero's display of self by hedging it about with ironies. But pride cometh before the fall, potency before deflation. The ironies can do their work only to the extent that Volpone wins the right to be their target. This he does by sheer personal magnificence: by being what Jonson calls him in the dramatis personae, "a Magnifico." He rises to this potent level (both socially and dramatically) largely because of his urgent and unstoppable desire to compete.

At the moment I want to defer discussion of the suppressed competition between Volpone and Mosca; it's one of the ironies that Jonson saves for the end, and I will do the same. For most of the play, Volpone is the undisputed master, Mosca the endlessly inventive but apparently selfless parasite. They have worked out a relationship based on mutual support (on teamwork, in fact), and they depend on the integrity of this relationship in competing against the sharpers and shysters of Venice. So long as Volpone and Mosca keep in check any suspicion of competition between each other, they remain in control. Working as a team they can predict and capitalize on the competitive urges which divide their antagonists into selfishly isolated competitors. "But am I sole heir?" asks Voltore, wishing to be reassured that he has outmaneuvered the other legacy-hunters. "Without a partner, sir," says Mosca; and Voltore's nervous legalism fades behind a smile of complacency: "Happy, happy me!" (I.iii.44–47). When Mosca turns to Corbaccio, he can use the smug departure of the lawyer as a competitive stimulus; only after Corbaccio knows that Voltore has left a handsome bribe does he offer his own bag of chequins which, he believes, "Will quite weigh down his plate" (I.iv.70). As Volpone says, all of the would-be heirs are determined to "counterwork the one unto the other," to "contend in gifts, as they would seem in love" (I.i.83–84). These opening scenes are alive with awareness of the malice which money provokes. To paraphrase L. C. Knights, Jonson had the clarity of mind to understand the capitalist system even while it was unfolding, and the honesty to admit what competition for gain can do to the human character.[33] For the men in Jonson's Venice, the game of getting and spending is a sophistication of the primitive need to assert manliness as dominance.

In the case of Corvino, competitive zeal expresses itself as violence, misogyny, possessiveness. Jonson allows the ugliness of these distor-

33. *Drama and Society in the Age of Jonson* (London, 1937), pp. 200–206.

tions to be felt in Corvino's threats to "chalk a line" beyond which his wife dare not move, or to restrict her motion so that she'll have "no pleasure . . . but backwards" (II.v.52–61). Corvino's laughable tactics of surveillance and custody are inherited from a long comic tradition of jealousy and cuckoldry, but the masterstroke is Mosca's (and Jonson's) ability to see the cause underneath the symptoms. When Mosca tells Corvino that Volpone now needs a young woman to coddle him, all he has to do to bring Corvino around is to present the case in competitive terms: "One o' the doctors offered there his daughter" (II.vi.60). Horrified at the thought of being outbid, Corvino indulges in a parody of thinking—"Wherefore should not I / As well command my blood and my affections / As this dull doctor?" (II.vi.70–72)—and reaches the triumphant conclusion that it's all right with him if Mosca uses his wife in the bartering.

Against this background of contemptible elbowing for advantage, both Volpone and Mosca present themselves as competitors on a grand scale. Mosca saves his claim to magnificence for his one soliloquy, where he dismisses the ordinary sycophant, who relies on the "bare town-art" of flattery as an opponent unworthy of the true parasite: "your fine, elegant rascal, that can rise / And stoop, almost together, like an arrow" (III.i.14–24). Even in formulating this hierarchy of parasites and sub-parasites, Mosca is imitating his master's economic snobbery: "I use no trade, no venture," Volpone says proudly, and he follows this advertisement of his dignity with a derisive list of "common" strategies for getting rich (I.i.33). In the mountebank scene he's equally anxious to insist that he's not one of the "rabble of these ground *ciarlitani*" (II.ii.48–49) but Scoto of Mantua, knower of "the rarest secrets" (II.ii.159), companion to cardinals, counselor of princes, the envy of all Italy, the cock of the walk.

Celia first sees Volpone when he's in this mood of self-inflation, and her perception of his manliness remains part of what might crudely be called their relationship. I'll return to Celia shortly, but first there are things that need to be said about Volpone's sex life. He's not married, of course, which is why he has no legitimate heirs. His property includes "A handsome, pretty, customed bawdy-house" (V.vii.12) which he mentions with the kind of affection you'd expect from a pimp who made a big enough killing to retire. Mosca's account of his illegitimate children—"Some dozen, or more, that he begot on beggars, / Gypsies, and Jews, and black-moors" (I.v.44–45)—may not be the literal truth, but it's part of Volpone's sexual image. According to rumor, the dwarf, eunuch, and hermaphrodite who live with Volpone are his children. "He's the true father of his family," Mosca says, "In all save me" (I.v.48–49). It's possible to read this last line as Mosca's claim to be one of Volpone's bastards, though not a "true" copy of the paternal image. There's no more than a hint to this effect, and that's how it should be; Jonson gives you just the murkiness of possible paternity, much as Beckett does in the pairing of Hamm and Clov in *Endgame*. What the innuendos add up to is a perverse and self-assertive potency for which a phrase like "dirty old man" is far too mild. Volpone is a man who loves nobody, but can seduce almost anyone and knows that he can.

So all Mosca has to do is mention the fair face and the white skin of Corvino's wife, and Volpone is ready for the old game. It can't be love—or even lust in any immediate sense—because Volpone hasn't so much as laid eyes on her. When Mosca explains that Celia is "kept as warily as is your gold" (I.v.118), Volpone's eagerness escalates from curiosity ("How might I see her?") to urgency ("I must see her"). Volpone's desire expresses itself as competitive potency: as the need to perform, to dominate, to violate, and (at his time of life) to prove that the old magic still works.

The actors who play Volpone and Celia will need to make assumptions like these to prepare for their first meeting. Volpone swaggers onstage in his showy mountebank disguise, plants himself under Celia's window, and begins a demonstration of circus patter that makes music out of nonsense. Then *"Celia at the window throws down her handkerchief"* (II.ii.218.1). The stage direction doesn't say how long Celia has been at her window, or whether Volpone has noticed her presence, or whether she drops the handkerchief naïvely, deliberately, coquettishly, or accidentally.[34] But the scene brings together a beautiful young woman whose life is a cloistered hell and an experienced magnifico in the full stride of his performance. However intended, the handkerchief is a meaningful sign. Corvino, basing his interpretation

---

34. R. B. Parker has shown how important these alternatives are by discussing the choices made by modern directors and actors in playing the scene; see "*Volpone* in Performance: 1921–1972," *RenD*, N.S. IX (1978), 158–160.

on observation instead of fantasy, is for once dead right: "You were an actor with your handkerchief" (II.v.40).

The next encounter between Celia and Volpone takes place in Volpone's bedroom. Corvino's part in the scene is yet another foolish and artless attempt to control his wife's behavior, though by now he's pushing and goading her in the direction of Volpone's bed, insisting that a man as old as Volpone can do her no harm. Having destroyed what little credit he may still have enjoyed in his wife's estimation, he allows Mosca to usher him out of the room. Alone with Celia at last, Volpone *"leaps off from the couch"* (III.vii.139.1–3) and the seduction begins in earnest. It includes Volpone's praise for the "miracle" of Celia's beauty which now raises him from his bed (III.vii.146), his performance of the song, "Come my Celia, let us prove" (III.vii.166–183), and his catalog of anticipated pleasures:

> Thou like Europa now, and I like Jove,
> Then I like Mars, and thou like Erycine;
> So of the rest, till we have quite run through,
> And wearied all the fables of the gods.
> Then will I have thee in more modern forms . . . .
>
> (III.vii.222–226)

Celia's part through most of this is infuriatingly passive. What little she does say is designed to keep Volpone at arms' length. I can find in the text no justification for the recurring belief of modern directors that Celia reaches a point of near-seduction.[35] Her one long speech indicates, I think, that Jonson is far more concerned with Volpone's responses than with hers. She begs to be released, appealing to his pity, and if he has none of that, she says, "Be bountiful and kill me" (III.vii.245). This is little more than an echo of patient Griselda, but what follows hits Volpone with the force of a challenge:

> Yet feed your wrath, sir, rather than your lust,
> It is a vice comes nearer manliness.
>
> (III.vii.249–250)

35. See Parker, "*Volpone* in Performance," p. 159, and especially the comment quoted here by Frank Hauser, who directed the Oxford Playhouse production in 1966: "The point I wanted to get across in the actual staging of it was that she *is* seduced, not wholly seduced, but tempted by it."

After hearing this provocation and appreciating the genuine counter-force of her resistance, Volpone calculates his chances, wonders what people will think about him if he fails, and threatens rape. Enter Bonario, with naked weapon drawn, sounding the battle cry: "Forbear, foul ravisher! libidinous swine!" (III.vii.267).

The ironies are beginning their work, and that is how Jonson has planned it from the start. You can't be a real emblem of manliness if you spend your days lying flat on your back, pretending to be virtually paralyzed, and submitting to a heavy treatment of makeup before allowing a visitor to enter. And you're not the Don Juan you thought you were if your carefully orchestrated love scene ends when somebody bigger and younger rushes in just when you're threatening violence. The anticlimax rankles when Volpone next speaks to Mosca, and it continues to hurt. Technically, the old partners make a brilliant recovery in the first courtroom scene by forging and gaining credibility for the big lie: it was all Bonario's fault—he was hoping to kill his father, he'd been openly screwing Celia for months—and in any case Volpone could never have been a real threat. To convince the court, *"Volpone is brought in, as impotent"* (IV.vi.20.1). Whatever loss of esteem Volpone may feel by publicly declaring impotence he claims to recover when the court accepts and endorses the lie: this is more satisfying, he tells Mosca, "than if I had enjoyed the wench" (V.ii.10). Perhaps. But if that's true, it says more than a man might care to admit about himself.

What brings Volpone down for the last time is the inability to stop competing. Just counting his winnings is no satisfaction; there must be victims for him to spurn, fools for him to scorn. So he invents a tactic to bring back all of the old contestants, because he needs them. He wants the rumor of his death spread through the streets of Venice, because:

> I shall have instantly my vulture, crow,
> Raven, come flying hither on the news
> To peck for carrion.

> (V.ii.64–66)

So Mosca gets to enter his name in the will, puts on the clarissimo's robe, and makes a point of holding onto the keys. For the first time, Mosca has the competitive edge, and that's enough to shatter the old partnership forever.

In the desperate tension of the final courtroom scenes, Mosca retains his advantage. When he enters, dressed in splendor, declared unbelievably rich, it seems that Volpone's manliness has been conferred on him as well. "A proper man," muses one of the judges, as he begins to plot the fortune of his marriageable daughter (V.xii.50–51). And in the surreptitious bargaining between Mosca and Volpone (disguised as a courtroom lackey) which occupies real stage center while the legal guardians of Venice are adjusting to a new set of lies, Mosca proves that he has become Volpone's match. His first offer is an even split: share the money equally, agree to a standoff. Volpone refuses this with contempt, thinks of the alternatives, and at last agrees. But by this time Mosca has caught the bargaining fever: "I cannot now / Afford it you so cheap" (V.xii.69–70). Between habitual competitors, equality is impossible. Mosca knows now that he's going to be the master in any new alliance. And Volpone, unwilling to see himself in a servile position, throws off his disguise.

Punishment is immediate, severe, and poetic. Mosca is to be whipped and condemned for life to service as a galley slave. Volpone's wealth is confiscated, and he's condemned to prison where he'll be "cramped with irons" until his body becomes "sick and lame indeed" (V.xii.123–124). Both sentences are external versions of what has already happened in each case to the inner man.

If you live in Volpone's Venice, as everybody does, you can choose not to compete. The price of this choice is to make you not only an outsider, but an impotent windbag. Sir Politic Wouldbe spends his days noting down the occasions when rats get at his spur-leathers or the places where he urinates. And when Peregrine pays a visit to Sir Politic's house, the comings and goings prompt him to say, "I see the family is all female here" (V.iv.14).[36]

If you do choose to compete—for as much of the world and the flesh as you can make yours—there's another price to be paid. It is illustrated allegorically in the entertainment put on by the freaks at the outset of the action. The soul of Apollo performs a bewildering series of transmigrations in this interlude, passing indifferently from whores to philosophers, from literal to figurative asses, and coming to rest at

---

36. For a comprehensive analysis of the Wouldbe household and its place in Jonson's scheme, see Jonas A. Barish, "The Double Plot in *Volpone*," *MP*, LI (1953–1954), 83–92.

last in the body of Androgyno, the hermaphrodite. This is what happens to the human soul if it's allowed to drift, without values, in a world where self-assertion is the only rule. The precise terror of this result can be measured, I think, against the ideal of the "manly soul" which Jonson saw reflected in the people he loved and admired.

Neither impotence nor androgyny is a tolerable condition for Jonson. Between them stands the good man, Bonario, described sneeringly by Corvino as "that piece of cedar, / That fine, well-timbered gallant" (IV.v.123–124). Here, if anywhere, is a moral point of rest. But Jonson is too much of a competitor himself, too much in love with the game he has created, and too honest an artist to give Bonario more than his nominal assent. So he's artistically stingy with Bonario (giving the poor actor almost nothing more than irate virtue to sustain him) and economically generous (giving him loads of money, as if to say, let's see if that won't corrupt you, too). And he reverses the proportions for Volpone. Economic disaster, imprisonment, immobility. But the artistic approval which lavishes on him the words of a theatrical magnifico, and reserves the last word for him as well. Volpone's final performance is an exercise in the art of competing for applause: "though the fox be punished by the laws," he comes forward to request that the spectators "fare jovially, and clap your hands" (V.xii.153–157). This ending feels like the work of a man who knows the human cost of competition, but knows as well that he won't and doesn't want to suppress the fighting spirit in himself.

The Alchemist picks up where *Volpone* left off, both artistically and morally. The plot begins with an elaborately vulgar cockfight in which the two male tricksters compete, not so much for the one available hen (whom they've agreed to share in any case), but for dominance within the "venter tripartite" (I.i.135) which unites them against a shared enemy—the world of law, society, and common sense. The real bond which holds this uneasy partnership of magus, pimp, and whore together is naked self-interest: when Face dissolves the agreement by kicking Dol Common and Subtle out the back door at the end of the play he's only admitting that competing strategies of self-interest no longer coincide. In *Volpone,* a lifelong partnership is blown apart when the truth is at last uncovered; in *The Alchemist* the precarious truth is obvious from the outset, and the spectators know that any serious imbalance of pressure is likely to cause an explosion.

From a moral perspective, the chicanery by which the world is run in *Volpone* goes through a further stage of refinement in *The Alchemist* and emerges as absurdity. When delusions are inflated well beyond the limits of ordinary credibility, some sane point of reference becomes not merely desirable, but necessary. It's a bit like moving from the satire of *Rolling Stone* (in its days of glory) to the orchestrated inanity of *National Lampoon*. In the first case you're free to pick and choose the issues that matter and the stances you'll take, but in the second you're boxed into a corner where all you can do is shout, "This is crazy!"

What happens to manliness in a world made over by alchemical fantasy is suggested, with emblematic authority, by Lovewit's allusion to "The boy of six year old, with the great thing" (V.i.24). This mental icon appears in Lovewit's list of the items that might well attract curious crowds to his otherwise vacant house. And it's the perfect image of what the men of the play look like when sexually aroused.

Sir Epicure Mammon's dream is an absurdly literal fantasy of how it would feel to be the complete man. [37] The great thing for Mammon is to be endowed with limitless potency:

> For I do mean
> To have a list of wives and concubines
> Equal with Solomon, who had the stone
> Alike with me; and I will make me a back
> With the elixir, that shall be as tough
> As Hercules', to encounter fifty a night.
>
> (II.ii.34–39).

Here the dream of potency discredits itself through rhetorical overkill, especially when Mammon adds to it special safeguards (such as gelding Face and all of the gallants who might be sexual competitors), self-conscious voyeurism (in wishing to see multiple mirror-images of him-

---

37. Here and elsewhere I am indebted to Alvin B. Kernan's discussions of Jonson, such as the observation that Jonson's fools, "both great and small, are men who cannot understand metaphor"; see *The Cankered Muse: Satire of the English Renaissance* (New Haven, Conn., 1959), p. 183. See also "Alchemy and Acting: The Major Plays of Ben Jonson," *SLI*, VI (1973), 1–22.

self, walking "Naked between my succubae"), and the joy of humiliation (as in his refusal to accept anyone but "fathers and mothers" to do his pimping and procuring). What Mammon wants to project as manliness is in fact childishness: the sort of potency appropriate to a six-year-old imagination. In describing the restorative properties of the elixir, Mammon gives himself away by claiming that "In eight-and-twenty days / I'll make an old man of fourscore a child" (II.i.52–53). That's as good a description as any of what Mammon has been able to do to himself. He puffs out his pretentious lust to Dol Common, supposing her to be the sister of some great lord, by announcing that she's made him "the happiest man in Europe" (IV.i.112). Minutes later he cowers in a corner, desperately afraid of losing his hope, appealing for Subtle's forgiveness on the grounds that he didn't mean to do it: "Nay, good, dear father, / There was no' unchaste purpose" (IV.v.44–45). The boy of six years old has been caught red-handed with the great thing.

Sir Epicure's fraudulent manliness is an extreme case, but not so different in kind from what happens to the lesser fools. Dapper thinks he can prove himself a man by mounting the Faery Queen, but all he earns is a symbolic unmanning: he's dressed in Fortune's petticoat and thrown into her "privy lodgings" (III.v.79) where he remains (utterly forgotten) until Subtle rescues him by accident in the rush of housecleaning at the end of the play. Even then he's willing to submit to further indignities. "Down o' your knees and wriggle," says Face (V.iv.21); Dapper, still seeing the Faery Queen instead of a mere Dol Common, continues his training in obedience.

Face himself, for all of his brilliance in exploiting the disproportionate desires of other men, isn't as clearheaded as he pretends to be. Dol Common doesn't threaten him: he's used to dealing with whores. But Dame Pliant—nineteen years old, rich, naïve, and gorgeous—does. Even before he sees her, he anticipates trouble; there will be sexual competition from Subtle, he correctly surmises, and he tries to forestall a crisis by getting Subtle to agree to drawing lots for her. But once he's seen and touched her, he's vulnerable: " 'Fore God, / She is a delicate dabchick! I must have her" (IV.ii.59–60). He now asserts his privileged right by claiming that Subtle is too old to be Dame Pliant's lover, and he tries to buy off his rival with offers of compensation. This time, however, Face can't avoid becoming a member of the company of fools. At the first emergency he loses Dame Pliant to the "common cause" (IV.iii.76): that is, he agrees to let Subtle persuade her to practice Dol's trade. And in the end he loses her again—because he needs a prize big enough to buy Lovewit's indulgence.

You'd expect that Surly—the one skeptic in a world of believers—would salvage at least his manliness. But he's the victim of Jonson's most contemptuous rhetorical strategies. When Surly masquerades as the Spanish Don, he protects his identity but not his character. Face predicts that Dol will make him as "tame / As the poor blackbirds were i' the great frost" (III.iii.45–46). The great thing loses its masculine character if Dol does her work properly, "For she must milk his epididymis" (III.iii.22). Although it's Dame Pliant who eventually does the job, Surly's manhood is unquestionably deflated. "Your fortunes may make me a man," he says with foolish optimism after he's rescued her virtue by refusing to act out the whorehouse fantasy which Face and Subtle have obligingly made possible (IV.vi.13). Surly has the kind of integrity that hardens the arteries; he'd rather denounce his enemies than sleep with his friends. It's this "want of putting forward" (V.v.55) that prevents him from becoming the man he'd like to be. Integrity is a cold bedfellow if it's the only one you have, as Surly at last admits: "Must I needs cheat myself / With this same foolish vice of honesty!" (V.v.83–84). Sir Epicure and Surly are neatly if improbably paired at the end as the big losers in a game where too much faith is as disastrous as too little.

To counterpoise the sexual anarchy in which men lose their manliness, Jonson offers something far better than brutish pedantry or sulky resentment.[38] He offers an example of the man who is capable of loving with wit. As William Blissett remarks: "Lovewit? You have to hand

38. I borrow the hostile phrases from two of the most celebrated attacks on Jonson the playwright. Shaw dismissed Jonson as a "brutish pedant" in *Our Theatres in the Nineties* (London, 1932), II, 183; and Edmund Wilson's essay, "Morose Ben Jonson," *The Triple Thinkers,* rev. ed. (New York, 1948), pp. 213–232, includes the claim that many of the comic fools are "the creation of Jonson's own envy, stimulated, no doubt, from two sources—first, the grievance of the man of good birth unjustly deprived of his patrimony, and, second, the sulky resentment of the man who can only withhold against the man who can freely lavish" (pp. 224–225). Shaw's attack is not the sort that requires a rebuttal. Wilson's has been temperately but decisively answered by Jones A. Barish in his "Introduction" to *Ben Jonson: A Collection of Critical Essays* (Englewood Cliffs, N.J., 1963), pp. 9–13, a collection in which Wilson's essay is reprinted (pp. 60–74).

it to him." [39] Since, like everyone else in *The Alchemist,* Lovewit enters a world where months of hoping and years of preparation can be blown up in a single exhalation of alchemical smoke, his success should be measured by the things he doesn't lose. The list is a long one: Lovewit doesn't lose the woman he wants, his home, his butler, his reputation as a good neighbor, his record as a decent citizen, his integrity, his patience, his sense of humor. These achievements may fall short of the completeness required by Jonson's ideal, but that shouldn't tarnish them. Remarkably, somebody has survived the chaos of Jonsonian comedy with his manliness intact.

Epicoene is a play of surfaces. Moral questions matter less in this play than they generally do in Jonson, and manners account for more. [40] Given Jonson's view of human character, this is only a change in emphasis—and a pragmatic change at that, since *Epicoene* was first performed by a boys' company, the Children of her Majesty's Revels—but a change it remains nonetheless. Distortions of character in this play have less to do with inner compulsions than with outward affectations. Morose himself, determined as he is to find a wife who will speak seldom, softly, and only when spoken to, is ingenuously open in declaring exactly what it is he wants. The play as a whole makes sense only if you recognize that caricature can become art in the hands of a great satiric writer.

So it's artistically right that manliness comes closer to the surface in this play than in any of the other comedies. In the final scene, Morose the bridegroom confronts his wife and the party of wedding celebrants with a shocking announcement: "I am no man, ladies" (V.iv.40). For Morose, this is the emotional climax of a wedding day on which everything has gone wrong, and I think it should be played as a mo-

---

39. "The Venter Tripartite in *The Alchemist,*" *SEL,* VIII (1968), 334.

40. L. G. Salingar argues, in "Farce and Fashion in *The Silent Woman,*" *E&S* (1967), pp. 29–46, that Jonson's concerns in the play are principally social rather than strictly moral; hence his "sharp, animated, farcical portrayal of the discomforts and vexations of metropolitan life" (p. 44). This goes a long way toward locating the tone of the play, though I think Salingar overstresses the realism of Morose in claiming that Jonson constructs his character out of "qualities appropriate to comedy of manners rather than farce" (p. 39). As my argument will imply, I believe Morose to be a conflation of both modes.

ment of great (comic) solemnity. The declaration isn't literally true, of course; Morose wants out of this marriage in the worst way, and he's now willing to take Truewit's advice to "confess yourself but a man unable, and she will sue to be divorced first" (V.iii.159–160). But there's a real sense in which Morose has spent the whole day revealing his impotence. He can't prevent Truewit from entering his house armed with a post horn and a sermon of such length and cynicism as to blight anyone's honeymoon for weeks. He can't stop the parade of wits, braveries, fops, and musicians which parodies the spirit of the marriage festival. He can't escape from the noise even by retreating to his acoustically insulated attic and sitting on the rafters, next to his "treble ceilings" (I.i.167). He can't prevent the silent woman, whom he has found only after a troublesome and expensive search, from turning into a talkative shrew as soon as she's married him. When Morose takes center stage at the end of all this to affirm his impotence, he's virtually acting out the scenario proposed by his nephew, Dauphine: "Marry, God forbid, sir, that you should geld yourself to anger your wife" (IV.iv.9–10). The next step in Morose's degradation is his acceptance of cuckoldry; he brays with approval when Daw and La Foole both pretend they've been getting it on with his new wife. And if this isn't enough, Jonson hides the final unmanning in the plot. When all else fails, when even the claims of absolute impotence and manifest cuckoldry don't secure the desired divorce, Dauphine pulls off Epicoene's peruke and says with a flourish: "here is your release, sir; you have married a boy" (V.iv.181–182). The tacit annulment which accompanies this gesture is enough to reclaim the solitude which Morose thought he had lost, but not to restore the manliness he's publicly given away.

If *Epicoene* is a play about manners, it follows (for Jonson) that it's also a play about language. This connection is implicit throughout Jonson's critical program. "*Language* most shewes a man," he writes in *Discoveries;* "speake that I may see thee. It springs out of the most retired, and inmost parts of us, and is the Image of the Parent of it, the mind. No glasse renders a mans forme, or likenesse, so true as his speech." [41] Just as manners are the art of man as a social being, so lan-

---

41. *H & S,* VIII, 625.

guage is the intellectual art. The connection is explicit in the Jonsonian judgment on the "effeminate person" which I've already discussed: "Wheresoever, manners, and fashions are corrupted, Language is."

The corruptions of language in *Epicoene* have been studied with great sensitivity by Partridge and Barish—the first critics since Dryden to understand the richness of surface that makes this play remarkable.[42] If I borrow from Partridge's account of the sexually ambivalent imagery, or from Barish's explication of the range of prose styles in the play, it's because these are true to the letter and spirit of *Epicoene*. Like *Volpone* and *The Alchemist,* this play is a proving-ground for manliness; more conspicuously than either of them, it's a verbal universe in which the manly style is put to the test.

Partly because Jonson is a satirist, partly because he's Jonson, it's always easier to begin with negative examples. If you need a flagrant offender against the ideal of manliness, try Sir Amorous La Foole. Listen to him talk for five minutes and you'll find yourself thinking about Osric. He can't say good morning without putting on airs. There's a breathy quality in his every phrase, which he supposes will mark him as interested in other people, but which anyone who's not tone-deaf can identify as the puff of self-importance. "Good faith," he says as he enters Clerimont's house, "it is a fine lodging, almost as delicate a lodging as mine" (I.iv.4–5). Conversation is a difficult art for Sir Amorous, though he thinks it's easy, largely because he makes no effort to listen to what anyone else is saying while he composes himself for the next installment of his serial recitation. When Clerimont tells him that he's likely to be beaten up for the "doubtfulness o' your phrase" (I.iv.14), Sir Amorous continues gushing just as if the insult had missed him completely: "It should be extremely against my will, sir, if I contested with any man" (I.iv.17). Mention any of his relatives to Sir Amorous, and you've got to prepare yourself for the aria which begins, "They all come out of our house, the La Fooles o' the north, the La Fooles of the west, the La Fooles of the east and south" (I.iv.34–36), and which won't end until you've heard more than you can stand about heraldry, dining on pheasant, getting knighted in Ireland, or

---

42. See, respectively, Edward Partridge, *The Broken Compass: A Study of the Major Comedies of Ben Jonson* (New York, 1958), pp. 161–177; and Jonas A. Barish, *Ben Jonson and the Language of Prose Comedy* (Cambridge, Mass., 1960), pp. 147–186.

what to wear if you're traveling to Cadiz. When Sir Amorous bustles offstage—at last—Clerimont turns to Dauphine and says: "Did you ever hear such a wind-fucker as this?" (I.iv.69). I suppose it's a sense of decorum that prompts editors to gloss this by pointing out that the windhover used to be known by a racier name, though I think some injustice is done here both to the noble bird and to Gerard Manly Hopkins. For me, "wind-fucker" is perfect as it stands; there could be no better image of the frenetic, self-absorbed, and yet aimless verbal pumping which La Foole tries to pass off as real speech.

Sir Amorous, a brilliant demonstration of the principle that too much pickedness isn't manly, is only one voice in a crowd of linguistic offenders. Jack Daw's masquerade as the man of letters lurches into bathos whenever he reads his own poetry or talks about the books he obviously hasn't read. Captain Otter's invective at his wife's expense melts into servile apology the moment he's confronted with his princess. The Collegiate ladies, artlessly exercising their wits "with most masculine or rather hermaphroditical authority" (I.i.72–73), are imperfect usurpers of manliness. Jonson is observing and re-creating in the society of the play a state of affairs he found threatening: namely, a world where epicene manners are dominant, where distinctions between male and female have been subverted, where the voice of manliness (when it tries to speak) is likely to sound the false notes of foppery, stridency, or androgyny.[43]

So the only real competitors are Truewit (seconded by Clerimont, supported by Dauphine) and Morose. The first meeting between them is a verbal joust where nothing is at stake except manliness. Pretending to be the bearer of news from court, Truewit elbows his way into Morose's house and begins to talk, and talk, and talk. He's chosen the perfect strategy for evading Morose's angry interruptions: "Alas, sir. I am but a messenger," he can say with a shrug; "I but tell you what you must hear" (II.ii.46–47). Before this confrontation occurs, the spectators have been told that the one thing Morose can't abide is noise, and

43. In this sense it's true, as Barbara J. Baines and Mary C. Williams point out in "The Contemporary and Classical Antifeminist Tradition in Jonson's *Epicoene,*" *RenP* (1977), pp. 43–58, that the satiric vision of the play depends on patriarchal assumptions: female authority in marriage is an abhorrent inversion (as in the Otter marriage contract), a real man is master in his own household, and so on.

they've seen for themselves the imperious conversational tyranny whereby Morose dictates expansively to a servant who must answer him only in rigidly prescribed gestures. Truewit gains the dramatic, moral, and verbal initiative simply by ignoring all the silly rules by means of which Morose manages to intimidate everyone else. He enters as if on a delightful social mission, pretends that his antagonist's rage is good-natured badinage, and invents new reasons for talking each time he's challenged. When Morose tries to gain the upper hand by launching into a tirade—"If I had made an assassinate upon your father, vitiated your mother, ravished your sisters"—Truewit checks him smartly with: "I would kill you, sir. I would kill you if you had" (II.ii.41–43). It's the old match-up between a fighter who's feared because he lunges hungrily at the smell of blood, and one who's admired because he dances adroitly out of reach until he's in just the right position to strike.

When Truewit accuses Morose of wishing to "mount the marriage-bed like a town-bull" (III.v.39–40), he's making a real point about Morose's approach to social life as a whole. Just as Sir Amorous hopes to get by with nothing but manners to recommend him, so Morose tries to construct a life in which manners will be irrelevant. Truewit understands the shallowness of the one position, the indecency of the other. As a social being, Truewit occupies an acceptably human position between the butterfly and the bull; as a speaker of the language, he avoids both fluttering and bellowing. I've already said enough about La Foole's effeminate style to distinguish it from genuine speech. But the contrast between the styles of Truewit and Morose is a subtler one, and for this reason I recommend listening to their voices in turn as they talk about one of the great subjects of comedy: how to choose a wife.

Morose gets his turn first. Epicoene has been delivered to him without the agony of courtship, and the scouting reports assure him that she's exactly what he wants. All that remains is for him to inspect the merchandise, which he does in the following lines:

Very well done, Cutbeard. Give aside now a little and leave   *He goes about*
me to examine her condition and aptitude to my affection.   *her, and views*
She is exceeding fair and of a special good favor; a sweet   *her.*

composition or harmony of limbs; her temper of beauty has the true height of my blood. The knave hath exceedingly well fitted me without; I will now try her within. Come near, fair gentlewoman; let not my behavior seem rude, though unto you, being rare, it may haply appear strange. *She curtsies.* Nay, lady, you may speak, though Cutbeard and my man might not: for of all sounds only the sweet voice of a fair lady has the just length of mine ears. I beseech you, say, lady; out of the first fire of meeting eyes, they say, love is striken: do you feel any such motion suddenly shot into you from any part you see in me? Ha, lady?—*Curtsy.*

(II.v.13–26)

If language best shows a man, what it reveals here is a person unfit for human companionship. Having cut himself off from the outside world, Morose has only one standard of measurement left: himself. Epicoene's attractive appearance means only that she's "well fitted" to "me." This pronoun, often in the possessive form, dominates the passage like a *basso continuo*: "my affection," "my blood," "my behavior," "my man," "mine ears," and finally, "any part you see in me." Here's a bridegroom having a first look at his prospective wife, and what strikes him as worth talking about is himself—dissected into psychological attributes, personal idiosyncrasies, parts of the body. When he mentions her, it's in general terms: she's fine "without," so let's "try her within." To give the woman a body and a soul would at least salvage her dignity, but for Morose an outside and an inside will do. There's an emotional coarseness in this procedure—a coarseness made harsher by the sexual insensitivity which allows Morose to speak of inspecting his bride "within" while apparently missing the gynecological flavor of the remark. Even when he tries to be courtly—as in the clumsy allusion to the "fire of meeting eyes"—all Morose can do is arouse disgust. And the coarseness of sentiment is matched by a roughness of grammar; fragments of thought are dumped into Epicoene's ears without the civility of a progressive order or the courtesy of connectives to ease the pain of listening. Each item in this list of rhetorical blunders is a small indication of the speaker's poor judgment. Sensationally poor judgment, in fact, because the speaker is a bull who makes a complete inspection of his "heifer" (II.v.60) without being able to distinguish between female and male.

To illustrate the Truewit style I've chosen a speech on a roughly similar theme. Dauphine has just expressed admiration for Truewit's knowledge of women, and an eagerness to learn from the master. Truewit replies:

Yes, but you must leave to live i' your chamber, then, a month together, upon *Amadis de Gaul* or *Don Quixote,* as you are wont, and come abroad where the matter is frequent, to court, to tiltings, public shows and feasts, to plays, and church sometimes; thither they come to show their new tires too, to see and to be seen. In these places a man shall find whom to love, whom to play with, whom to touch once, whom to hold ever. The variety arrests his judgment. A wench to please a man comes not down dropping from the ceiling, as he lies on his back droning a tobacco pipe. He must go where she is.

(IV.i.50–59)

In Jonson's terms, this speaker merits praise for manly composition—for choosing the stones with care and fitting them precisely so that the structure as a whole stands square and strong. How can a man find a wench to please him? "He must go where she is." The concluding sentence is the central idea which both justifies and completes the knitting and binding of the speech as a whole. It's worth remembering that for Jonson the writer, language is like stone, not brick. When Truewit constructs a series, for example, the items needn't be mechanically regular. The final item in the series—"to court, to tiltings, public shows and feasts, to plays, and church sometimes"—has the offhand casualness of an afterthought, and the rightness of a perfectly relevant afterthought. What's true of the small units is true of the larger ones as well. The sentences in this speech range from the long and artfully subordinated introductory sequence, to the six monosyllables which announce the conclusion.

Despite the solidity of the construction, there's an easy naturalness in Truewit's speech. He achieves this conversational tone partly through sheer dexterity, as in the wonderful image of the bachelor droning on his pipe and expecting the woman of his dreams to drop from the ceiling. When you're as skillful a speaker as Truewit is, you can hide art with art. But there's an additional dramatic quality that contributes to the tone. Truewit isn't so much making a speech as talking to someone whose literary tastes and cultural preferences he knows well enough to make them part of the conversation.

Unlike Morose, Truewit is a man of superior judgment. He's fallible, of course, conspicuously fallible in being no better than anyone else at guessing the secret of Epicoene's gender. But he's the sharpest and most discerning judge of character in Jonson's London. While John Daw is collecting a reputation as a poet and a scholar, Truewit trusts his experience and his independence of mind to tell him that the man is a fool. As the trickster of the comedy, Truewit relies on a practiced eye for seeing in advance how the fools and gulls are going to behave. And his language is alive with the kind of intelligence that isn't afraid of deciding "whom to touch once, whom to hold ever."

Both Truewit's position in the play and his style are in one sense privileges conferred on him by Jonson; he's a discerning observer and speaker because Jonson wants him to be. Since *Epicoene* is a play of surfaces, privileges of this kind are permitted to characters who happen to be born with the right names. In the dedicatory letter which offers *Epicoene* to the attention of Sir Francis Stuart, Jonson describes the ability to exercise wise and impartial judgment as "that noblest and manliest virtue" (ll. 7–8). There's no good reason to blame Jonson for coveting this virtue himself, or for allowing Truewit to express it in manliness of speech.

The concluding action in each of Jonson's major comedies is provoked by a symbol of impotence. In *Volpone,* the magnifico is carried into the courtroom *"as impotent";* in *The Alchemist* a great explosion deflates the psychological priapism of Sir Epicure and his fellow-dreamers; in *Epicoene* Morose declares that he's not a man only to find that his wife isn't a woman. The radical paradigm of this pattern occurs in the puppet play at the end of *Bartholomew Fair.* Zeal-of-the-land Busy brings the puppet play to a halt with the last of his thundering denunciations: "Down with Dagon, down with Dagon!" (V.v.1). In the disputation which follows, the puritan's "main argument" against the miniature players "is that you are an abomination; for the male among you putteth on the apparel of the female, and the female of the male" (V.v.86–88). The perversity of the players is threatening to Busy's patriarchal notion of exact sexual walking. The Puppet Dionysius has a ready answer: "It is your old stale argument against the players, but it will not hold against the puppets; for we have neither male nor female amongst us" (V.v.91–93). And with that, *"The puppet takes up his garment"* (V.v.94.1) to reveal the absence of the great thing. Confronted by sexlessness, Busy knows he must resign: "I am confuted; the cause hath failed me," he admits. As for the puppet play, "Let it go on" (V.v.101–104).

I think that the puppet's derisive gesture is an accurate measurement of the relationship between *Bartholomew Fair* and the comedies which precede it. On the one hand, *Bartholomew Fair* expands and enriches what has gone before: the world of the fair is itself a hotbed of desire in which the competing interests and jargons of the vendors and seekers of pleasure are absurdly orchestrated. But *Bartholomew Fair* is also an outrageously comprehensive act of self-parody.[44] The Induction is a piece of writing which only someone with a whimsical awareness of his reputation for self-assertion could have produced. "These master-poets, they will ha' their own absurd courses," says the Stage-keeper by way of apology for an author who has "kicked me three or four times about the tiring-house, I thank him, for but offering to put in, with my experience" (ll. 23–26). The elaborately technical contract between playwright and audience which follows, solemnly read out by the Scrivener, is the closest thing in Jonson to a genuinely collective agreement. Like all such agreements, it follows a tacit admission that authoritative paternalism hasn't been an entirely blessed arrangement.

I'm not proposing that *Bartholomew Fair* be read as a Jonsonian recantation; the master-poet of the Induction, however he may have changed, "prays you to believe his ware is still the same" (l. 143). But there is in this play an uncharacteristic letting-go, a feeling for the world as a circus of appetites which won't be controlled by calling on principle. Zeal-of-the-land Busy typifies the new Jonsonian mood which is willing to say, "Let it go on."

The new mood is what allows Jonson to tolerate, forgive, and enjoy the two great spirits of the fair—Ursula the pig-woman and Bartholomew Cokes—both of whom transcend the distinction between male and female as surely as the puppets do. Ursula is technically female, and most of the references to her nourishing capacities make her explicitly maternal. To Overdo she's "the very womb and bed of enormity" (II.ii.101); to Knockem "she's mother o' the pigs" (II.v.70). But her femaleness defies heterosexual conventions; as Quarlous observes, embracing her would be "like falling into a whole shire of butter" (II.v.90). And when Ursula talks or drinks (as she does incessantly), her style is a parody of manliness: "two stone o' suet a day is my propor-

---

44. See Barish, *Prose Comedy,* pp. 212–215.

tion. I can but hold life and soul together with this (here's to you, Nightingale) and a whiff of tobacco, at most. Where's my pipe now?" (II.ii.77–80). Dripping with sweat and fat, presiding greedily over her passionately roasting pigs, Ursula stands for appetite at a level more primitive than sexual desire. She is the sexless goddess whose nature it is to offer the promise of limitless indulgence.

The ideal consumer in the fair world is Cokes, for whom every desire is a whim of the moment: each new hobbyhorse or ballad or gingerbread man eclipses whatever it was he bought last, so he buys them all. Though he's nineteen years old and comically tall, Cokes can't be trusted to visit the fair except in the company of his "dry nurse," Humphrey Wasp (I.v.45). Even so, his childishness makes him the easiest mark for every purveyor and snapper-up of trifles. The litany of items he loses includes his money, his cloak, his hat, his sword, his sister, his fiancée, but above all "my bargain o' hobbyhorses and gingerbread, which grieves me worst of all" (IV.ii.78–79). For an experienced cutpurse like Edgworth, Cokes is too innocent to be a challenge: "Purse? a man might cut out his kidneys, I think, and he never feel 'em, he is so earnest at the sport" (IV.ii.39–40). Like Ursula, Cokes represents asexual desire: in his case, the caprices which lead him from one trinket to the next keep him blissfully unaware of adult responsibilities. He's hopeless at defending either himself or his engagement to Grace Wellborn, but in his view of things, these are not matters worth caring about.

Despite the greasy sensuality of the one and the vacuous simplicity of the other, Ursula and Cokes are the spirits whom Jonson is indulgently celebrating in *Bartholomew Fair*. I'd be less confident about making this claim if it weren't for Michael Bogdanov's energetic and thoughtful production at the Young Vic in 1978.[45] The authority given to Ursula in this modern-dress interpretation was earned in part by the actress (Laura Cox). But it was supported by the mannishness of her costume, the dominant placing of her booth at the center of the set, and even by the icon which decorated the program—*"the pig's head with a large writing under it"* (III.ii.53–55)—appropriately modeled

45. The review by Gillian Reynolds in *Plays and Players,* Aug. 1978, pp. 16–17, does not do justice to the vitality of the production, but it includes accurate information and two fine photographs.

on Jonson's stage direction. Cokes, as played by Phillip Bowen, was a faultless fool. Ostentatiously overdressed for a circus, indelibly upper-class in language and manners, he danced through his disastrous day at the fair without for a moment losing his conviction that nothing could go wrong. In the puppet play at the close, Cokes's insipid commentary was greeted with laughter and applause of the kind you reserve for the artless comic who makes the best jokes when he doesn't understand them himself.

The representatives of manliness who encounter the desires of the fair get harsher treatment from Jonson than either his amorphously female provider or his promiscuously childish consumer. In various ways, Adam Overdo, Zeal-of-the-land Busy, Quarlous, Edgworth, and a handful of lesser competitors adopt the stances and the styles of manliness either to defend themselves against the perils of desire or to exploit the fair to their own advantage. Overdo, the justice who hopes to smell out enormities by visiting the fair in disguise, could have emerged for a younger Jonson as a voice of sanity, comparable to Lovewit or Truewit. But in *Bartholomew Fair* the "manliest virtue" of justice is helpless; the only person who places absolute trust in the warrant of Justice Overdo is a certifiable madman, Trouble-all.

Jonson the man may have felt that in *Bartholomew Fair* he had gone too far in allowing desire to dissolve the potency of the manly soul. If this is the case, then it appears he tried to set matters right by including the virtuous but clumsy character, Manly, in his next comedy, *The Devil is an Ass.*[46] But whatever his private thoughts, Jonson the comic artist was aware of the limits of manliness. In *Bartholomew Fair,* more completely than anywhere else, he understood that manliness, in a world of desire, can be self-defeating, fraudulent, ridiculous. That wasn't Jonson's only or final view of the matter, but it was the deepest and most frightening admission he would make.

---

46. See G. R. Hibbard, "Ben Jonson and Human Nature," *A Celebration of Ben Jonson,* ed. William Blissett et al. (Toronto, 1973), pp. 78–79.

Unfashioning the Man of Mode: A Comic Countergenre in Marston, Jonson, and Middleton

WILLIAM W. E. SLIGHTS

R OSALIE COLIE argued in the 1972 Una Lectures "that literary invention—both 'finding' and 'making'—in the Renaissance was largely generic, and that transfer of ancient values was largely in generic terms, accomplished by generic instruments and helps."[1] Assertions like this have opened a broad area of debate among students of Jacobean comedy about the generic forms and antiforms used by the playwrights to convey not just moral and aesthetic values but also political and financial ones relevant to the tough city world they lived in. The attempt to relate genre to human value systems has launched us into some very deep, sometimes murky water. Was John Marston really recommending traditional Christian humanist values at about the same time that Thomas Middleton was busily dismantling the happy communities of the New Comedy in order to expose their irrelevance to capitalist London?[2] And if two such divergent enterprises were thriv-

1. Rosalie L. Colie, *The Resources of Kind: Genre-Theory in the Renaissance,* ed. Barbara K. Lewalski (Berkeley, Calif., 1973), p. 17.

2. See George L. Geckle, *John Marston's Drama: Themes, Images, Sources* (Rutherford, N.J., 1980), and George E. Rowe, Jr., *Thomas Middleton and the New Comedy Tradition* (Lincoln, Neb., 1979).

ing under the sign of comedy, what was it in the new urban culture that generated those distinctive currents of comic turbulence that make this drama so challenging? As critics like Brian Gibbons, Alexander Leggatt, and George Rowe have realized, we need keener-edged "generic instruments" to locate and measure the real generative sources in Jacobean culture that made such radically new comic art possible.

The artist who works within a generic frame relies on both imitation and innovation. The creative atmosphere remains relatively clear so long as the literary models for imitation are remote and revered as authoritative. The Bible and a limited group of classical texts stand at just such a safe distance from medieval and sixteenth-century drama. The creative situation becomes more volatile as the models become more proximate and less sacred, as for instance sixteenth-century Italian short stories and Marlowe's plays stood in relation to Shakespeare's plays. Authors react strongly to a taste—or a distaste—for recent art. The result is a rapid fragmentation within formerly fixed genres. The pressure in the Jacobean theater to be current and innovative produced an enormous variety within comedy and even within a single author's output in the kind.

Generic commentators on English Renaissance drama have just begun to recognize that their acts of interpretation extend beyond the varieties of identifiable literary imitation into an entire network of cultural events and assumptions that conditioned those acts of imitation. Stephen Greenblatt has isolated a particularly significant development in Renaissance culture that is fully documented in its drama. He calls it "self-fashioning."[3] By the term he means the enactment of a conviction, apparently shared by men and women of all classes, that an individual might consciously set out to shape a coherent but many-sided self capable of controlling the explosion of social experiences in the courts, cities, and outposts of the known world. Greenblatt proposes that the ideal of the consciously fashioned self is a vital link between literature and other expressions of contemporary Renaissance culture. He sets out to interleave several highly influential texts of the period

3. Stephen Greenblatt, *Renaissance Self-Fashioning From More to Shakespeare* (Chicago, 1980).

from More to Shakespeare with nonliterary and preliterary accounts
of Renaissance attitudes toward power so that, in his words,

> we may interpret the interplay of their symbolic structures with those perceiv-
> able in the careers of their authors and in the larger social world as constituting
> a single, complex process of self-fashioning and, through this interpretation,
> come closer to understanding how literary and social identities were formed
> in this culture. That is, we are able to achieve a concrete apprehension of the
> consequences for human expression—for the "I"—of a specific form of pow-
> er, power at once localized in particular institutions—the court, the church,
> the colonial administration, the patriarchal family—and diffused in ideologi-
> cal structures of meaning, characteristic modes of expression, recurrent narra-
> tive patterns.
>
> (p.6)

The chronology of texts places *Tamburlaine, The Jew of Malta,* and
Othello at the end of Greenblatt's study. The popular drama provides
him a fitting climax because it is necessarily so responsive to the form
and pressure of the age and so deeply committed to the notion of the
invented self, the dramatis personae. For these reasons, if for no others, the generic study of Jacobean comedy will do well to take account
of the concept of self-fashioning that did so much to vitalize the persons, fictional and real, of the immediately preceding age.

Greenblatt's work on Tudor authors is extremely rich in its strategic
deployment of noncanonical texts to attack the problem of how historical and fictional personalities imitate one another in the prose and
nondramatic poetry of the period. Time and again he shows us exactly
which attitudes from a diplomatic communiqué or a martyr's death or
a soldier's diary are being mirrored in a Wyatt lyric or a Tyndale guide
to holy living. The book loses some of its precision, however, in dealing with dramatic texts, perhaps because the immense variety of
voices and dispositions represented in any given Renaissance dramatic
cast of characters can never be precisely identified with the individual
dramatist's sources and motives for imitation. There is, however, an
excellent starting point for a study of Jacobean satiric comedy in some
of Greenblatt's remarks about the self-fashioning urge among Marlowe's heroes. Commenting on the drive of these characters to define
themselves without regard for any institutional influence, Greenblatt
remarks that "the effect is to dissolve the structure of sacramental and

blood relations that normally determine identity in this period and to render the heroes virtually autochthonous, their names and identities given by no one but themselves" (p. 213). In this way Marlowe creates a form of heroic tragedy that glorifies self-fashioning, though it must be recognized that his self-made men expend their energies in tragic illusions. In the drama of the early seventeenth century, I believe we can detect a reaction against Marlowe's version of self-fashioning.

Of course a degree of skepticism about shaping the self is built into the drama from its beginnings, as the metatheatricians among us will be quick to point out. When Plautus's Mercury decides to make himself into, and hence to displace, Amphitryo, there can only be trouble. Likewise, in tragedy, Oedipus's efforts to shape his fate independently of divine forces are hideously self-destructive. But the more precise phenomenon of Protean identity-shifting does not become the special focus for moral and social comment until we reach the comedies of James's reign, where the gulls dissipate their energies in dreams and the tricksters eventually reveal the self-canceling, uncentered selves that so perfectly illustrate the seductive illusion of their own theatrical delights.

Jonson, Marston, and Middleton, each in his own terms, admit that a kind of power continues to reside in the self-fashioning urge that earlier had dominated the stage careers of Tamburlaine, Faustus, and Barabas, but that power nearly always stumbles comically into imitations of current fashions and passing fancies. Even such an apparently clear-sighted trickster as Volpone values ephemeral fantasies of power above all the substantial objects with which he imagines he has displaced the world's Prime Mover. In his world, where one enthusiasm instantly replaces another and where envious man competes to displace his rival, violence is an inevitable result. I wish to look with particular care at this violence and the forms of personal power-brokering that the Jacobean dramatists found ripe for comic exploitation.

I

The authors of *The Obedience of the Christian Man, The Book of the Governor, The Court of Civil Courtesy,* and other sixteenth-century handbooks of self-fashioning put great stock in linguistic artistry as a builder of personality and culture. Mercury, the quicksilver wit, and Proteus, the great shifter of identities, were often invoked as lords of language in both its creative and its potentially destructive aspects.[4] In his first stage comedy, *Every Man In His Humour,* Ben Jonson helped to transfer the high value of verbal artifice from the ages of Cicero and Quintillian to his own recalcitrant generation. Because the play traces the successful education of the aspiring poet, Lorenzo (Knowell, Junior, in the revised version), to its triumphant fulfillment, it can be seen as the legitimate child of the preceding Christian humanist age and of the forms of New Comedy, significantly anglicized by Jonson but still largely intact. *Every Man In* may well be the last major triumph for these values and forms on the English stage. I cannot, then, agree with Joel Altman when he claims that the ending of the play "marks the emergence of a new hero—the humane wit—capable of supposing himself other than he is in order to judge more equitably the problems of our common life."[5] For a line of enlightened disguisers such as Altman here proclaims we must look not to the tricksters of Jonson, Chapman, Middleton, or Brome but to a small group of heroines in Shakespeare's romantic comedies. The remaining voices of Jacobean, Caroline, and Restoration comedy generally pronounce a harsher sentence on masters of disguise and fast-talk, those two most easily stageable marks of a fashioned self.

Writing for an audience of Londoners surrounded by what he thought to be thoroughly debased models of linguistic self-fashioning, Ben Jonson located the ideal of poetic eloquence at a considerable remove from the world of his comedies. Although rhetorical grace and power were well within the reach of the speakers in his masques and poems, comedy required of him a more brazen style, one that could feelingly remind his audience how far they had strayed from the set forms of civilized expression. Even in his epistles and prologues, speaking in the voice of the author, Jonson became increasingly shrill over the course of his career. His artistic program—announced boldly

4. Compare Mercury as satiric presenter in Jonson's *Cynthia's Revels* and the account of Proteus in A. Bartlett Giamatti, "Proteus Unbound: Some Versions of the Sea God in the Renaissance," in *The Disciplines of Criticism,* ed. Peter Demetz et al. (New Haven, Conn., 1968), pp. 437–475.

5. Joel B. Altman, *The Tudor Play of Mind: Rhetorical Inquiry and the Development of Elizabethan Drama* (Berkeley, Calif., 1978), pp. 194–195.

in the comparative safety of his commonplace book—to make the poet the acknowledged legislator of the world, though it led to limited victories in the fictional courts of Gargaphie *(Cynthia's Revels)* and Augustan Rome *(Poetaster),* finds heavy going in the middle comedies. In *Volpone,* for example, poetry is at best a remote ideal, at worst the garbled mass of Lady Pol's misreadings. While in *Poetaster* there were strong purgatives to control what Thomas Dekker called "this ages phantasticknesse" and "the inflammation of vpstart fashions,"[6] the fantastic outpourings of Sir Epicure Mammon cannot be squelched by the bluff reformer, Pertinax Surly. Though Jonson makes Surly a fool, he is a fool such as Jonson recognized himself to be. There is more than a bit of the plain-speaking reformer's frustration in the carefully studied Jonson-persona that emerges from the *Conversations with Drummond.* He was fighting a losing battle against the language of the city magpie, that wizard at picking up flashy words of whatever value and promising new, easily accessible kinds of wealth, a currency formerly undreamed of by the masters of vast lands and courtly eloquence. Independence from fixed structures of society and personality, fed by racy forms of street language, became the pet illusion of the Win-the-Fight Littlewits, Herod Frappatores, Ephestian Quomodos, and other curiously named self-fashioners of the Jacobean stage.

However much he was the poet of the London gutter-cheat, Jonson began his stage career writing for and about those heirs of sixteenth-century humanism whom he chastized for squandering their enormous socioeconomic power. Their problems, as defined in Jonson's comedies, have less to do with man's timeless depravity than with a particular culture's glamorization of the urge to fashion the self into a power to be reckoned with—in the terms of seventeenth-century London, a gentleman. Abandoning those feudal, colonial, and ecclesiastical structures that fifty years before had given significance to every activity from scholarly drudgery to voyages of discovery, the new Londoner was scrambling to win a game that was comic for Jonson precisely because its stakes, by any time-tested standard, were so low. Once a Kastrill had moved to the city and learned to conduct his quar-

6. See Dekker's mock-manual of verbal and sartorial gallantry, *The Gul's Horne-booke,* in *The Non-Dramatic Works of Thomas Dekker,* 5 vols. (1885; rpt. New York, 1963), II, 214.

rels according to the latest fashion, what would he have, even if he were not bilked of his entire inheritance?

In the comedies, then, Jonson challenges the wisdom of those champions of culture who for years had been divesting themselves of family estates in order to follow the fashions of Elizabeth's and then James's court. As Lawrence Stone points out in his analysis of the English aristocracy in crisis,

Under Elizabeth their capital holdings in land and their incomes deteriorated, both relatively and absolutely, as a result of which respect for their titles and their authority was diminished. . . . The cure for this financial crisis was sought in vigorous reorganization and exploitation of the estates which were left, the result of which was to contribute to this second and graver crisis, the crisis of confidence which came to a head in the reign of Charles I.[7]

Certainly "confidence" would be the last word to describe an audience's attitude toward one such aristocrat in Jonson's *Epicoene,* Sir Amorous La-Foole. In his predictably extravagant style he boasts of a career that, thirty years earlier, would have seemed far less foolish as a way to cut a fine figure in courtly London, "the eye o' the land."

We are as ancient a family, as any is in *Europe*—but I my selfe am descended lineally of the *french* LA-FOOLES—and, wee doe beare for our coate *Yellow,* or *Or,* checker'd *Azure,* and *Gules,* and some three or foure colours more, which is a very noted coate, and has, some-times, beene solemnely worne by diuers nobilitie of our house—but let that goe, antiquitie is not respected now. . . . I haue beene a mad wag, in my time, and haue spent some crownes since I was a page in court, to my lord LOFTY, and after, my ladies gentleman-vsher, who got mee knighted in *Ireland,* since it pleas'd my elder brother to die—I had as faire a gold ierkin on that day, as any was worne in the *Iland*-voyage, or at *Caliz,* none disprais'd, and I came ouer in it hither, show'd my selfe to my friends, in court, and after went downe to my tenants, in the countrey, and suruai'd my lands, let new leases, tooke their money, spent it in the eye o' the land here, vpon ladies—and now I can take vp at my pleasure.[8]

(I.iv.39–68)

7. Lawrence Stone, *The Crisis of the Aristocracy, 1558–1641* (Oxford, 1965), p. 164.

8. Throughout I have used Herford and Simpson's *Ben Jonson* (Oxford, 1925–1952).

Despite a few hair-raising lapses like the obliging withdrawal of his elder brother from this life, La-Foole has outlined the courtly ideal of a generation earlier: noble genealogy, foreign soldiering, conspicuous consumption, estates leased for ready money, attendance at court, easy credit. La-Foole's degenerate and silly version of self-fashioning is sneered at by Jonson's young gallants, Clerimont and Dauphine, who simply exploit the fool's lavish banquet to make a painful charivari for Morose. Though they condescend to the would-be courtier, their own pastimes are no less trivial (I.i.23–41), the values behind their own acts of self-fashioning no sounder than those of La-Foole. Clerimont, Dauphine, and Truewit unconsciously imitate the petty rivalry between La-Foole and Jack Daw as each tries to gain advantage of the other two by usurping their imagined positions of power. Such acts of displacement through improvisation—though admittedly more suavely executed—were practiced regularly in the heyday of self-fashioning at Elizabeth's court. By having his characters improvise at cross-purposes to achieve the goal of tormenting Morose into awarding his nephew an inheritance, Jonson generates an elaborate dramatic action at the conscious expense of audience sympathy for his frenetic and self-absorbed characters. Truewit, for example, tries to dissuade Morose from marrying and hence disinheriting Dauphine, but this act of diplomacy does more to show off his own pyrotechnic wit than to aid his friend. Indeed, Truewit almost wrecks Dauphine's secret scheme to marry Morose off to a reputedly silent woman who later proves to be neither silent nor a woman. Clerimont, the third gallant, becomes the sole object of affection for that band of "perfect courtier[s]," the Collegiate Ladies, who, acting "in aemulation of one another, doe all . . . things alike" (V.ii.32–33; IV.vi.68–69).

In *Epicoene* we can observe Jonson's hostile but humorous response to a mode of self-fashioning that had made the entire city effeminate and effete, in his view. The constant joking about uncertain sexual identities creates a queasiness that had its origins and chief institutional model in the royal court. As Stone says, "It was the Court that led the fashion, and a philandering queen followed by a homosexual king no doubt gave an added incentive to the movement: both Elizabeth and James had an eye for the well-dressed young man"[8] (p. 564). The movement toward courtly and aristocratic licentiousness became a prime target for stage satirists during the reign of James. They mocked not only the excesses of courtly pretenders, but the basic ideal of self-fashioning at all levels of society.

Nowhere is the folly of a self-fashioning, theatrical conception of the self so clearly realized as in the rise and fall of Jonson's Venetian magnifico. Volpone rehearses so diligently to "cocker vp [his] *genius*" for improvisation that he displaces a loyal son from his father's last testament and a jealous husband from his closely guarded wife. Both acts of displacement result in violent beatings as men battle to defend their honor and, more important, their property. The brilliance of Volpone's theatrical skill in empathizing with, imitating, and displacing others receives the ultimate praise in Mosca's metaphysical conundrum after the mountebank scene:

> VOLPONE
> But, were they gull'd
> With a beliefe, that I was SCOTO?
> MOSCA
> Sir,
> SCOTO himselfe could hardly haue distinguish'd!

(II.iv.34–36)

But for Jonson the actor's skill is finally self-canceling and produces a man "forgetfull of himselfe" because his integrity has been so fragmented by constant revision in the self-fashioning process that he has no central, believable identity. Stepping back critically from his own art in *Discoveries,* Jonson writes:

> I *haue* considered, our whole life is like a *Play:* wherein every man, forgetfull of himselfe, is in travaile with expression of another. Nay, wee so insist in imitating others, as wee cannot (when it is necessary) returne to our selves: like Children, that imitate the vices of *Stammerers* so long, till at last they become such; and make the habit to another nature, as it is never forgotten.

(ll. 1093–1099)

The elements of willful mimicry and self-conscious performance, present in comedy from earliest times,[9] become the most deeply ironic moral perspective in Jacobean comedy and its most persistent generic characteristic. In this drama the ingenuity of the "quicksilver wit" and

---

9. See Leo Salingar, *Shakespeare and the Traditions of Comedy* (Cambridge, Eng., 1974), pp. 1–27.

the fine manners of the fop are widely suspect, as are all vestiges of *sprezzatura* in Protestant England.[10] Jonson's strategy at the end of *Volpone* is to turn the audience against the facile trickster, however distressing that may be after we have taken such delight in his fantastic improvisations. As Greenblatt argues in his essay on "The False Ending in *Volpone*," the trickster's cynical triumph in the fourth-act courtroom scene is more than the audience's comic sensibility can endure. The truly satisfying end is to see Volpone dismissed from the mirror world of illusion that he has created.[11]

The pressure to keep performing in a world of self-proclaiming illusion is no less intense for the triumvirate of tricksters in *The Alchemist* than it had been for Volpone and Mosca. Their jealous infighting reflects a larger struggle to establish fresh identities with which to control both the law and their fellow outlaws. What the blunt reformer, Surly, is unable to affect, is finally accomplished by the ironic workings of the characters' own self-canceling identities. The struggle for power within this microcommonwealth—as in the Commonwealth at large—is decided not by the Protean wit but by the noncomic, everyday man, Lovewit, who is a spectator of the human scene. As Jonson commented in another context, someone has to stand apart and look "downe on the Stage of the world, and [condemn] the Play of *Fortune*. For though the most be Players, some must be *Spectators*" (*Discoveries*, ll. 1107–1109). The real value of his art exists for those who can observe it steadfastly from a distance and judge correctly the futility of the ideal of self-fashioning that it mocks.

II

If Jonson took his writing seriously as an instrument for gaining moral perspective on the world, he also understood that comedy written for his age had to be partly self-mocking. In his personal life he knew how to fashion a tough, abrasive image of himself, but it was al-

10. The premium placed on industry in the period caused the courtly ideal to be regarded as "a kind of aesthetic magic" or "cult of the 'too easy.' " See Greenblatt, *Self-Fashioning*, p. 190.

11. Stephen Greenblatt, "The False Ending in *Volpone*," *JEGP*, LXXV (1976), 90–104. See also Alexander Leggatt, "The Suicide of Volpone," *UTQ*, XXXIX (1969), 19–32.

ways tinged with a humorous, self-deprecating irony, as in the verbal self-portrait of his "mountaine belly" and "rockie face" or in the mock-heroically conceived military skirmishes that raged around his big toe one memorable night.[12] In his plays, characters blithely mutilate poetic grace and truth. They exercise specious power through mimicry, and they stretch to its limits the world of fantasy that he created for them to bustle in.

The life and comic art of Jonson's professed *"amico . . . candido et cordato,"* John Marston, also helped to define the limits of self-fashioning for the Jacobean age.[13] Marston emerges from history as an odd blend of orthodox moralist and scofflaw. He drew heavily on moral emblems and apothegms in his plays, and he always exacted punishment and often full repentance from transgressors in his comedies. At the same time, he was jailed twice for satirizing James and his court before he was apparently forced to take orders and retire from the stage to a remote parish in Hampshire.[14] Marston made a noteworthy, brief career of creating satiric personae only to subvert them in narratives of retiring or disappearing selves. Although he studied to enter his father's profession, the law, he used his experience in the Middle Temple mainly to cultivate a sharply anti-authoritarian wit. His satiric persona from *The Scourge of Villanie,* W. Kinsayder, was sufficiently conspicuous in the last years of Elizabeth's reign to draw fire from several rival poets. Not satisfied with the persona of the foul-mouthed defiler of fashionable opinion, Marston attacked two characters of this very sort, Quadratus and Lampatho Doria, in his early comedy *What You Will.* Their coarse vituperations seem far in excess of what would be required to denounce such lightweight folly as that of Simplicus Faber and the "Frenchyfied" fop, Sir Laverdure. The latter is no more or less silly than Jonson's La-Foole or Etherege's man of mode, Sir Fopling Flutter. He is, however, perceived as a threat to the stability of the play's society because he may captivate the good Mistress Celia, whose husband has apparently been drowned on some foreign venture. A ri-

12. See *"My Picture Left in Scotland,"* from *Under-wood,* and *Conversations with Drummond,* ll. 322–324.

13. The Latin phrase is from the dedication to *The Malcontent.*

14. See Philip Finkelpearl, *John Marston of the Middle Temple: An Elizabethan Dramatist in His Social Setting* (Cambridge, Mass., 1969), pp. 256–258.

val for the supposed widow's hand conspires to fashion the local per-
fumer into a copy of the missing husband, Albano, in order to scare off
the competition. The layers of displacement by mimesis merge into
chaos when the real Albano reappears and, unable to impress the
world of fakes with his genuine identity, stutters in comic frustration:

> I was her husband and was call'd *Albano* before I was drown'd, but now after
> my resurrection I am I know not what indeede brothers, and indeede sisters
> and indeede wife I am: *What you will,* do'st thou laugh, dost thou ge, ge, ge,
> gerne; a p, p, p, perfumer, a fiddler, *a Diabalo, matre de Dios,* lle f, f, f, firk
> you by the Lord now, now I will.[15]

The speaker is a comic affront to anyone raised on classical and Renaissance rhetoric as he gives bumbling testimony that genuine identity
counts for nothing in a world of fraudulent self-fashioners, experts in
"slie dissemblance" (II, 259). Jonson later went on to explore the same
ironic source of civilization's discontents in *The Devil is an Ass,* where
a genuine devil can command no recognition or respect in Jonson's
world of scheming engineers and supersubtle adulterers. Indeed, fictions that stress lost personality and radical inconsistency of character
are legion in the comedy of the Jacobean period. Time after time we
find playwrights like Marston and Middleton stressing inauthenticity
and discontinuity of character in order to question the efficacy of
comic transformation in a society where the ideal of self-fashioning
has degenerated into foppishness and sharp practice.

It is not surprising, then, that Marston chooses fictions of self-oblit-
eration for his two most successful comedies, the pair that most directly reflects on the fops and manipulators who found a safe haven in
the transitional court of the early seventeenth century. The heroes of
The Malcontent and *The Fawn* go underground to expose the folly of a
court shot through with superficial imitation, and both men learn
something about themselves in the process. Malevole, the malcontent,
is a useful persona for the prince who must fight his way back from en-
forced retirement, a fight that Albano in *What You Will* barely won
and that Kinsayder/Marston apparently lost. Malevole's imitation of

---

15. *The Plays of John Marston,* ed. H. Harvey Wood, 3 vols. (Edinburgh, 1934–1939),
II, 283. References to this nonlineated text are by volume and page number.

decadence and violence is so convincing that it threatens at times to upset the generic structure of the play, which is designated on the 1604 title page as *"Tragiecomedia."* His antithesis, the persona of the fawning cur assumed by Duke Hercules in *The Fawn,* attacks the corrupt court of Gonzalo along its soft underbelly. Nymphodoro, the resident courtly lecher who would so perfectly imitate all courtiers as to claim all their amorous victories for himself, boasts a current string of "threescore and nine ladies" (I.ii.55) and a talent for totally flexible affectation:

> For mine own part, I am a perfect Ovidian, and can with him affect all. If she be a virgin of a modest eye, shamefac'd, temperate aspect, her very modesty inflames me, her sober blushes fires me. If I behold a wanton, pretty, courtly, petulant ape, I am extremely in love with her, because she is not clownishly rude, and that she assures her lover of no ignorant, dull, unmoving Venus. Be she sourly severe, I think she wittily counterfeits, and I loue her for her wit.[16]
>
> (III.i.27–35)

And so on through the catalog of all sizes, manners, and ages of women. Truly a man for all ladies, but, as inevitably turns out, for none. The man simply dares not compete with his invented self. Though Nymphodoro boasts, "I count all in the way of honor" (III.i.66), the fountainhead of foolish honor is the Duke himself, who witlessly proclaims the time and place where his daughter and young Tiberio may meet to violate the Duke's "panderiz'd" honor (III.i.412). Marston's play amply prepares the way for Gervase Markham's lament for a lost age of genuine nobility, written in the closing years of James's reign:

> Tell the phantasticke Mimmickes of honour, those which are caried away with euery shadow of fauour or fashion, that neuer fixe vpon any thing that is constant or serious; that alwaies hunt after vanities, and thinke no exercise in Armes so meritorious, as tossing a Shyttelwike: tell them the study of vaine things is a toilesome Idlenesse, and a painfull Folly . . . and belieue it, there is nothing more dishonourable or daungerous either to Court or Commonwealth, then an Ignorant great one.[17]

Philip Finkelpearl has made a convincing case for the particular "Ignorant great one" of Marston's *The Fawn* being none other than James I

---

16. *The Fawn,* ed. Gerald A. Smith (Lincoln, Neb., 1965).
17. Gervase Markham, *Honour His Perfection* (London, 1624), p. 39.

of England.[18] No wonder Marston had to pull a disappearing act of his own. He was gouging too deep to be regarded as the loyal and entertaining opposition.

Marston's last comedy, *The Dutch Courtesan,* deserves to be looked at more closely than it has been, both for its view of a culture becoming disenchanted with the idea of self-fashioning and as a challenge to our usual ideas of comedy. He makes his work highly culture-specific in time and place. The theological, courtly, and mercantile issues of the day mentioned in the play range in seriousness from debates over free will and conscience to courtly kissing and "spigott-frigging," which sounds terrible but actually has to do with brewers who, in the words of Lear's Fool, "mar their malt with water." The Cocledemoy/ Mulligrub underplot locates the action within a moral topography specific to London, naming the most notorious places of sin (Clerkenwell, Cheapside, the Paris Gardens) and punishment (Bridewell, Newgate). The French sources of narrative (Nicholas de Montreulx's *Les Bergeries de Juliette*) and sentiment (Montaigne's *Essais* in Florio's translation) are completely readjusted to an urban society that is making its rules ad hoc, in accordance with the lessons of immediate experience, and without reference to any model of self-fashioning in James's or any other court.

Why, one wonders, is such an aggressively English play of the early Jacobean period named *The Dutch Courtesan*? The foreign villainess, however base her morals, is decidedly no ordinary English tart. Because Franceschina is Dutch, her accent guarantees a laugh right from her first line ("O mine aderliver love, vat sall me do to requit dis your mush affection?" [I.ii.79–80]), and she is Dutch, perhaps, because Marston, like his hero, "would have married men love the stews as Englishmen lov'd the Low Countries: wish war should be maintain'd there lest it should come home to their own doors" (I.i.62–65).[19] This strategic, early linking of sexual politics with the preceding monarch's foreign policy of battling the Spanish on Dutch soil rather than at home introduces the particularly Marstonian problematics of what Greenblatt calls "a specific form of power, power at once localized in particular institutions—the court, the church, the colonial administra-

18. Finkelpearl, pp. 220–237.
19. *The Dutch Courtesan,* ed. M. L. Wine (Lincoln, Neb., 1965).

tion, the patriarchal family—and diffused in ideological structures of meaning, characteristic modes of expression, recurrent narrative patterns" (*Self-Fashioning,* p. 6). The Dutch courtesan is a powerful fallen woman, a "fair devil" (V.iii.44) who gets her "living by the curse of man, the sweat of [her] brow" for "every man must follow his trade, and every woman her occupation" (I.i.93–95). The phrase sardonically links her with the countercourtly, Puritan value of industry so central to the Renaissance sense of self. As the *Homilie Against Idlenesse* admonished:

God did cast [man] out of paradise into this wofull vale of misery, enioyning hym to labour the ground that he was taken out of, and to eate his breade in the sweate of hys face all the dayes of hys life. It is the appointment and will of God, that euery man . . . shoulde giue him selfe to some honest and godly exercise and labour.[20]

Franceschina's labors are not women's curse for Eve's transgression but the lucrative reenactment of that transgression. Her brand of Puritanism is associated with what Englishmen regarded as the worst excesses of the evangelical Lowlands, embodied in the Family of Love sect to which the bawd Mary Faugh and the "spigott-frigging" tapster Mulligrub belong.[21] The Familists had earned a reputation among defenders of established morality both for sexual promiscuity and outlandish moral self-righteousness. It would seem that a bizarre inversion was taking place on the Jacobean stage as the idle Virgin of Rome receded as the chief threat to society and the hardworking Protestant whore of Holland emerged in that role.

In any case, Marston presents lust as an alien force to be controlled by native authority. The self-styled "wise man" (II.i.94), Malhereux, violently proclaims such moral authority, but it crumbles on his first encounter with the seductress. Sexual repression proves in his case to be as foreign and potentially murderous as imported libertinism. Malhereux plots with the Dutch courtesan to murder his friend—and her ex-lover—Freevil. The latter then pretends to have been killed by the

---

20. *The Seconde Tome of Homilies* (London, 1595), sig. Hh5 ʳᵛ

21. See Wine's note on I.i.139–140 and also Thomas Middleton's spoof on the Familists in *The Family of Love.*

conspirators, thus removing himself from the scene in yet another version of Marston's disappearing reformers. In doing so, Freevil effectively increases the power of his moral authority. He now has the power to become invisible, the victim of a violent crime that calls out for punishment of the lust-ridden Malhereux. Freevil can die, be mourned, cause his friend to repent, and then come back to marry the heavenly Beatrice. His is the positive version of the self-cancellation orchestrated by Volpone and by Middleton's equally unfortunate trickster, Quomodo. But there are problems in Marston's moral vision. The violence of lust and also its remedy exceed what is customary in stage comedy. The audience must listen patiently to the auricular confession of a relatively unimaginative sinner. Finally, the self-righteous but duplicitous reformer makes an unattractive comic hero. A meticulous self-fashioner who casts off his whore, tries his friend's chastity with the whore's wiles, and then gloats over contrasting his own holy marriage with his friend's lustful torments, simply lacks the integrity demanded of reformers in any age.

The problems with *The Dutch Courtesan* result from a kind of overflow of resentment generated in the defense of a specific cultural value—chastity in this case. Greenblatt describes the recoil effect of this kind of deep-seated cultural defensiveness: "The power generated to attack the alien in the name of the authority is produced in excess and threatens the authority it sets out to defend" (*Self-Fashioning*, p. 9). Because Marston frequently combines reflexive authoritarian satire with outrageous libertine sentiments, he actually undercuts the Protestant critique of sexual pleasure that he evidently set out to uphold. His overreaction to a perceived cultural threat may account for the sense of many good readers that Marston loses control of his moral vehicle, delighting in what he deplores. After all, what I have called the problematics of Marston are also the special signature of his most notable triumphs in the form of comedy. However disconcerting his conscious disregard for sexual and linguistic taboos, the quality of his comic irony is often similar to that of Swift's *Modest Proposal*.

If Marston's moral vision seems to us blurred at times, it may be because he is a product, as well as a would-be reformer, of seventeenth-century English culture, and we are not. He is violently opposed to the artificial conception of self that characterizes the moral snobs of his society, censorious "wise men" like Malhereux. At the same time, he harbors a view of morality closely resembling the Renaissance conception of diplomacy and trade that "posited a severely limited substance (power or wealth [and we might add virtue]) and hence assumed that the gain of one party is inevitably the loss of the other" (*Self-Fashioning*, p. 141). To many modern ears, the result is a sporadic, testy, and often unconvincing vindication of creaky old saws like: "Providence all wicked art o'ertops" (*The Dutch Courtesan*, IV.iv.95). Finally, there is little room in Marston's plays for what Altman calls "The Tudor play of mind." The rather nasty and brutish lessons of experience replace the flexibility of self available earlier to a courtier-poet like Wyatt or even to a corrupt diplomat like Marlowe's Barabas. Marston himself worked in an arena of public morality as unforgiving in its way as the entertainment world of the bear pits. Whether in his contention with rivals like Jonson or with ecclesiastical and civil authorities, Marston tried to fight against the ideal of the fashioned self, but some extremely powerful people apparently resented his satire and saw him retired from the stage after only ten productive years.

III

In the highly power-conscious entertainment circles of Jacobean London, Thomas Middleton seems to have found it expedient to maintain a lower personal profile than Marston had. Though he acknowledged authorship of his plays, they are marked by an extreme version of authorial evasiveness.[22] Not only was Middleton, so far as we know, never harassed or imprisoned by the authorities, he was appointed city chronologer in 1620 and received sizable stipends for writing and producing public pageants. The pageants are closely linked with the power struggles of James's and Charles's reigns and have too often been placed in the "You-Had-to-Have-Been-There" section of scholarly inquiry. The comedies have remained more accessible, at least within the academy, although they are just as closely tied to Jacobean London as the pageants.

A critical problem with Middleton's comedies, and one that has been only half-perceived, is knowing what the author wants us to

22. Dorothy M. Farr, *Thomas Middleton and the Drama of Realism* (London, 1973), p. 1.

make of the witty and unscrupulous tricksters who invariably get the lead roles in these plays. Is their keen interest in self-image-making their forte or their flaw? Middleton himself is at least partly responsible for the critical uncertainty, as his personal views remain largely unknown. Still, a pattern begins to emerge in the repeated failure of his Follywits and Easys to pull off the traditional comic hero's trick of "supposing himself other than he is in order to judge more equitably the problems of our common life."[23] These communal heroes, though they occasionally copy the mythic Proteus's talent for external transformation, never achieve his genius for fostering civic cohesiveness.

    Proteus was a familiar-enough figure in Renaissance drama, but Middleton uses the legend for a special purpose. He goes beyond Jonson's mockery of Volpone's Protean boasting to Celia that he can transform himself into any Ovidian shape. Instead, Middleton glances ironically at an earlier interpretation of Proteus as resolver of civilization's tensions. According to A. Bartlett Giamatti,

The Renaissance principle of tolerance, of amending oneself to the necessities of life, of adapting oneself to one's sense of the contingencies in things, underlies the proper government of the city of man. And Proteus, whose various forms signify the wise man's ability to influence men for the good, is a proper figure for this principle of flexible civility.[24]

A successful statesman such as Thomas More fully exemplified this "principle of flexible civility" as he precariously balanced criticism with compliment amid the greatest aggregations of power in Europe. But principled tolerance and peaceful coexistence are never achieved by Middleton's comic characters, who, instead, see only "the contingencies in things," never their constant truths. While Jonson and Marston attack the fundamental idea of self-fashioning, Middleton attacks only those characters who would fashion, or be fashioned by, others.

    The five gallants of Middleton's play by that name gather passively around Fitsgrave in Act V waiting to be assigned armorial devices that

---

23. Altman, p. 195. Although Altman does not use the phrase to describe Middleton's plays, it identifies an important set of assumptions behind much English Renaissance comedy.

24. *The Disciplines of Criticism*, pp. 471–472.

they hope will socially establish themselves and their heirs but that actually serve only to expose their blockishness, immoral excesses, and poor Latin. This is not exciting dramaturgy, but it makes the point that for Middleton folly means substituting mere response to contingency for any self-initiated purpose. The young hero of *Michaelmas Term,* Richard Easy, is definitely the gull until Quomodo's wife is attracted to him and shows him how easily he has let himself be fashioned by the unscrupulous cloth merchant and his cronies. Middleton casts the concept of the fashioned self into a commercial context in which Easy, a landed gallant from Essex, instantly demands a "gentleman's credit in town" (II.iii.159).[25] The word "credit" here and elsewhere in the play means the credence that one can generate in his ability to repay loans, but Middleton also uses it in its more general sense of "personal influence based on the confidence of others; power derived from character or reputation."[26] Easy's reputation as a well-to-do landed heir has preceded him to London, but his *lack* of the other key element, character, is clearly established by his eagerness to fit the fashionable mold defined by Quomodo's disguised assistant, Shortyard: "There's a kind of bold grace expected throughout all the parts of a gentleman. . . . [A] man must not so much as spit but within line and fashion" (II.i.91–93). One of the things that Easy is encouraged to do "for fashion's sake" (II.iii.246–247) is to countersign a rigged bond that leads him to forfeit his lands to Quomodo. Easy's willingness to follow the fashion rather than fashioning himself into a resilient city-dweller has lost him his credit with lenders and also with Middleton's audience. By taking it easy, as his name implies, he forfeits the personal power entailed in Middleton's word "credit," at least until Thomasine takes pity on him and gives him the evidence he needs to control his own life.

The most basic kinds of economic and emotional self-control are missing in the majority of Middleton's characters and in none so completely as Allwit from *A Chaste Maid in Cheapside.* He is not a person at all but a figurehead that hangs onto a family institution founded and supported, financially and sexually, by Sir Walter Whorehound. Allwit

25. *Michaelmas Term,* ed. Richard Levin (Lincoln, Neb., 1966).
26. *OED,* definition 6.

is initially delighted to remain a nonentity, praising his benefactor and drinking his wine.

> The Founders come to Towne . . .
> . . . .
> I thanke him, h'as maintain'd my House this ten yeeres,
> Not onely keepes my Wife, but a keepes me,
> And all my Family, I am at his Table,
> He get me all my Children, and payes the Nurse,
> Monthly, or weekely, puts me to nothing,
> Rent, nor Church duties, not so much as the Scavenger,
> The happiest state that ever Man was borne to.[27]
>
> (I.ii.12–22)

Ironically, this personal cipher is morally enraged when Sir Walter repents his adulterous ways and withdraws support from the fools' paradise. Middleton thus neatly demonstrates how easily standard morality rushes in to fill the vacuum left by the "Founder" or creator of those indifferent to self-fashioning.

In Middleton's world of comedy the bonds of family, land, and law are systematically broken in men's scramble to adopt whatever contingent face will produce immediate profit. His characters take very seriously the ironically intended advice of Philibert de Vienne's *Philosopher at Court,* who recommends "some understanding of the state and affayers of the Realme, as of warres, of practizes, of marchandice, and howe we maye honestly robbe, deceyue, and make our best profite."[28] A century after these sentiments were translated into English, as least one English author, Richard Head, was still complaining that "these *Protei* of this loose age can turn themselves into any shape, so that the conversion of the form will produce any profit or advantage.'[29]

27. *A Chaste Maid in Cheapside,* ed. Charles Barber (Berkeley, Calif., 1969).

28. Philibert de Vienne, *Le philosophe de court* (1547), trans. George North, *The Philosopher at Court* (London, 1575), p. 30. Daniel Javitch has argued that the translator failed to see Philibert's persistent irony because the Elizabethans were so bemused by the forms of courtliness that, unlike the original French author, they had no comic distance on their ethic of deviousness. See "*The Philosopher at Court:* A French Satire Misunderstood," *CL,* XXIII (1971), 97–124.

29. Richard Head [?], *Proteus Redivius: Or the Art of Wheedling, or Insinuation* (London, 1675), p. 5.

Middleton's Quomodo handily accumulates the "profit" spoken of by Philibert and Head, but he so distrusts the socially stabilizing bonds of marital fidelity and family inheritance that, like Volpone, he advertises his own death, secretly witnesses his own betrayal, and loses everything. Quomodo's basic skepticism about inheritances ("cozenage in the father wheels about to folly in the son" [IV.i.83–84]) troubles even such honest characters as the goldsmith Yellowhammer *(A Chaste Maid)* and Sir Bounteous Progress *(A Mad World)*, both of whom fear the spendthrift tendencies of youth. The latter case is especially relevant to our concerns with comedy, since it highlights the differences between Middleton's views of self-fashioning and comic craftiness, and those of Jonson and Marston. The hero of *A Mad World, My Masters,* Richard Follywit, is denied his uncle's inheritance because that ordinarily generous old man suspects that his nephew is a dull-witted prodigal who would squander any money he got. Through a series of disguises and deceptions, Follywit established his credit with his uncle as a genuinely flexible and inventive trickster. Whereas such tricksters are uniformly *dis*credited in Jonson's and Marston's comedies, Middleton rewards his, thereby implicitly approving the comic formula that has enlisted the sympathies of Western audiences ever since Odysseus pulled the wool over the Cyclops's eye. Follywit's slightly awkward execution of his final trick (he is caught when his uncle Bounteous's stolen alarm-watch goes off in his pocket and when his virgin bride turns out to be Bounteous's cast-off whore) adds another dimension to Middleton's humor. A condition of approving his Protean trickster is that he have good humor enough to laugh at the imperfections of his own created selves. This assures that he has the "centered self" that Volpone lacks. Middleton, then, was adapting the older, Elizabethan dramatic mode of celebrating flexibility of self to the new urban world of credit, profit, and fashion.

IV

Post-Jacobean comedy continued to explore the topics of sex and money, but it did so with a notable reduction in the Elizabethan enthusiasm for celebrating fertility, community, and self-fashioning. A new and persistent note had been struck in plays such as Middleton's *A*

Chaste Maid, in which fertility is as much a curse as a blessing and the comic society exists in fragments as remote and often uninviting as Wales, Cambridge, and the stews of London. If, as George Rowe argues in his book on Middleton, the values of Roman New Comedy suffered a drubbing during James's reign, so too did the pervasive Renaissance ideal of the imaginatively fashioned self. The self-made men of Caroline and Restoration comedy bear an unsavory resemblance to Jonson's cheats, Marston's whining moralists and disappearing reformers, and Middleton's shady new-money men and purveyors of credit. Massinger's Luke Frugal *(The City Madam),* for instance, combines entrepreneurial flair with the language of the tyrant to make himself a petty demon akin to Middleton's Hoard, Dampit, Quomodo, and Whorehound. The once-noble ideal of self-fashioning is reduced to theatrical gimmickry in the masques, parades, and pageants of *The City Madam.*

The titular heroes of Marlowe's tragedies and the self-generating impulse that they glorified are reduced still further in the nonheroic drama of the Restoration. While Dryden could keep alive a self-conscious imitation of earlier Herculean heroes, Etherege openly mocked such playing at manliness in *The Man of Mode or, Sir Fopling Flutter.* Young Bellair dubs Sir Fopling "the Pattern of modern Gallantry," an epithet emended by Dorimant to "the pattern of modern Foppery" (I.i.349–51).[30] The alien Parisian fashions have spawned a race of men who, lacking any integral sense of self, live only in their mirrors.

> SIR FOPLING
> In a glass a man may entertain himself—
> DORIMANT
> The shadow of himself indeed.
> SIR FOPLING
> Correct the Errours of his motions and his dress.
> MEDLEY
> I find Sir *Fopling* in your Solitude, you remember the
> saying of the wise man, and study your self.

$$\text{(IV.ii.87–92)}$$

In this travesty of self-knowledge, the satiric glass has become a vehicle for superficiality and self-regard. Playing, itself, becomes a primary

---

30. *The Man of Mode or, Sir Fopling Flutter,* ed. John Conaghan (Edinburgh, 1973).

metaphor for all kinds of sexual toying, trivial art, and vacant personalities. Not only is Sir Fopling a "Sheer Mimick" and "Ape" (V.i.99–100), his chief critic, the romantic hero, Dorimant, has "been us'd to deep Play" (by which he means sex), and "mak[ing] one at small Game" in "the Play-House" (III.iii.70–75). When he taunts a lady with "how wantonly [she] play'd with [her] head" while watching a play and in turn being watched by the fops, she turns the insult around and *"Acts him,"* as the stage direction puts it (III.iii.99–104). Far from fashioning a unique and flexible personality, Dorimant plays a highly imitable character-part.

The more explicitly Etherege's fictional world presents itself as stage play and its characters as imitators of actors, the more we are asked to feel contempt for them and their medium of expression. Comedy begins to scoff openly at its own illusions and to mock its own methods in this way because the Restoration dramatists, unlike Shakespeare, relegated all serious self-fashioning to heroic tragedy. No Restoration version of Faustus or his satiric counterpart, Volpone, could find a resonant ideal of personal identity to embody or to parody on the comic stage. Not until the nineteenth century did the Marlovian hero reemerge in a style that provoked another comic genius, G. B. Shaw, into his own version of the countergenre I have tried to delineate.

Identity and Acting in Elizabethan Tragedy

THOMAS HYDE

Eᴠᴇʀʏ ᴘʟᴀʏ places itself or moves among modes of representation that, at one pole, are realistic, random, apparently artless, as yet uninterpreted and, at the other, emblematic, patterned, artificial, already meaningful. More than the playwrights of other eras and traditions, Shakespeare and his contemporaries incorporated an extraordinary range of modes within single plays, and we are accustomed to notice the counterpoint of modes in these plays and discuss its function and significance. Playwrights choose what scenes to represent, of course, and in what modes to represent them, but in accord with conventions of probability and coherence going back to Aristotle, plays that include a variety of modes often present a change in mode, especially a change to a more artful or patterned mode, as willed by their characters. By appearing to cede choice to his characters, a playwright complicates the relation between the poles defined above and those simpler polarities—illusion and reality, art and life. The theatrical illusion becomes no longer exterior and contingent to a play; it does double duty, signifying as well as presenting. When Hamlet stages *The Murder of Gonzago* or Prospero his wedding masque, the plays imitate how in reality men impose meaning on experience or test it through

93

hypothesis, how they subdue or conceal disorder within game or cere-mony—in short, how life is always imitating art.

We are used to these ideas and to some of their echoes and implica-tions in light of Elizabethan polemic about the morality and utility of drama. But one situation remains where an artful, patterned, ceremo-nial mode of representation, especially when it appears to be the choice of the chief character, causes modern audiences discomfort or even antipathy—that is, the deaths of tragic heroes. The tragedies whose ends work best for us are those like *King Lear* where all pattern lies in ruins, and art and ceremony have exhausted their capacities to convey or control or falsify tragic experience. Othello's last speech, in contrast, raises problems even if we reject the view that its artful self-dramatization is really self-deception. And Cleopatra stage-managing her suicide similarly leaves us unsure whether she dies illuminated or illusioned.

Some of our problems with these endings, as with others like them, no doubt derive from anachronism, from reading a modern sense of identity into old plays. Stephen Greenblatt reminds us, for example, that not only in Elizabethan plays were deaths theatrical:

The truly remarkable death scenes of the age, on the scaffold, at home, or even on the battlefield—Sir Thomas More, Mary Queen of Scots, Sir Philip Sidney, John Donne, Ralegh, Charles I—were precisely that: *scenes,* presided over by actor-playwrights who had brilliantly conceived and thoroughly mastered their roles. [1]

Robert R. Hellenga has recently argued that many of the hoariest char-acter problems in Shakespeare's plays yield easily to a historical con-ception of human identity and thus neither call for nor warrant the in-genuities of modern psychology. [2] The case is convincing, but it needs to be extended beyond traditional character problems to account for the general shape of many tragedies and for some of their most striking details of language and action.

1. *Sir Walter Ralegh: The Renaissance Man and His Roles* (New Haven, Conn., 1973), p. 40.

2. "Elizabethan Dramatic Conventions and Elizabethan Reality," *RenD*, N.S. XII (1981), 27–49.

In its barest outline, one might describe the shape of plays that end in a conspicuously theatrical mode as regressive: the main plot finds resolution only as it recedes into some small work of art or illusion designed and performed by the chief character—that is, into some kind of play-within-the-play. This pattern appears to reverse a basic principle of artistic composition—that major, foreground figures seem lifelike partly by contrast with more conventionally or "semiotically" represented background figures.[3] One might think of this pattern as the opposite of the movement that ends masques with players and audience mingling and the fiction dissolving into the court setting that it was designed to reflect and adorn. In contrast, tragedies often isolate players from the audience by interposing an additional layer of fiction or artifice in the form of final theatrics—playlets, monologues, masques, duels, or other ceremonies. These withdrawals or regressions have often been noted and their presence accounted for by their technical function: to close or frame a plot, to give the audience a detached and cathartic view of the action, to produce the sense of an ending, a dramatic analogue for the cadences that mark the close of musical compositions. To these undoubted technical functions I want to add a mimetic function, to suggest that these closing artificialities signify *as* artificialities, that they bear upon the question of tragic identity, and that they should often be understood as unfolding into action the Renaissance arch-image of men as actors on the stage that is the world.

I

The best entrance upon this argument is close study of an early and influential example: the last act of *The Spanish Tragedy,* in which the regressive pattern is clearest and most problematical. Hieronimo finally achieves his revenge by performing in deadly earnest a play-within-the-play, and even a sympathetic critic finds something wrong with this regressive movement.

3. See Boris Uspensky, *A Poetics of Composition: The Structure of the Artistic Text and Typology of a Compositional Form,* trans. Valentina Zavarin and Susan Wittig (Berkeley, Los Angeles, and London, 1973), pp. 155–165.

The play within and the play without dissolve into each other . . . [wrote Leslie Fiedler]. The pivot of revenge upon which the whole structure turns, the climactic action of the whole fable, falls within the inner play, so that the outer play has no true ending but trails off into superogatory and unconvincing horrors.[4]

As if this regressive shape of the plot were not enough, two further oddities in the final act of *The Spanish Tragedy* call attention to the larger problem and also, as will appear, suggest its solution.

The first of these oddities is Hieronimo's plan to have his fatal play-within-the-play "in unknown languages," one part in Latin, one in Greek, one in Italian, and the fourth in French. His own cast protests that "this will be a mere confusion," and the printer seems to have agreed, since he prefaced the text of the playlet with a note:

Gentlemen, this play of Hieronimo in sundry languages, was thought good to be set down in English more largely, for the easier understanding of every public reader.[5]

Yet when Hieronimo steps forward to conclude his play and his revenge, he begins: "Here break we off our sundry languages / And thus conclude I in our vulgar tongue" (IV.4.74–75). Can the play-within-the-play have been given in sundry languages, and if so, why? That is the act's first oddity.

Hieronimo's conclusion in our vulgar tongue runs to some eighty uninterrupted lines in which he reveals the body of his murdered son and explains the grounds and means of his revenge. Little remains to be explained, but—and this is the scene's second oddity—neither the king nor the fathers of the dead actors are satisfied. "Now I have thee, I will make thee speak," says the king after his officers prevent Hieronimo's suicide, "Why hast thou done this undeserving deed?" (IV.iv.164–165). And the fathers echo this demand: "Why hast thou murdered my Balthasar?" "Why hast thou butchered both my children

---

4. "The Defense of Illusion and the Creation of Myth," in *English Institute Essays,* 1949. Quoted from W. K. Wimsatt, ed., *Literary Criticism: Idea and Act* (Berkeley, Los Angeles, and London, 1974), p. 103.

5. Thomas Kyd, *The Spanish Tragedy,* ed. Philip Edwards, The Revels Plays (London, 1959), IV.i.173,180; IV.iv.10 ff.   I cite this edition throughout.

thus?" In seven lines, Hieronimo repeats his reasons, but the king and Castile continue the interrogation: "Who were thy confederates in this?" "Why speak'st thou not?" Hieronimo's only confederate, as he has already explained and as the viceroy recognizes, was Castile's daughter Bel-imperia, who killed herself in the play-within-the-play. But Hieronimo has already explained and now asks only for the liberty of silence: "Sufficeth I may not, nor I will not tell thee." The king threatens tortures, and Hieronimo replies: "Never shalt thou force me to reveal / The thing that I have vowed inviolate." He makes good this resolution by biting out his tongue. The play's best editor summarizes the problem posed by these speeches:

That the king should be violently moved and strangely bewildered is only to be expected, but that his passion should take the form of insisting on information which he already has is almost as odd as Hieronimo's vowing to conceal what he has already told.[6]

Behind both of these odd details in the action of the final act lies the generative image of the *theatrum mundi,* which begins to emerge when Hieronimo steps forward to deliver the epilogue to his play of *Soliman and Perseda:*

> Haply you think, but bootless are your thoughts,
> That this is fabulously counterfeit,
> And that we do as all tragedians do:
> To die today, for fashioning our scene,
> The death of Ajax or some Roman peer,
> And in a minute starting up again,
> Revive to please tomorrow's audience.
>
> (IV.iv.76–82)

These words have a double effect. Even as Hieronimo's royal audience on the stage begins to suspect the truth of his deadly play, we in the theater are reminded that all of the corpses now fallen and yet to fall will in a minute revive to take our applause. Yet we cannot be complacent. Theatrical illusion has proven true, if only within the bounds of an encompassing illusion; who is to say for certain where illusion ends and reality begins? That epistemological quandary will be deeper for

6. *Ibid.,* p. xxxv.

an audience that hears in Hieronimo's lines a reversal of an ancient commonplace:

[Death] comes to no more than the murder of one of the personages in a play; the actor alters his make-up and enters in a new role. The actor, of course, was not really killed; but if dying is but changing a body as an actor changes a costume, or even an exit from the body like the exit of an actor from the boards when he has no more to say and do—though he will still return to act on another occasion—what is there so very dreadful in this transformation of living beings into one another?[7]

That is Plotinus, arguing that all the world's a stage and our lives and deaths as illusory and insubstantial as the actions of a play. Even Sancho Panza had heard this commonplace many times.[8] By reversing the commonplace, Hieronimo stresses the truth of the deaths just enacted, but no less stresses the theatricality of the plot and actions that have produced them. More than a witty device for accomplishing revenge, the play-within-the-play implies that all revenge is theatrical in the sense of requiring resolute performance of deliberated actions. "The plot's already in my head," Hieronimo himself declares (IV.i.53).

So far I have said nothing that has not been said many times before about the plays, duels, masques, or dances that end so many revenge tragedies influenced by Kyd. But the mode of Hieronimo's revenge has implications that seem to have gone unrecognized, perhaps because Hieronimo's long speech of explanation has been seen as extraneous to his play, as an abandonment of the theatrics of revenge.[9] Hieronimo sees it differently; the speech begins "Now break we off our sundry languages," but the play does not end till the end of the speech some eighty lines later:

> And princes, now behold Hieronimo,
> Author and actor in this tragedy
> Bearing his latest fortune in his fist:
> And *will* as resolute *conclude his part*
> As any of the actors gone before.

7. Plotinus, *The Enneads,* trans. Stephen McKenna, 4th ed. (London, 1969), III.ii.15.

8. *Don Quixote,* II.12.

9. See, for example, Anne Righter [Barton], *Shakespeare and the Idea of the Play* (1962; rpt. Harmondsworth, 1967), p. 74.

And gentles, *thus I end my play:*
Urge no more words, I have no more to say.
                    (*He runs to hang himself.*) [my italics]

The play-within-the-play does not end, then, until this speech
which is its epilogue, the last words of the author and actor before he
exits from the stage of this world. Death, Plotinus and countless others
had said, is "like the exit of an actor from the boards when he has no
more to say or do"; Hieronimo will enact that adage. Silence is the end
of every play, and Hieronimo is determined to make his own death as
theatrical as any of the others. He runs to hang himself again in character as the bashaw who, as he told Bel-imperia, "moved with remorse of
his misdeeds, / Ran to a mountain-top and hung himself" (IV.i.129–130).
But there is an even surer sign of the meaning of Hieronimo's last acts.
Before his play began, he had locked the stage doors apparently to prevent interference, but by the end of the epilogue the locked doors
have come to express Hieronimo's choice to lock himself within his
play, within the inescapable theatrics of the revenge he plotted and
acted. The locked doors turn out to express Hieronimo's determination better than they prevent interference, for the royal audience or
their attendants immediately act upon the Viceroy's command:
"Break ope the doors, run, save Hieronimo" (IV.iv.156). External authority breaks in to save the actor from his role and deprive the author
of his authority. He must not die resolute as a revenger, but live to perform as a "traitor, damned bloody murderer" in a final scene to be produced by the king's justice (l. 163). He must, the king, viceroy, and
duke all demand, speak more than is set down—set down in his epilogue and condensed in the argument which he gave to the king before
the play began and which Castile may still be holding. Hieronimo does
speak, but only to rehearse his epilogue in brief and then to beg the liberty of silence. Rather than speak more than is set down, he will bite
out his own tongue; rather than write more than he has written already, he will stab himself and Castile with a penknife.

Critics have disparaged the "meaningless savagery" of Hieronimo's
last acts, but the author of the additions to the scene first printed in
1602 discerned a meaning. [10] In the first quarto, Hieronimo bites out

10. Philip Edwards, *Kyd,* Writers and Their Work, no. 192 (London, 1966), p. 38.
Text of 1602 additions in *The Spanish Tragedy,* ed. Edwards, p. 135, emphasis added.

his tongue upon the line, "First take my tongue, and afterwards my heart." The second quarto glosses this line by adding a new one: "Now *to express the rupture of my part,* / First take my tongue, and afterward my heart." Like the locked stage doors, Hieronimo's refusal to speak more than he had set down, to be put out of his part, expresses his irrevocable self-commitment to the tragic role he has authored and enacted. So does the death of Castile, whom Hieronimo kills as much in character as the murderous bashaw of his play as in his own character.

If this view is accepted, it becomes one of the ironies of *The Spanish Tragedy* that its hero would have agreed with some of his (and Kyd's) harshest critics. "A situation inspired by the true genius of tragedy collapses into a series of blood-curdling incidents," judged Frederick Boas; "Never has the maxim *finis cororat opus* been more disasterously violated." [11] Hieronimo might agree and yet maintain that the unsatisfactory end was not *his* design; it was what he locked the stage doors against. It was Kyd's design, however, and G. K. Hunter is surely right to defend the unraveling of Hieronimo's design as significant in itself—measuring "the gap between the dream of justice and the haphazard and inefficient human actions that so often must embody it." [12] Hieronimo's silence, if I may summarize, makes both psychological and thematic sense; it is not a problem requiring explanation as either a failure of Kyd's art or an instance of textual corruption.

Some further implications of Hieronimo's silence remain to be explored, however, particularly those that bear upon the first oddity of Kyd's last act, the unknown languages of the play-within-the-play. Hieronimo began his epilogue by varying the commonplace that likens death to an actor's exit from the stage. He ends the epilogue by varying another commonplace. "Princes, now behold Hieronimo," he concludes, "*Author and actor* in this tragedy" (IV.iv.147–148; emphasis added), yet it was commonplace that, to quote Raleigh, "God is the author of all our tragedies, [and] hath written out for us, and appointed us all the parts we are to play." [13] Hieronimo makes good his claim to

---

11. *The Works of Thomas Kyd* (Oxford, 1955), p. xxxix.

12. "Ironies of Justice in *TheSpanish Tragedy,*" *RenD,* N.S. VIII (1965), 103.

13. Sir Walter Raleigh, *The History of the World,* ed. C. A. Patrides (Philadelphia, 1971), p. 70.

authorship, as I have already suggested, by refusing to speak after the princes have broken in upon his play. He will no longer react to others' designs, or reply to their questions; he will act only the part, speak only the lines, he has authored himself. But can a man presume to be author of his own tragedy without infringing God's prerogative?

Hieronimo wavers on this question, as on its corollary the morality of revenge, until finally he comes to a resolute ambivalence, an ambivalence willing to act despite doubts and willing also to bear the consequences. One might cite many instances of wavering or ambivalence, but two are especially relevant to the issue at hand. At the beginning of the last act, Bel-imperia's vow of revenge persuades Hieronimo "that heaven applies our drift, / And all the saints do sit soliciting / For vengeance on those cursed murderers" (IV.i.32–34). But is he still persuaded a few moments later when he urges the princes to accept their parts in his play by citing a classical precedent? If "Nero thought it no disparagement" to act in tragedies, he tells Lorenzo and Balthazar, why should they? The precedent should not be flattering and would hardly comfort the princes if they remembered that Nero liked to act in tragedies in which he could personally kill condemned men who were cast in fatal parts. [14] But the allusion also calls into question Hieronimo's conviction of divine sanction for his vengeance. He can believe, of course, that Providence made use of Nero's wickedness, but can he believe also that all the saints sit soliciting for his plan to imitate Nero, to give a renaissance to Nero's brand of justice?

A still clearer instance of Hieronimo's ambivalence about divine sanction for his authorship is the confusion of languages in his play. Twenty years ago, S. F. Johnson resolved the problem of the play in sundry languages by seeing it as a dramatized allusion. Noting Hieronimo's own brief explanation—"Now I shall see the fall of Babylon, / Wrought by the heavens in this confusion"—Johnson argued that Hieronimo's revenge imitates God's justice against both Babylon and Babel. "Like the Lord, Hieronimo has arranged to confound language"; his revenge, too, will be wrought by the heavens. [15] But the al-

14. IV.i.87, and see Arthur Freeman, *Thomas Kyd: Facts and Problems* (Oxford, 1967), pp. 62–63.

15. IV.i.195–196; Johnson, "*The Spanish Tragedy,* or Babylon Revisited," in Richard Hosley, ed., *Essays on Shakespeare and Elizabethan Drama in honor of Hardin Craig* (Columbia, Mo., 1962), p. 27.

lusion to Babel cuts simultaneously the other way. The Lord punished with confusion of tongues, not murderers, but the builders of Babel, men whose tower encroached upon the heavens, who aspired above the human. That is the crime, less of Lorenzo and Balthazar than of Hieronimo himself who, though otherwise no Marlovian overreacher, does encroach upon the divine prerogative of vengeance and presume to be the author of his own fate. As at Babel, displacement of God as author leads to the babble of sundry languages. Hieronimo himself seems conscious of the ambivalence of his allusion to Babel, for if he confounds the languages of the play as author, as actor he suffers the confusion along with the rest of the cast. His presumption punishes itself; his punishment is the crime. Acceptance of this reciprocity is a large part of Hieronimo's dignity at the end of the play. He bites out his tongue, not in a "berserk resolve to have done with language forever," as some have argued, but because he remains "resolute," accepting responsibility for his authorship, which means acting the part he has authored and no other.[16] Hieronimo's biting out his tongue is both an act and a figure.

II

My purpose is not so much to explicate these two famous cruxes in *The Spanish Tragedy* as to show how they suggest a theatrical sense of human identity, an unfolding into action and speech of the idea of the world as a stage, and therefore how they help to explain the regressive movement of this and other plays which locate the resolution of their plots only within an inner play, a game, or other artificial form. If Herionimo had his way, *The Spanish Tragedy* would end with his resolute acting of the last death in the play-within-the-play. Life—that is, the outer play—will not submit so completely to his authorship, but his refusal to speak and his gratuitous murder of Castile, though they depart from his script, further emphasize its crucial idea: that men can

---

16. Jonas A. Barish, "*The Spanish Tragedy,* or The Pleasures and Perils of Rhetoric," in John Russell Brown and Bernard Harris, eds., *Elizabethan Theatre,* Stratford-upon-Avon Studies 9 (London, 1966), p. 82. See also Carol McGinnis Kay, "Deception through Words: A Reading of *The Spanish Tragedy,*" *SP,* LXXIV (1977), 20–38.

author their own parts, but cannot then think to escape the consequences of acting them in full. The world is a stage on which each man
must play a part, but the part, whether of his own or another's authorship, is the man. A man is free to determine his own character, but
once determined, character is fate.

If these implications can be drawn from the last act of *The Spanish
Tragedy,* they present a pessimistic or tragic variant of the *theatrum
mundi* image that characterizes the most optimistic phase of Renaissance humanism. Pico della Mirandola, we may remember, wrote this
optimistic view into a speech for God to Adam in Eden:

We have made thee neither of heaven nor of earth, neither mortal nor immortal, so that with freedom of choice and with honor, as though the maker and
molder of thyself, thou mayest fashion thyself in whatever shape thou shalt
prefer. [17]

In his *Fable about Man* Vives made the theatrical metaphor explicit. [18]
Man, the arch-actor, can play all the parts on the world's stage and, as
star of the show, can choose or revise his roles at will. In the end, so
well can he impersonate even the gods themselves that they invite him
to leave the play and join them in the audience. It is worth noting how
thoroughly Vives's fable reverses the myth of Babel, where a jealous
God pretends to fear that "nothing that [men] propose to do will now
be impossible for them" and so confuses their tongues to punish aspi-
ration and curb precisely the freedom and flexibility that Pico and
Vives extoll (Genesis 11:6). More to the point, the optimistic Renaissance view of man as arch-actor counters the fatalism that survives in
Raleigh's medieval version of the theater of the world, where God "is
the author of all our tragedies, [and] hath written out for us, and appointed us all the parts we are to play."

17. *Oration on the Dignity of Man,* trans. Elizabeth Livermore Forbes, in *The Renaissance Philosophy of Man,* ed. Ernest Cassirer, Paul Oskar Kristeller, and John Herman
Randall, Jr. (Chicago and London, 1948), p. 225. In the following discussion, I am indebted to two essays from *The Disciplines of Criticism,* ed. Peter Demetz, Thomas
Greene, and Lowry Nelson, Jr. (New Haven and London, 1968): Thomas Greene's "The
Flexibility of the Self in Renaissance Literature" and A. Bartlett Giamatti's "Proteus Unbound: Some Versions of the Sea God in the Renaissance."
18. Trans. Nancy Lenkeith in *Renaissance Philosophy of Man.*

Hieronimo's claim to be author and actor of his tragedy stands para-doxically in both these camps. He affirms the author-actor's freedom to write out his own part, but chooses to imitate an old story of divine retribution for such hubris and in the end refuses to leave the inner play and join its audience. Man, Hieronimo's actions suggest, is a Pro-teus whose flexibility consumes itself, who is free to choose his identity, but whose choice dwindles as it is exercised. He ends in a role which he has chosen and authored, but which is not for that more authentic, less fabricated or artificial.

I have considered [wrote Ben Jonson] our whole life is like a play: wherein ev-ery man, forgetfull of himselfe, is in travaile with expression of another. Nay, wee so insist in imitating others, as wee cannot (when it is necessary) returne to our selves: like Children, that imitate the vices of *Stammerers* so long, till at last they become such: and make the habit to another nature. [19]

Jonson's discursive use of the play image, like Kyd's dramatic one, ac-cepts the premise of Renaissance humanism that, in Erasmus's phrase, men are not born but made, and are made chiefly by *imitatio,* by speaking in another's voice, playing another's part. [20] But if they ac-cept the premise, Jonson and Kyd reflect skeptically that the result will likely be a false or fabricated identity, a parody for which one will have irrevocably traded the genuine self, the detached and uncommit-ted will that fabricated it. Though far from the medieval fatalism that saw God as the author and casting agent of all our tragedies, this pessi-mistic version of man as the arch-actor comes close to another medi-eval tradition, one best exemplified in the *Inferno.* The principle of *contrappasso* that allots sinners their punishments in Dante's hell might be described by way of a theatrical metaphor. Some human acts are inescapable, requiring the man who performs them in life to con-tinue for eternity playing out some version of the fatal original. *The Spanish Tragedy,* with its chorus of Andrea and Revenge, begins and ends with such an idea of "endlesse tragedy" (IV.v.48).

19. *Discoveries,* 1093–1099, in *Ben Jonson,* ed. C. H. Herford and Percy and Evelyn Simpson (Oxford, 1925–1952), VIII, 597.
    20. On Renaissance *imitatio* see Thomas M. Greene, *The Light in Troy: Imitation and Discovery in Renaissance Poetry* (New Haven and London, 1982), esp. chap. 4.

I shall shortly suggest some ways in which the regressive shape of the last act of *The Spanish Tragedy* may be glimpsed also in several other plays and may illuminate some of their recurrent features, but first I must distinguish this pattern from a kindred pattern—kindred because it also accepts the humanists' premise that men are free to shape their own characters and destiny, distinct because it supposes different consequences of the act of shaping. Marlowe's Dr. Faustus can represent this second tragic pattern. Lucifer gives him a book with the injunction, "Peruse this book, and view it thoroughly, / And thou shalt turn thyself into what shape thou wilt," yet Faustus ends with no shape at all, merely "limbs / All torn asunder by the hand of death."[21] The "fearful shrieks and cries" that attend Faustus's death will contrast sufficiently with the silence Hieronimo insists on in his last words— "Urge no more words; I have no more to say"—the silence of identity petrifying as opposed to the violence of dismemberment. Man's Protean flexibility can lead to two bad ends in these pessimistic, English revisions of earlier Renaissance optimism: either to an endlessly shifting identity that is no identity at all, or to an alien, assumed, or made-up identity from which the hero is detached, but without hope of escape. This second pattern, that of *The Spanish Tragedy,* I believe to be the more prevalent in the tragedies of Shakespeare and his contemporaries. It appears explicitly in the title and conception of Middleton's *The Changling,* where comic and tragic versions of self-transformation oppose each other in the two plots, and the murderer De Flores reminds his accomplice Beatrice Johanna that she must forget her prior identity as given by social position and parentage because she has become "the deed's creature."[22] And these same ideas about the consequences of self-fashioning also inform, I shall go on to argue, the many Elizabethan and Jacobean tragedies that end with self-consciously theatrical, artificial, or unreal forms or modes.

---

21. *The Complete Plays of Christopher Marlowe,* ed. Irving Ribner (New York, 1963), II.ii.168–169; V.iii.6–7. See Stephen J. Greenblatt, "Marlowe and Renaissance Self-Fashioning," in *Two Renaissance Mythmakers: Christopher Marlowe and Ben Jonson,* Selected Papers from the English Institute, 1975–1976, N.S. I, pp. 41–69.

22. *The Changling,* ed. Patricia Thomson, The New Mermaids (London, 1971), III.iv.137.

My brief survey of four of these forms or modes—plays-within-plays, parodies of earlier scenes, dreams, and narratives—cannot pretend to be either exhaustive or conclusive, but will suggest how thoroughly Renaissance ideas of identity had forced these dramatists to revise the ancient commonplace that only at death does playing stop and the true self emerge from behind the mask. "Nam . . . eripitur persona; res manet," wrote Lucretius.[23] But the terminal artifices of these various plays imply that the *persona* may have so grown into *res* that death itself cannot part them. "Only we die in earnest—that's no jest," wrote Raleigh in the Tower, but these overt artifices imitate or represent arts of self-fashioning that make earnest out of jest in a way that death merely ratifies. If these are self-conscious artifices, they are not reflexive, but rather use the dramatic mode and its devices to figure and to understand, as well as to present, the course and fate of tragic identity.

III

Many, perhaps most, Elizabethan and Jacobean revenge tragedies end with masques or playlets, and this familiar fact is usually explained as simple imitation of the device that proved so successful for Kyd. Occasionally it is more than this, more also than the morally satisfying irony of plots fallen on the inventors' heads that Marlowe had popularized in *The Jew of Malta*. Revenge tragedies necessarily stress the plotting of the revenger and often also of the villain, so that potentially their masques or playlets may have the mimetic significance of Kyd's, suggesting by their artificiality the plotter's self-transformation into the part he authors and acts. Two examples must suffice. The fatal masque that ends *Women Beware Women* extends this potential onto a social plane. The characters all die in roles ironically appropriate to their past actions—the panderess as Juno, and so forth—and the contrivance of the masque, both artful and fatal, shows the self-destructive end of all the seductive social arts of the play. Tourneur achieves something closer to fulfillment of the masque's potential in *The Revenger's*

23. *De rerum natura,* 3.57. See Montaigne, *Essais,* I.18; Raleigh, "What Is Our Life? A Play of Passion," l. 10.

Tragedy. Vindice, unlike Hieronimo, has concealed his role in the murders and the masque that have carried off his enemies. He would be safe among the audience of survivors except that he cannot suppress his pride of authorship. " 'Twas somewhat witty carried though we say it: / 'Twas we two murder'd him." [24] Arrested and condemned, Vindice does not protest, but his final speech stresses in rhyming couplets the maxim "murder will out." Only one line—" 'Tis time to die when we are ourselves our foes"—hints at recognition that the revengers have lost their true, or at least their original, selves in the bloody roles they have played. But it hints only and does not enact that recognition as does Hieronimo's silence.

A parody scene, for my purposes here, is a special kind of mirror scene. It repeats an earlier scene with distortions or extravagances that call attention to its artificiality. I shall give only one example, a familiar one, from *Richard II.* At the beginning of Act IV, Aumerle and Bagot appear before Bolingbroke to charge each other with treason. The scene parodies the first scene of the play, in which Bolingbroke and Mowbray had charged each other with treason before Richard. Act I's solemn rites of knighthood have given way, however, to farce, as so many lords throw down their gages that Aumerle likens the scene to a dice game and must appeal to onlookers for more gloves. The parody here emphasizes the inauthenticity of this action rather than, as playlets usually do, its overdetermination, and it works as part of the reciprocal, up-and-down movement of the play. Richard loses his royal identity as Bolingbroke gains his, but, as constant theatrical imagery makes clear, Bolingbroke's identity as king is only a role. He will always be a player king, and the scenes in which he first monarchizes are therefore parodies, as he himself comes to recognize.

The later scene in which the Duke and Duchess of York plead extravagantly and unnecessarily for and against their son Aumerle is like a ballad, Bolingbroke says: "Our scene is alt'red from a serious thing, / And now chang'd to 'The Beggar and the King.' " [25] On his deathbed in *Henry IV, Part 2,* he finds that "all my reign hath been but as a scene /

24. *The Revenger's Tragedy*, ed. Lawrence J. Ross, Regents Renaissance Drama (Lincoln, Neb., 1966), V.iii.96–97.

25. (V.iii.79–80); my texts for Shakespeare throughout are those of the Riverside edition.

Acting that argument," but he plays his part resolutely to the end
(IV.v.197–198). Indeed, Henry recognizes the end by fulfillment of the
prophetically scripted death in Jerusalem, and his death, though otherwise entirely unlike Hieronimo's, bears out the commonplace analogy of death to an actor's exit when he has no more lines to speak.
After noting that "strength of speech is utterly denied [him]," Henry
dies offstage, so that his exit from the stage marks the end of his part
(IV.v.217). Richard, by contrast, has no part to play to the end. Having
helped to destroy the old world in which inherited roles shaped men's
identities, he cannot then successfully shape himself. Deposed, thrust
from his part, he knows not what name to call himself and meditates in
prison on the instability of identity: "Thus play I in one person many
people" (V.v.31). But to play many people is to *be* none. *Richard II* in
its twin protagonists illustrates the fates of both Hieronimo and Faustus, both bad ends that men can come to in a world where they must
shape themselves. Like Hieronimo's playlet, parody in *Richard II* enacts one of those ends: an increased artificiality and loss of authenticity which correspond to and imitate Bolingbroke's assumption of a
role not his own as well as the monarchy's loss of legitimacy.

Dreams are among the oldest metaphors for fiction, and it is not surprising therefore to find them among the kinds of withdrawal or re-
gression that recur toward the end of Elizabethan and Jacobean tragedies. Like plays-within-plays, dreams usually suggest both constriction
and inauthenticity of action. Two examples must suffice, both familiar
enough to need little more than mention, both suggesting, like Hieronimo's playlet, that human flexibility consumes itself when abused and
ends at last confined in an alien or made-up identity. *Richard III* is the
clearest example. In *Henry VI, Part 3,* he began his intimacy with the
audience by proclaiming his flexibility as an actor:

> Why, I can smile, and murther whiles I smile,
> And cry "Content" to that which grieves my heart,
> And wet my cheeks with artificial tears,
> And frame my face to all occasions.
> . . . .
> I can add colors to the chameleon,
> Change shapes with Proteus for advantages,
> And set the murtherous Machevil to school.

> Can I do this, and cannot get a crown?
> Tut, were it farther off, I'll pluck it down.
>
> (III.ii.182–185, 191–195)

Richard III bears out these talents only until Act IV, when his past deeds begin to exert a kind of repetition compulsion: "Murther her brothers and then marry her—/ Uncertain way of gain! But I am in / So far in blood that sin will pluck on sin" (IV.ii.62–63). He can urge the mother of his intended bride to "plead what I will be, not what I have been," but he cannot himself believe in this future change, and for her possibly feigned flexibility in hearing his suit, he judges the queen a "relenting fool, and shallow, changing woman" (IV.iv.414,431). The flexibility that won him the crown would now be weakness; he must lay aside his sardonic humor and resolutely act the part he has authored and cast himself in. Richard's authorship comes increasingly in question, however, as player after player dies remembering Margaret's curse, which comes to seem almost a script controlling the actions of the later acts.

These developments culminate in Richard's dream before Bosworth Field. Like other dreams in the play, it is premonitory, but where earlier dreams presented events to come, Richard's, with its procession of his victims, reckons up the past, the events of the play itself. They cannot be escaped or amended, and they will determine the next day's battle. Richard starts from his dream self-divided:

> Cold fearful drops stand on my trembling flesh.
> What do I fear? Myself? There's none else by.
> Richard loves Richard, that is, I [am] I.
> Is there a murtherer here? No. Yes, I am.
> Then fly. What, from myself? Great reason why—
> Lest I revenge. What, myself upon myself?
>
> (V.i.181–188)

Like Hieronimo's playlet, this dialogue of one dramatizes the alien being Richard has made of himself, but it does so by giving voice, for once in the play, to an original self or conscience which has survived his self-transformation, though only in dreams. With its doubling of the character, the speech is itself dreamlike and suggests that Richard and England have been living a nightmare from which Richmond has come to awaken them.

Macbeth is of course my second example. From the beginning, its hero understands, better than Richard III ever did or Lady Macbeth could conceive, the irrevocable self-transformation implicit in murdering Duncan. From the beginning to the end, he frames his actions to the weird sisters' prophecies, a more compelling script than Margaret's curse. And from the "happy prologues to the swelling act / Of the imperial theme" (I.iii.128–129) to the "poor player, / That struts and frets his hour upon the stage" (V.v.24–25), a subdued strain of play imagery sustains Macbeth's theatrical viewpoint on his own tragedy. Like Hieronimo or Bolingbroke or Richard III, Macbeth has presumed to act a part in history not his own, but ends staked like a bear in the unreal spectacle of his own tragedy.

Still, this theatrical viewpoint is secondary. The play produces a more inclusive and more powerful sense of unreality by stressing dreams and nightmares. According to Plato, during sleep, when a man's rational faculties relax their control, a bestial and savage part awakes and, freed from all sense of shame and all reason, stops at no atrocity or murder. A tyrant, Socrates concludes, is a man who lets this savage part rule even while he is awake, so that "he is the waking reality of what we dream."[26]

Macbeth offers ample warrant for invoking this passage from the *Republic,* but it will be enough to mention Banquo's prayer, "Merciful powers, / Restrain in me the cursed thoughts that nature / Gives way to in repose," and, of course, the restless ecstasy that Macbeth and his lady have exchanged for innocent sleep (II.i.7–9). By murdering Duncan, Macbeth has murdered sleep and condemned himself, like Plato's tyrant, to live out a waking nightmare, a nightmare that not only expresses his own guilty, impotent detachment from his crimes, but also gathers to itself the weird sisters, the riddling prophecies, and their dreamlike fulfillments. Where Hieronimo diminished himself at last to act in the play of his own revenge, Macbeth gives himself up to the nightmare of a tyrant's ambition.

The fourth and last of the kinds of mimetic artifice or unreality I am sketching is narrative, which emerges at the end of tragedies not only to tie up loose ends in the characters' knowledge of events but also to suggest that men consume their choices as they exercise them until at

26. *Republic,* 571b–576b; this passage, 576b, trans. Jowett.

last the drama of choice recedes into the past. At death a man becomes a character in a story, and this occurs whether or not he lays claim to be that story's author. For that reason, narratives are more flexible than plays-within-plays, parodies, or dreams. Although they, too, present actions at a remove from the immediacy of drama, that remove may be simply temporal and need not imply artifice or inauthenticity. Final narratives can therefore suggest characters' self-possession even as they mime them ceding possession of themselves to the stories in which they will survive. When spoken by tragic heroes, final narratives normally enact this kind of self-possession. When spoken by onlookers, they more often suggest contrivance and ironic distance, as do playlets, parodies, and dreams. The conversion of the events of *Romeo and Juliet* into a story at the close, for example—

> For never was a story of more woe
> Than this of Juliet and her Romeo—
>
> (V.iii.309–310)

seems of a piece with the fathers' promise to raise golden statues of their dead children. It may be the last word, but it is not an adequate one.

For the normal function of self-possession, *Hamlet* and *Othello* come first to mind, but I should like to mention *Titus Andronicus* for an example of a villain permitted at the end to possess himself through narrative. At the beginning of Act V, Aaron the Moor, from the top of a ladder with a noose around his neck, relates his own and the other villains' "murders, rapes, and massacres" (V.i.63). He takes credit as the inventor of all the play's atrocities and repents nothing but that he cannot invent ten thousand more. He presents himself not only as author and actor in these hideous events, but also as their most appreciative audience, describing how he laughed at one or related another to amuse the empress. Once he pried through a crevice in the wall to watch Titus receive the heads of the sons whom he had cut off his own hand to save. "[I] beheld his tears," he says, "and laugh'd so heartily / That both mine eyes were rainy like to his" (V.i.116–117). Aaron begins this speech by relating the events of the play, but turns quickly to self-characterization and finally looks forward with relish to everlasting pain in hell so long as it will permit him eternally to torment others by repeating this same tale. Death by hanging would mean nothing against the appalling self-possession Aaron achieves through his narrative, and Lucius can only cry, "Stop his mouth, and let him speak no more" (V.i.151). It is too late, for the force of Aaron's character, here concentrated in his narrative, outweighs Titus's grotesque imitation of mythical patterns of revenge or Lucius's own pale, self-justifying narrative at the end.

Aaron's triumph in his artistry of evil, expressed and symbolized by this narrative, is unique in Shakespeare. Both Richard III and Macbeth die resolutely but inarticulately in combat, alienated from the identities they have shaped and from the stories in which those identities will live on. Iago, though more like Aaron than the villain-heroes Richard and Macbeth, adopts Hieronimo's tactic: "Demand me nothing; what you know, you know: / From this time forth I never will speak word" (V.ii.303–304). Iago's silence leaves the final narrative to Othello and avoids unbalancing the play, but it also has a mimetic dimension. Hieronimo lost himself in grief and madness so that he could regain heroic resolution only by committing himself utterly to the part he acts in his play. His silence expressed his determination not to be put out of the part he had authored and acted. Iago, too, will not be put out to answer the demands of an author other than himself. But unlike Hieronimo, Iago has been playing parts from the beginning, and the identity he refuses to betray at the end is really no identity at all. "'Tis in ourselves that we are thus and thus," he says, but also, "I am not that I am" (I.iii.319–320; I.i.65). Where Hieronimo became nothing but the part he played, Iago becomes nothing at all.

The hero, of course, has the final narrative in *Othello,* a speech even more consciously concerned with narrative than Aaron's:

> I pray you, in your letters,
> When you shall these unlucky deeds relate,
> Speak of me as I am; nothing extenuate,
> Nor set down aught in malice. Then must you speak
> Of one that lov'd not wisely but too well;
> Of one not easily jealous, but being wrought,
> Perplexed in the extreme; of one whose hand
> (Like the base [Indian]) threw a pearl away
> Richer than all his tribe; of one whose subdu'd eyes.
> Albeit unused to the melting mood,
> Drop tears as fast as the Arabian trees

> Their medicinable gum. Set you down this;
> And say besides, that in Aleppo once,
> Where a malignant and a turban'd Turk
> Beat a Venetian and traduc'd the state,
> I took by th' throat the circumcised dog,
> And smote him—thus.

(V.ii.340–356)

Eliot and others have condemned Othello for adopting an aesthetic attitude in this speech, for dramatizing himself rather than responding "genuinely," and in a sense they are right.[27] The narrative of the past incident in Aleppo becomes suddenly a drama in which Othello plays both himself, loyal servant of the state, and another, its malignant enemy. But Eliot is wrong, I think, simply to attribute the aesthetic attitude to Othello without seeing its mimetic significance. The speech enacts both a self-possession or self-recovery through narrative and a profound self-alienation through its artificiality. "Oh bloody period!" Lodovico says, his pun continuing Othello's contrivance, and his judgment ought to stand against Gratiano's uncomprehending "All that is spoke is marr'd."

Hamlet responds more specifically than any other play to Hieronimo's claim to be both author and actor and to the pattern Kyd devised to sustain that claim, but my purposes here are more general and my treatment of *Hamlet* therefore brief. No less than Othello, Hamlet nears death concerned for the story in which he will live on. At first he thinks to tell the tale himself, but, "as this fell sergeant, Death, / is strict in his arrest," he must turn to Horatio: "Thou livest. Report me and my cause aright / To the unsatisfied" (V.ii.336–340). Horatio proclaims himself more an antique Roman than a Dane, and Hamlet must wrest the cup away to prevent Horatio's suicide. This exchange, if it adds a final color to Horatio's characterization as a foil to Hamlet, has at least two other effects. It allows Hamlet to dilate further on his need to provide for the narrative of these events, and it makes Horatio, like Hieronimo, a man saved from suicide for the sole purpose of speaking.

---

27. Eliot, "Shakespeare and the Stoicism of Seneca," in *Selected Essays,* 3d ed. (London, 1951), pp. 130–131. See also F. R. Leavis, "The Diabolic Intellect and the Noble Hero," in *The Common Pursuit* (Harmondsworth, 1962), pp. 151–153.

> O God, Horatio, what a wounded name,
> Things standing thus unknown, shall I leave behind me!
> If thou didst ever hold me in thy heart,
> Absent thee from felicity a while,
> And in this harsh world draw thy breath in pain
> To tell my story.
>
> (V.ii.344–349)

The play ends just before Horatio begins the tale. *Hamlet,* then, emphasizes a final narrative and its displacement from the hero to his spokesman, but only to postpone it till after the end of the play. The effect is quite opposite to that of *Othello* or, more generally, of the other tragedies mentioned above. The audience feels privileged to have witnessed the actual events rather than their narrative re-presentation. Horatio's brief prospectus adds to this effect:

> So shall you hear
> Of carnal, bloody, and unnatural acts,
> Of accidental judgments, casual slaughters,
> Of deaths put on by cunning and [forc'd] cause,
> And in this upshot, purposes mistook
> Fall'n on th' inventors' heads: all this can I
> Truly deliver.
>
> (V.ii.380–386)

After such an advertisement, one wonders whether Horatio's tale will report Hamlet's cause aright and gains a further impression of the authenticity of the events as the play itself has presented them. So, too, for the hero. After all his various roles and stories, Hamlet appears at the end free of them all, neither self-dramatizing nor yet fixed in the story he knows he will become, but simply as himself. Hieronimo's opposite fate can suggest some reasons for Hamlet's, for though he has toyed with authorship and put on more roles than just his antic disposition, Hamlet ends believing that "There's a divinity that shapes our ends, / Rough-hew them how we will" (V.ii.10–11). Making no claim to authorship and willing to act only the part Providence will provide, Hamlet escapes completely the self-imposed mimetic artifices that limn the ends of other tragic heroes.

The Structural Uses of Incest in English Renaissance Drama

LOIS E. BUELER

INCEST IS one of the distinctive motifs of Jacobean and Caroline theater because it is sensational. Such at least is the impression given by
most brief summaries of the drama of the period. Further, the presence
of incest has often been considered a sign of that "falling off in the general discipline"[1] once seen by critics as a moral characteristic of the
age and an artistic characteristic of its drama. Considerable reference
has been made to the sensational aspects of incest in its two best-
known examples, Beaumont and Fletcher's *A King and No King* and
Ford's *'Tis Pity She's a Whore*. Little systematic attention has been

1. The phrase is that of G. B. Harrison in *A Companion to Shakespeare Studies,* ed.
Harley Granville-Barker and G. B. Harrison (New York, 1934), p. 183; the decline the
result of James I's insufficient attention to state affairs. The tradition of regarding the
presence of incest as morally and artistically suspicious is exemplified by M. C. Bradbrook's lack of surprise at finding in Beaumont and Fletcher "a taste for the more extraordinary sexual themes (rape, impotence, incest) combined with a blurring of the aesthetic difference between tragedy and comedy and the moral distinction between right
and wrong" (*Themes and Conventions of Elizabethan Tragedy* [1935; rpt. Cambridge,
Eng., 1960], p. 243). Robert K. Turner, Jr., though he is objecting to the handling of incest rather than to the motif itself, attributes the popularity of *A King and No King* to

paid, however, to the way incest is used in other plays throughout the English Renaissance, and none to the relation between the wide variations in patterns of incest and the structure and character development of the plays. [2] A survey of the several dozen English Renaissance plays in which incest occurs (see table 1) suggests that, although unquestionably there is at least the possibility of sensational ramifications in them all, playwrights recognized from the first two more significant dramaturgical virtues of the incest motif: (1) its structural usefulness in complicating and unraveling plots; and (2) its peculiar economy for probing the moral relationship between individual passions and social well-being. In the following pages, I wish to identify and consider these uses and economies.

Incest, which is sexual attraction or activity within a forbidden degree of consanguinity or affinity, appears in English Renaissance plays in an unexpectedly wide number of variations: an incestuous relationship may be biological or only legal; it may take place within or outside the nuclear family and within or between generations; the passion may be one-way or reciprocal; it may be consummated or frustrated;

---

the effectiveness of its projection of the viewer's "licentious fantasies. . . . Not only was it titillating, but it must have been rather a relief to be told that there was a world where the standards of Christian humanism did not hold—where technicalities existed which permitted one to lie with one's sister or perhaps to gorge on such other exotic emotional confections as suited one's palate without having to pay with a moral illness that might last an eternity" (*A King and No King* [Lincoln, Neb., 1963], pp. xxv–xxvi).

2. The few good comments on incest in individual plays, and on the larger dramatic possibilities of the theme, are all too brief. See, particularly, Robert Ornstein, *The Moral Vision of Jacobean Tragedy* (Madison, Wis., 1960), pp. 203–207; Alan Brissenden, "Impediments to Love: A Theme in John Ford," *RenD*, VII (1964), 95–102; R. J. Kaufmann, "Ford's Tragic Perspective," in *Elizabethan Drama: Modern Essays in Criticism*, ed. R. J. Kaufmann (New York, 1961), pp. 356–372, especially pp. 370–371; and for a single paragraph that goes straight to the heart of the dramatic uses of the incest motif, Kenneth A. Requa, "Music in the Ear: Giovanni as Tragic Hero in Ford's *'Tis Pity She's a Whore*," *PLL*, VII (Winter 1971), 21–22. The structural uses of incest naturally vary according to literary genre and period. W. Daniel Wilson, who is at work on a study of incest in at least thirty English, French, and German works, primarily novels, finds that unlike the Renaissance the most common eighteenth- and early-nineteenth-century pattern is one of unwitting sibling incest which is often consummated and in which a primary concern is the philosophical grounds for the incest taboo itself ("Science, Natural Law, and Unwitting Sibling Incest in Eighteenth-Century Literature," *Studies in Eighteenth-Century Culture*, XIII [1984], 249–270).

TABLE 1
Some English Renaissance Incest Plays

Title	Author	Date*
Patient and Meek Grissill	Phillip	1559
Cambises	Preston	1561
David and Bethsabe	Peele	1587
Mother Bombie	Lyly	1589
A Looking Glass for London & *England*	Lodge & Greene	1590
The Comedy of Errors	Shakespeare	1592
Patient Grissil	Dekker, Chettle, & Haughton	1600
Hamlet	Shakespeare	1601
The Family of Love	Middleton	1602
The Phoenix	Middleton	1604
Parasitaster, or The Fawn	Marston	1605
The Revenger's Tragedy	Anonymous (Tourneur? Middleton?)	1606
The Turk	Mason	1607
The Devil's Charter	Barnes	1607
Pericles	Shakespeare	1608
The Atheist's Tragedy	Tourneur	1609
A King and No King	Beaumont & Fletcher	1611
The Captain	Fletcher	1612
No Wit, No Help Like a Woman's	Middleton	1613
The Duchess of Malfi	Webster	1614
The Witch	Middleton	1615
The Devil's Law-case	Webster	1617
Thierry and Theodoret	Fletcher & Massinger (w/Beaumont?)	1617
Women Pleased	Fletcher	1620
Women Beware Women	Middleton	1621
The Spanish Curate	Massinger & Fletcher	1622
The Fair Maid of the Inn	Fletcher (w/Massinger? others?)	1626
The Unnatural Combat	Massinger	1626
The Deserving Favorite	Carlell	1629
The Broken Heart	Ford	1629
The Inconstant Lady	Wilson	1630
The Jealous Lovers	Randolph	1632
'Tis Pity She's a Whore	Ford	1632

*For the sake of consistency, the dates used here are from Alfred Harbage, *Annals of English Drama, 975–1700*, rev. Samuel Schoenbaum (Philadelphia, 1964).

TABLE I (cont.)—Some English Renaissance Incest Plays

Title	Author	Date*
The Shepherd's Paradise	Montague	1633
The Guardian	Massinger	1633
The Shepherd's Holiday	Rutter	1634
The Lady of Pleasure	Shirley	1635
Aglaura	Suckling	1637
The Lady's Trial	Ford	1638
The Lovesick Court	Brome	1639
Sicily and Naples	Harding	1640
The Unnatural Tragedy	Cavendish	1658

*For the sake of consistency, the dates used here are from Alfred Harbage, *Annals of English Drama, 975–1700*, rev. Samuel Schoenbaum (Philadelphia, 1964).

characters may actually be related or only think they are; and they may or may not recognize their passions as incestuous. In some plays two different kinds of incest occur, in several plays characters are falsely accused of incest, and in a few the author suggests an incestuous attachment that his characters do not openly admit. Of the variations in types of incest, the most dramaturgically complicated are the distinctions between actual and fictional incest on the one hand and witting and unwitting incest on the other. By actual, I mean that characters are actually related by blood or law; by fictional, that the assumed consanguinity or affinity turns out not to exist. By witting, I mean that the perpetrating character recognizes his or her passion as incestuous; by unwitting, that he or she does not so recognize it.

The way these distinctions are combined can best be clarified by a quick resort to examples. In *'Tis Pity She's a Whore* (Ford), Giovanni loves Annabella. He thinks her his sister, and she is so indeed. The consanguinity is actual and the incest witting. In *A King and No King* (Beaumont and Fletcher), Arbaces loves Panthea. He thinks her his sister, but she is not. The consanguinity is fictional and the incest witting. In *The Lovesick Court* (Brome), Philocles loves Eudina. He thinks her unrelated, but she is his sister. The consanguinity is actual and the incest unwitting. In *No Wit, No Help Like a Woman's* (Middleton), Philip loves Grace. After he has married her, he comes to believe that she is his sister, though she is not. The consanguinity is fictional and the incest unwitting. These two pairs of types work dramatically in strikingly different ways. The distinction between *witting* and *unwitting* incest is an ethical one which may have the profoundest effect upon the dramatist's portrayal of character. The distinction between *actual* and *fictional* incest has virtually no effect upon the portrayal of character; instead it operates upon the structure of the plot and especially upon the possibilities for manipulating the denouement.

The distinctions between witting versus unwitting and actual versus fictional incest go far toward identifying the differences in tone and effect among our plays. (Tables 2 and 3 organize the plays under these rubrics.) So to a degree do a number of other distinctions—the matter of whether the incest is based on a biological or merely a legal relationship, for instance, or whether it takes place beyond or within the nuclear family or between parent and child or siblings. In terms of plotting, the most significant of these other variables involve the related factors of reciprocity and sexual consummation. Reciprocity is primarily a moral and psychological matter: a mutually incestuous passion has the moral virtue of not victimizing the unwilling and the psychological disadvantage of being that much more difficult to resist. Consummation, though morally and psychologically the grounds on which the dramatist may most easily distinguish a will to evil from an evil act, also is a structural matter, for it affects the reversibility of the dramatic action. Its presence is a signal, though not the only signal, for the ethically significant destruction of the incestuous characters. Where a playwright wishes to manage the denouement by successfully matching his incestuous lovers with other partners, he does not allow consummation, and the story of its prevention, whether through the self-control of the lover or lovers, the resistance of the would-be victim, or the revelation of a familial relationship to the unwitting, is the story of the play.

With these terms in hand, let us turn to three groups of plays which exemplify the most common uses of the incest motif. In considering these groups, and the characterizations they include, it is helpful to remember the strictures of Northrop Frye about the relation between character and dramatic shape: "In drama, characterization depends on function; what a character is follows from what he has to do in the

TABLE 2
Cases of Witting Incest

	ACTUAL		FICTIONAL	
	Legal	*Biological*	*Legal*	*Biological*
	Hamlet C N—wife & brother-in-law	Cambises C X—cousins ♂ ♀	S. Curate U N—wife & brother-in-law	Bombie U N—brother & sister
	Fawn C N—wife & brother-in-law	David & Beth C N—brother & sister		King/No King U N—brother & sister
	R. Tragedy C N—stepmother & stepson	Looking Glass U N—brother & sister		L. Court U N—brother & sister
	A. Tragedy U N—father & daughter-in-law	Family of Love U X—uncle & niece (accusation only)		
	A. Tragedy C N—stepmother & stepson-in-law	Phoenix U X—uncle & niece		
	D. Law-case U N—mother & son-in-law	Turk U X—uncle & niece		
	Aglaura C N—wife & brother-in-law	D. Charter C N—father & daughter		
	Aglaura U N—father & daughter-in-law	D. Charter C N—brother & sister		
		Pericles C N—father & daughter		
		Captain U N—father & daughter		
		Duchess U N—brother & sister		
		Witch C N—mother & son		
		D. Law-case U N—brother & sister		
		W. Beware W. C X—uncle & niece		

Fair Maid U N—brother & sister ↕

U. Combat U N—father & daughter ↕

B. Heart U N—brother & sister (accusation only) ↕

'Tis Pity C N—brother & sister ↕

Lady of Pleasure U X—aunt & nephew ↓

L. Trial U X—cousins ♂♀

↕ reciprocal
↓ unreciprocal

♂ male
♀ female

KEY   N nuclear   C consummated
         X extranuclear   U unconsummated

(Within each category, titles are listed in chronological order.)

TABLE 3
Cases of Unwitting Incest

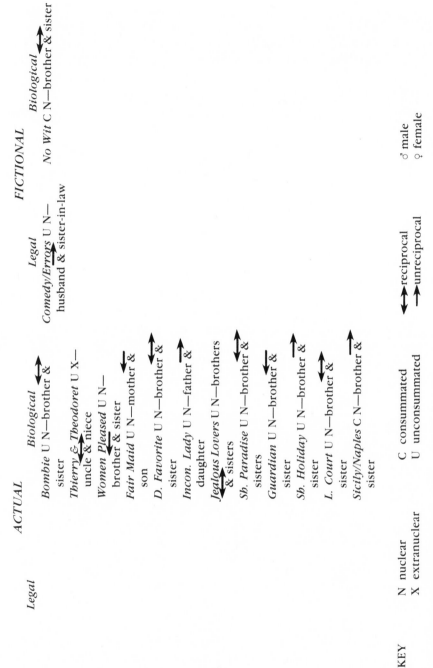

ACTUAL

Legal

Biological

- *Bombie* U N—brother & sister →←
- *Thierry & Theodoret* U X—uncle & niece →
- *Women Pleased* U N—brother & sister →
- *Fair Maid* U N—mother & son →
- *D. Favorite* U N—brother & sister →←
- *Incon. Lady* U N—father & daughter →
- *Jealous Lovers* U N—brothers & sisters →←
- *Sb. Paradise* U N—brother & sisters →←
- *Guardian* U N—brother & sister →
- *Sb. Holiday* U N—brother & sister →
- *L. Court* U N—brother & sister →
- *Sicily/Naples* C N—brother & sister →←

FICTIONAL

Legal

- *Comedy/Errors* U N—husband & sister-in-law

Biological

- *No Wit* C N—brother & sister →←

KEY
N nuclear
X extranuclear

C consummated
U unconsummated

→← reciprocal
→ unreciprocal

♂ male
♀ female

122

play. Dramatic function in its turn depends on the structure of the play; the character has certain things to do because the play has such and such a shape."[3] In Renaissance plays, incest is a device to clarify dramatic shape at least as much as to expose human passions. This shaping purpose is particularly apparent in plays involving unwitting incest, some of which we will consider first.

Unwitting Incest—Giving and Receiving

Unwitting incest is primarily the tool of the historically and socially restricted coterie drama of the Caroline court. Eight out of the twelve examples of actual, unwitting incest in our plays (see table 3) fall after 1628 and are with two exceptions the work of Cavalier dramatists who specialized in "love and honor" plays notable for their elaborate complications of personal relationships and their long-winded expositions of high-minded motives. (*The Lovesick Court* of Brome, not a court writer, is a high-spirited parody of the type.)[4] One of the most characteristic of Cavalier plots is what Alfred Harbage calls the Rival Friend Dilemma, and it is this plot that is chiefly served by the device of unwitting incest. Harbage describes the linkage succinctly:

In its perfected form the situation is as follows. A noble stranger becomes the friend and ally of a princely brother and sister. The princess falls in love with the noble stranger, but he falls in love with the prince's sweetheart. The friends become rivals, love clashes with honor, ethical and emotional stresses assume such a complexity that hearts ache among the characters, heads among the readers. Then the noble stranger discovers to his dismay that he is the

3. *Anatomy of Criticism* (Princeton, N. J., 1957), p. 171.

4. Alfred Harbage, his sensibilities understandably dulled by reading vast numbers of smotheringly awful plays, takes Brome straight in the course of recounting incompletely and slightly inaccurately the plot of *The Lovesick Court* (*Cavalier Drama* [1936; rpt. New York, 1964], pp. 158–159). G. E. Bentley, *The Jacobean and Caroline Stage*, III (Oxford, 1956), suggests mildly that the play is "possibly a satirization" (p. 77). I find the satiric interpretation supported not only by Brome's career, but by the doubling of the incest motif, the broadly comic characterization of the nurse Garrula, the practical (not ethical) incapacities of Eudina, and, most tellingly, the use of the subplot in which Doris's skeptical, manipulative, warmly sly treatment of her suitors undercuts in a way highly atypical of Cavalier drama the lovesick agonies of her betters.

brother of the prince's sweetheart; thus freed from his ill placed attachment in this quarter, he suddenly reciprocates the love of the princess and brother and sister wed brother and sister.[5]

Lodowick Carlell's *The Deserving Favorite,* one of the earliest and most readable of these plays, shows that the purpose of the characteristic complications is to multiply the opportunities for the demonstration of nobility and generosity. With the exception of Jacomo the necessary villain, all the characters seek—in fact, they go out of their way to create—occasions for honor. Thus Clarinda, who loves Lysander and is loved by the Duke, sees through Lysander's pretense of dishonorable lust for her and refuses to recoil in disgust and turn to a more advantageous match. Cleonarda, the King's daughter who falls in love with Lysander while secretly tending his wounds, refuses to take advantage of her position and the wounded man's growing love for her, and both urges him to remain loyal to Clarinda and tells Clarinda where to find him. The Duke, who is thought to have been killed by Lysander in a duel, reveals his identity rather than profit from his rival's execution. Lysander, who commences the play honorably loving Clarinda and only pretends dishonorable lust so that she may honorably break her engagement and ally herself with the more highly placed Duke, remains faithful to her although he reciprocates Cleonarda's passion. The way out of the tangle is through the device of unwitting incest: once Clarinda and Lysander are revealed to be brother and sister, Lysander is free to marry Cleonarda, and Clarinda, who has been impressed by the Duke's noble deeds, to marry him. Since in this type of play love is the response to great virtue as well as great physical attractiveness, the competition in virtue creates the justification for the shifting allegiances. Love does not so much "clash with honor" as follow from it: a character's selflessness increases desirability though it temporarily blocks attainment.

Why, we must ask, is incest of just this sort so frequent in these plays? The essential feature of unwitting incestuous attachments is that they allow the playwright to hold pure the honor of the characters who engage in them: thus Carlell's Clarinda and Lysander are in no way tainted by their courtship. In a drama in which the game of honor

5. *Cavalier Drama,* p. 32.

is played on the field of love, unwitting incest may in fact be the ideal complicating and unraveling device. It increases the number of possible love combinations while cutting down the number of actual characters. It increases discussion of plot complications and social relationships but reduces psychological probing, since no explanation is required for why a decent person ceases to desire a sibling once the consanguinity is known. And it makes the relationship between Love and Honor as simple and clear as may be. An honorable person should love another who is honorable. Not only should one, but by an operation of right-minded Nature, one does. On the other hand, an honorable person should not engage in morally reprehensible actions. Once the love is revealed to be incestuous, the characters' instant abandonment of it demonstrates precisely the necessary point, that true love, which results from the urge to seek honor, is responsive to the demands of honor.

But the action brought about by the revelation of incest is not merely negative. When brother and sister respond to moral law by giving up their sexual love for each other, they promptly bestow themselves on others. Rival Friend/Unwitting Incest plays are not about romantic triangles but about romantic quadrangles. Something more than the attraction of dramatic economy explains such symmetry. In the world of Cavalier drama, the establishment or maintenance of friendship and of family relationships is as essential to social cohesiveness as is sexual love. Such cohesiveness is created by acts of giving and receiving: Lysander attempts to give up Clarinda to the Duke, Cleonarda tries to give Lysander to Clarinda, the King (after a heart-stopping threat designed "to encrease / The joy"–V.3225)[6] gives Cleonarda to Lysander, Clarinda accepts the Duke, the Hermit receives Lysander as his son, and so on. Characters have their obligations to family and friends, and their rights as family and friends, as well as their rights and obligations as lovers.

6. *The Deserving Favourite,* ed. Charles H. Gray (Chicago, 1905). Other quotations below are from the following editions: *'Tis Pity She's a Whore,* ed. N. W. Bawcutt (Lincoln, Neb., 1966); *The Revenger's Tragedy,* ed. Lawrence J. Ross (Lincoln, Neb., 1966); *The Witch,* in *The Plays of Thomas Middleton,* ed. Havelock Ellis (London, 1890); *The Unnatural Combat,* ed. Robert S. Tefler (Princeton, N.J., 1932); *Women Beware Women,* ed. Roma Gill (New York, 1969); *A King and No King,* ed. Robert K. Turner, Jr. (Lincoln, Neb., 1963).

Portrayed here is the exchange that Claude Lévi-Strauss identifies as
the essence of culture.[7] The origin of culture, he maintains, lies in the
exchange of women as marriage partners, and the proof of this origin
lies in the prohibition of incest. The desire to acquire women in marriage must be coupled with the willingness to give up the marriageable
women already in one's possession in order for the exchanges that create a social entity to operate. The mechanism of exchange is most directly threatened by incest—that is, monopoly of the sexual services
of one's own family—and most directly facilitated by giving one's
available family members to others who then acquire obligations in return.[8] Hence, perhaps, the attraction of the incest device to this drama
which Harbage characterizes as one of the civilizing pursuits of a court
obsessed with its social behavior.[9] The moment when, unwitting incest having been revealed, the affected characters turn their attentions
outward to establish bonds beyond themselves is the culturally stabilizing moment. Brother and sister—Lysander and Clarinda—are not
thereby lost to each other. Quite the contrary. They gain, though they
may not monopolize, each other. Because they are brother and sister
and will henceforth act accordingly, not only are old families reconsti-
tuted and old friends reconciled, but new friends won and new families created.

7. Lévi-Strauss's theories of kinship, in which the incest prohibition is made the
uniquely revelatory center, appear most fully in his 1949 work *Les structures élémen-
taires de la parenté* and its revised 1967 edition. My citations are from the English translation of that second edition, *The Elementary Structures of Kinship,* ed. Rodney Need-
ham, trans. James Harle Bell and John Richard von Sturmer (Boston, 1969). For all its
problems, a brief, readable, highly critical review of which may be found in Edmund
Leach's *Claude Lévi-Strauss* (New York, 1970), chap. 6, Levi-Strauss's basic view of incest seems to illuminate Renaissance drama most helpfully. The criticism that he confuses sex rules with marriage rules (see Leach, pp. 110–111) causes little problem in relation to a literature which does precisely the same thing. In Tudor and Stuart plays, the
confusion is only practical, though, not theoretical. One may not marry where one may
not have sex; although the converse is not, practically speaking, true, for one may certainly have sex where one may not marry—the precise point of such activity is always its
risk.

8. *The Elementary Structures of Kinship,* esp. pp. 42–68.

9. *Cavalier Drama,* p. 45.

Witting Incest—Manifestations of Evil

Unwitting incest plays tend to be plays about virtue, in which the triumph of good or at least good luck is actually aided by the aborted threat of incest. Witting incest plays, on the other hand, are about evil, the evil of an aggravated selfishness which takes that portion of one's own which is intended for others and reserves it for oneself. Incest, which Renaissance playwrights are unanimous in assuming is not nor cannot come to good, expresses this selfishness in perfect dramatic form, through the action of dramatic characters. Its evil is sometimes deliberate and calculating, sometimes compelling, but unsought and unsettling. The delineation of deliberate evil is by far the more common use of witting incest, and the one we shall consider first.

After her first sexual encounter with her brother Giovanni, Annabella of *'Tis Pity She's a Whore* shares her exultation with her nurse:

ANNABELLA

Guardian!

PUTANA

Child, how is't, child? Well, thank Heaven, ha?

ANNABELLA

O guardian, what a paradise of joy
Have I pass'd over!

PUTANA

Nay, what a paradise of joy have you pass'd under! Why, now I commend thee, charge: fear nothing, sweetheart; what though he be your brother? Your brother's a man, I hope, and I say still, if a young wench feel the fit upon her, let her take anybody, father or brother, all is one.

(II.i.41–49)

This exchange reveals the two possible and opposite significances of witting incest. Annabella has just sworn to live to her brother and to no other (II.i.26–28). Her love for him is focused and specific: union with Giovanni is all her purpose and her joy. Such specificity does not occur to Putana. For her, the incestuous passage she has abetted is a convincing demonstration of the very indiscriminateness of Annabella's sexual nature. Young wenches are subject to fits, and fits must be laid by men. But men are only bodies, and any body will do. All is one.

128 LOIS E. BUELER

Putana no more understands Annabella than she understands the action in which she finds herself. Her blindness will cost her her eyes. But, like the vulgar spectator of a conventional play, she knows the customary dramatic use of witting incest. It is a manifestation not only of lust but of indiscriminate, hence completely beastly, lust. This beastliness can have either tragic or comic application. *The Revenger's Tragedy* portrays it grimly. "Then thou know'st / I'th'world strange lust?" (I.iii.55–56) Lussurioso asks Vindice-Piato. In affirmation, Vindice chooses the example of incest:

> O, Dutch lust, fulsome lust!
> Drunken procreation, which begets so many drunkards,
> Some father dreads not (gone to bed in wine)
> To slide from the mother, and cling the daughter-in-law;
> Some uncles are adulterous with their nieces,
> Brothers with brothers' wives. O, hour of incest!
> Any kin now, next to the rim o'th'sister,
> Is man's meat in these days: and in the morning,
> When they'are up and dress'd, and their mask on,
> Who can perceive this?—save that eternal eye,
> That sees through flesh and all.
>
> (ll. 56–66)

In *The Atheist's Tragedy,* on the other hand, Levidulcia's indiscriminateness is farcical. In Act II she is sexually aroused by the departure of a newly wedded couple to bed, hastily arranges a tryst with her stepson-in-law Sebastian, and turns hotly to the servant Fresco before Sebastian has time to keep his appointment. Sebastian's legal kinship to her merely stresses the all-inclusiveness of her appetite. Indiscriminate lust finds its most grotesque reduction in the relationship between Hecate and her son Firestone in Middleton's *The Witch.* The son has asked to borrow the family night-mare to carry out a sexual intrigue.

> HECATE
> And who shall lie with me, then?
> FIRESTONE
> The great cat
> For one night, mother; 'tis but a night:
> Make shift with him for once.

HECATE
You're a kind son!
But 'tis the nature of you all; I see that
You had rather hunt after strange women still
Than lie with your own mothers.

(I, pp. 129–130)

The son gets his means of conveyance, Hecate presumably settling for the great cat. The casual comicality of the whole conversation is Middleton's point. Sex of every variety is the witches' profession; they advise other characters on sexual matters and create incubi for their own satisfaction. Complete lack of discrimination marks their activities: cats and incubi substitute for men, and sons are indistinguishable from lovers.

Since incest manifests indiscriminate lust, hence accomplished depravity, it is characteristically combined in its perpetrator with a variety of other sins. Thus Cambises of Preston's play is intemperate, headstrong, and bloody, his incestuous marriage with his cousin merely one example of his villainy. Claudius of *Hamlet* is a drunkard, a murderer, and a usurper, as well as an incestmonger. Lelia of Fletcher's *The Captain* is appallingly unfilial even before she conceives her incestuous passion for her father. Ammon of Peele's *David and Bethsabe* multiplies the evil of his rape on his sister Thamar by his rejection of her. Frederick of Shirley's *The Lady of Pleasure* demonstrates the depths of his descent into debauchery by his sexual approach to his aunt. Often the very motive for incest is not only sexual interest but revenge or greed. Herod Frappatore of Marston's *The Fawn* lies with his sister-in-law as much out of hatred and envy of his brother as out of sheer concupiscence. The characters of Massinger and Fletcher's *The Spanish Curate* use incest for revenge, as does the bastard Spurio in *The Revenger's Tragedy* who lies with his stepmother to wrong his father. [10] The motive of greed—for money, for position, or for political power— occurs in *The Spanish Curate, Hamlet, Cambises, Pericles, The Dev-*

---

10. Necessarily, the incest in these episodes of revenge is legal rather than biological. Spurio's chief interest is to cuckold the man who disinherited him. Were the Duchess his own mother, the sin would injure him more than it would his father. Despite ecclesiastical dogma, Renaissance audiences, like modern ones, clearly felt the bond of blood to be closer than the bond of sacrament.

il's Law-case, and Mason's *The Turk,* where Borgias woos his niece for
her political inheritance. The synthesizing of varieties of evil and indiscriminate sexuality through incest is particularly neat in *The Phoe-
nix,* where Middleton's juvenile preachiness clarifies his handling of
convention. Judge Falso solicits his niece because of a genital itch: he
needs a woman. But he picks this woman because by so using her he
would save the expense of a wife at the same time as, through prevent-
ing her marriage, he would retain control of her dowry. His lust is finally at the service of his greed, a greed adept to any crime, any breech
of promise, any offense against nature and hospitality. Falso's venality
is totally impersonal, incest ironically the appropriate indication of
how far that impersonality extends.

Finally, a perverse sort of family pride or solidarity is a suggested
motive for the incest of *Pericles, The Witch,* D'Amville's attack on his
daughter-in-law in *The Atheist's Tragedy,* and especially that repository of Renaissance family horrors, Barnes's *The Devil's Charter; or,
The Tragedy of Pope Alexander Sixth.* Barnes's play, about the Borgias, epitomizes drama in which incest is only one of the evils—for example, blasphemy, diabolism, sodomy, murder—perpetrated by the
protagonist. Here the incest is multiple, for not only does Pope Alexander sleep with his daughter Lucretia, but she with her brother Caesar. Indiscriminate lust indeed. But family pride as an additional motive for incest, as for all the actions of Pope Alexander, is to be found
both in Barnes and in his sources.[11] The historical Alexander was impelled on his ignoble course by the desire to immortalize himself
through aggrandizing his progeny. Renaissance understanding of the
Borgias was ill-served by the fact that salient portions of the most reli-
able historical source, Guicciardini's *History of Italy,* were expurgated
by the Roman See and remained largely unpublished until the eigh-
teenth century.[12] Nevertheless, common opinion was certain that not

11. R. B. McKerrow, Barnes's editor in the *Materialien zur Kunde des älteren Englis-
chen Dramas* (Louvain, 1904), cites appropriate passages from the Fenton translation of
Guicciardini's *History of Italy* (McKerrow, pp. 104–105). A discussion of Borgia family
relations, undoubtedly known to Barnes, occurs also in Innocent Gentillet's *Anti-Ma-
chiavel.* See the reprint of the 1576 edition edited by Edward Rathé (Geneva, 1968), pp.
338–339.

12. See the comments of Sidney Alexander, pp. xvi–xviii, in the preface to his recent
translation of the *History* (New York, 1969). The most salient expurgated passage occurs in book 3, pp. 123–124, of Alexander's edition.

only greed and arrogance, but also, in Guicciardini's words, "tender and boundless love," [13] held the father to his children. [14]

The interest—I will not say the importance—of *The Devil's Charter* in the handling of incest lies not in its propagation of gossip about the Borgias but in its tantalizing failure to exploit the psychological possibilities inherent in the motif. Where incest is a variety of evil it is rarely the center of the dramatic action. So long as it is only a single example of unexamined nastiness it seems hardly enough on which to build a play. But the story of the Borgias provides multiple examples of a potentially very revealing sort of nastiness. The play's treatment of the rise and death of Roderic Borgia suggests that, behind the collection of iniquities, Barnes almost perceived the governing selfishness of the man—a selfishness not equivalent simply to greed, lust for power, sensual indulgence, or any other of the foibles of all men, but an absolute property of self-regarding, an absolute incapacity for emotional contact with others. Either Barnes did not see that he had such an organizing principle, or he did not care. Certainly the play exploits the multiplicity and variety of Borgia family transgressions rather than their psychological similarity. But the incestuous sexual concentration that runs through the history of such a family lies available to other writers seeking to dramatize the catastrophic results of solipsism.

Witting Incest—The Failure of Exchange

There are a few plays in which a witting incestuous attraction either overtakes characters otherwise portrayed as good or results in so powerful an upheaval that it becomes the chief means of creating the character's personality. The effects of such a use of incest are twofold.

13. *The History of Florence,* trans. Mario Domandi (New York, 1970), p. 241. This history was unknown to the Renaissance, having reposed in the Guicciardini family vault for 350 years after it was written. But the sentiments of the author here seem to express the general opinions of the Borgias' contemporaries.

14. In discussing suspicions of incest in *The Duchess of Malfi,* William Empson refers to the common understanding of Elizabethans about the Borgias. "Elizabethans believed that Lucrezia Borgia went to bed with her brothers because, owing to her intense family pride, which was like that of the Pharoahs, she could find no fit mate elsewhere." " 'Mine Eyes Dazzle,' a review of Clifford Leech's *Webster: 'The Duchess of Malfi,' " Essays in Criticism,* XIV (1964), 85.

Since these characters are not mere degenerates, the collision between passion and moral norms causes a potentially revealing anguish. And since the passion cuts off a usual and necessary form of social exchange, it threatens to consume the family and cripple the society in which it takes place. The anguish and the threat do not always take stage center. In Ford's *The Lady's Trial,* where a minor character entertains a circumspect and unrequited love for his married cousin, the hint of incestuous passion merely flavors one of the play's many examples of ethical discrimination and control. In Lyly's *Mother Bombie* and Brome's *The Lovesick Court,* where quite subsidiary to the main unwitting incest plot are the agonies of characters in love with supposed siblings, the way out of the fiction as well as the fact of incest is revelation of the distant fostering of a baby or two, and in both plays clues to this changeling device proliferate from the moment the prospect of incest is introduced. For Lyly and Brome, witting incest is a minor piece of structural complication made dramaturgically easy by the main unwitting incest plot. It is hard to tell where the focus lies in Fletcher's *The Fair Maid of the Inn.* The potential for psychological complexity inherent in the intimations of long-standing sexual interest between Cesario and his sister is forgotten in the complexity of unwitting incest which follows when the mother, to save him from a family feud, maintains that Cesario is not her son. The evidence of these several plays suggests that witting incest, except as a manifestation of pervasive evil, is too potent a motif to be used with any great success in a minor strain. Ford soft-pedals the theme almost to nonexistence, Brome and Lyly undercut it from the start, and Fletcher (and, it may be, collaborators) simply loses his way, introducing a striking and significant idea that goes nowhere.

There are several plays, however, which do not lose their way. *A King and No King, Women Beware Women, The Unnatural Combat,* and *'Tis Pity She's a Whore,* to give them in their most likely order of composition, are the most interesting of the few English Renaissance plays that set witting incest squarely in the center of the action. Massinger's *The Unnatural Combat* is the least good of the four, in part because it is caught halfway between the use of incest as a manifestation of general evil and its more sophisticated use as the prime indicator of specific personality disorder and social malaise. Judging from his actions, Malefort the protagonist is a thoroughly bad man. Some years preceding the play's action, he lusted after the mistress of his friend Montreville and poisoned his wife to marry her. During the play he self-righteously and savagely kills in a duel the son of that first marriage who seeks to avenge his mother, and he breaks his promise to give Montreville the hand of his daughter Theocrine in order to bestow her more advantageously. Then, increasingly consumed with passion for his daughter, he delays her marriage and is on his way to rape her when he is forestalled by Montreville's own rape upon her and her ensuing death. Lest we mistake the nature and degree of Malefort's wickedness, Massinger kills him with a stroke of lightning that leaves his body black and putrifying, the fate also visited on Antiochus, the incestuous father in *Pericles,* and Remilia, the incestuous sister in *A Looking Glass for London and England.*

Malefort's passion for Theocrine is certainly a manifestation of evil. But it is neither indiscriminate nor calculating, at least one of which descriptions applies to those incests we have labeled under the "manifestation of evil" category. Malefort loves his daughter, as Montreville loves her, because she is the image of her dead mother. And, far from welcoming his lust or seeking to gain by it, he struggles against it with all the fury and hopelessness of his uncontrollably passionate nature. In fact, Theocrine falls into Montreville's hands precisely because her father has demanded, in a despairing effort to quell his longing, that his friend lock her away from him.

Incestuous love, then, represents a culpable passion which Malefort recognizes and despises but is unable to resist. But there are culpable passions aplenty in the lives of Renaissance characters, as of men and women generally. Why incest? What does this degree of focus on this particular rebellion of body, mind, and spirit give Massinger that he cannot get any other way? The very prohibition against incest may of course be provocative to the arrogant character who is tempted to think himself above the law. "The *fact of being a rule,* completely independent of its modalities, is indeed the very essence of the incest prohibition," Lévi-Strauss maintains.[15] To be told that there is something he may not do, or may not have, simply because society says so,

---

15. *The Elementary Structures of Kinship,* p. 32.

can be enough to whet the proud man's appetite. Proud Malefort certainly is, and he eventually rationalizes his passion in the utterly conventional vein and with the utterly conventional examples of the Renaissance "sinner-as-free-thinker" which constitutes a veritable trope:
the gods do it, the beasts do it, why should not I do it? (V.i.19–42). [16]
Thus he seeks by co-opting a position in the hierarchical order at once
above and below his own to evade his human status and with it the
rules that bind human culture. There are other rules, certainly, against
murder, false dealing, slaying one's own children, and Malefort breaks
them all. But the rule against incest is a particularly good indicator of
moral attitudes because it is not challengeable on the grounds of expe-
diency or self-preservation but is challengeable only on the grounds of
self-will, and for that reason its violation is Malefort's culminating
antisocial act.

In addition to the formal fact of being a rule, the incest prohibition
involves as we have seen the maintenance of a system of culture-creating
or culture-enhancing exchange. Following Lévi-Strauss's analysis, the
character who engages in incest takes for his own consumption the
goods that should be available for exchange; by monopolizing his family, he fails to create the social obligations of others toward him that
knit up the social fabric. Massinger dramatizes this failure of social ex-

16. Ovid's *Metamorphoses* serves as a *locus classicus* for this as for so many other Renaissance tropes on the relations between man and nature. "The gods do it" is the ra-
tionalization of Byblis debating her love for her brother Caunis (Ninth Book, ll. 590–
597, of Arthur Golding's 1567 translation); "the beasts do it" is the refrain of Myrrha in
defense of her love for her father Cinyras (Tenth Book, ll. 357–367). Myrrha (ll. 367–
372) also has recourse to the example of other realms where incest, far from forbidden,
is preferred. Donne, in his metamorphic fragment "Metempsychosis," provides the Ju-
deo-Christian version of those other realms in his reference (ll. 201–203) to the time before men "tooke laws which made freedome lesse" when incest "Till now unlawfull,
therefore ill, t'was not." The laws are first and foremost those of Leviticus, chaps. 18
and 20. Among our plays, the example of the gods provides the excuse in *A Looking
Glass for London and England* (I.i.71–119); the beasts are the example in *The Atheist's
Tragedy* (IV.iii.127–130), *The Lovesick Court* (III.iii), *Aglaura* (II.iii.5–18), *A King and
No King* (IV.iv.131–138); and a more generalized appeal to Nature figures in *The Turk*
(I.iii.76—Nature "thou art my God"), *The Captain* (IV.iv.194–195—if Nature does not
approve, "Our organs / will not fit"), and *'Tis Pity She's a Whore* (I.i). Ornstein, pp. 203–
207, discusses the Renaissance argument about nature and incest in reference to its use
in *'Tis Pity*.

change in both variety and detail. Malefort's initial impulse is to give his daughter away, promising her first to Montreville and then to Beaufort Jr. This second offer, the only one of which Theocrine is aware, is the healthy one: young Beaufort woos her ardently, though modestly, and she responds in kind. It is, however, this very courtship that brings Malefort's incestuous attachment into the open. From the moment (II.iii) that Beaufort Jr. accepts the opportunity to seek Theocrine's consent, the father grows increasingly doting, increasingly jealous, increasingly cognizant of his own desires. He cannot give his daughter to Beaufort Jr., though the match would be appropriate and advantageous for all. He cannot even give her to Montreville, his alter ego and nemesis, though he would thereby effect a kind of exchange, however suspect, for the woman he took from his friend. Montreville takes her anyway, and performs the rape her father would perform, savagely breaking in upon Malefort's family. Montreville is himself broken in on by the outside world in the persons of the avenging Beauforts, and the tragedy ends with every social connection Malefort has ever made totally annihilated.

We should expect other plays in which witting incest is central to include these essential concerns: the temptation of the prohibited act and the collapse of social exchange. The social-exchange system is a particular focus of *Women Beware Women,* in which incest forms the second plot. The family of that plot is a foursome, the brothers Fabritio and Hippolito, their sister Livia, and Fabritio's daughter Isabella who dotes upon her uncle Hippolito as he on her. As the play opens, Fabritio is urging his daughter to marry the obscene and dim-witted Ward, who repels her. At the same time, she is shaken by her uncle's despairing admission of his long-standing passion for her. Though she enjoys his company above that of all others, she rejects incest with a horror-stricken vigor. Now sister Livia, pitying her brother's distress, undertakes to procure Isabella for him. When Isabella suddenly appears joyfully acquiescent, Hippolito does not pause to inquire the reason, but takes her to him with a maximum of eagerness and a minimum of qualms. What has made the difference is in terms of our schema of types of incest the most ingenious convolution in the canon: Livia has misinformed Isabella that she is not Fabritio's daughter but the result of her mother's adultery. Thus we have a case of actual incest that is witting for Hippolito but unwitting for Isabella, who in fact regards the incest as fictional, believing that the assumption of their consanguinity is erroneous.

Middleton makes maximum plot capital out of this discrepancy between witting and unwitting incest. And he clearly seeks a degree of ambiguity in his audience's response to Isabella. Her willingness to accept a lover who believes he is committing incest and to contract a covering marriage of convenience with the disgusting Ward bespeaks an unsavory casuistical opportunism. Nevertheless, the merchandising of Isabella by her father and her husband-to-be is so unspeakable as to suggest, at least as far as our immediate emotional reactions are concerned, that Isabella is as much sinned against as sinning. Perhaps we have here an explanation of Middleton's rather unusual use of extranuclear incest as a major plot focus, for the fact that this relationship is between uncle and niece, not sister and brother or parent and child, unquestionably weakens its moral repulsiveness. The essence of the witting/unwitting discrepancy, however, lies in the issue of reciprocity. Isabella shares Hippolito's passion but not his willingness to commit incest. When Livia's lie is revealed, Isabella understands that she has been subjected to a kind of rape. But it is the familial relationship, not the sexual act, the label, not the deed, which appalls her. She turns on her aunt, not her uncle, in revenge. To Isabella, Hippolito is the source of her love; it is Livia who is responsible for her sin.

Livia is in fact the heart of this plot altogether. An accomplished bawd, she has made Bianca available to the Duke; making her niece available to her brother is in part merely one more professional challenge. That accomplished, she is herself suddenly smitten and buys with her gold and her attentions Leantio, Bianca's cast-off husband, as her lover. The round of utterly inappropriate unions is complete. The Duke has acquired as mistress the wife of a man who stole her from her family and has lived in fear of discovery since; Leantio out of frustration and spite has become the gigolo of an aging court intriguer; Hippolito is sleeping with his niece; the Ward has acquired as bride a woman who uses him as cover for a continuing affair and ensuing pregnancy. With the exception of the prior marriage of Leantio and Bianca, all these unions have been facilitated by Livia. The inevitable collapse is also triggered by Livia. Hippolito, affronted in his family pride by his sister's liaison with a mere factor, slaughters Leantio. The enraged Livia turns on her brother by telling the truth about their relationship to Isabella, who plots to avenge herself on her aunt, Livia at the same time plotting against Hippolito with the assistance of the guardian avenging his cuckolded Ward. The inappropriateness of his liaison with Bianca has also been insisted upon to the Duke by his brother the Cardinal, whom Bianca now fears and seeks to poison. Various combinations of poetic error and justice bring all to their end in the final masque, an elaborate denouement accomplished with a precision and economy that excite the admiration.

Incest, then, is one of the many corrupt, unnatural, abortive, and doomed sexual transactions of this sexually most mercantile of plays.[17] Again, as in *The Unnatural Combat,* it is the culmination of a family's inability to bestow its members appropriately and hence to create the fruitful exchanges necessary to social well-being. Livia herself makes that point when she first reacts to Hippolito's confession of his incestuous affection:

> Must thy eye
> Dwell evilly on the fairness of thy kindred,
> And seek not where it should? It is confined
> Now in a narrower prison than was made for't:
> It is allowed a stranger; and where bounty
> Is made the great man's honour, 'tis ill husbandry
> To spare, and servants shall have small thanks for't.
> So he Heaven's bounty seems to scorn and mock,
> That spares free means, and spends of his own stock.
>
> (II.i.8–16)

The analogy is with the prestige- and obligation-creating bounty of the gentlemanly householder to his neighbors and retainers (the Renaissance version of the potlatch), and its relation to incest and sexual exchange is precisely the one argued by Lévi-Strauss.

But Livia also is trapped in this narrow prison of a family. It is not certain that Middleton wishes us to see her deep affection for Hippo-

---

17. The best treatment of the play's emphasis on "the corruption of life and love by money" is by Christopher Ricks in "Word-Play in *Women Beware Women*," *RES,* N. S. XII (1961), 238–250.

lito as overtly incestuous, as critics have argued. [18] It *is* certain that Middleton reminds us, as do so many Renaissance playwrights, how close panderism is to the act of sex itself, how frequently the pandering of one family member by another is an act of incest at one remove. [19] Once Livia has served her brother's and her niece's sexual interests and turns to serve her own, she triggers Hippolito's possessiveness, which would sell her for the kind of marital preferment the Duke pretends to offer but which denies her her arrangement with the man of her choosing. Leantio's death is a brief and sudden diversion from what is essentially an erotic familial triangle. The tightness with which uncle, aunt, and niece are bound together is emphasized by the orchestration of their deaths. Livia throws down her flaming gold to smother Isabella; as Hippolito leans over Isabella's body, Livia dies poisoned by her niece's incense; and as Hippolito, who has escaped Guardiano's trap, kisses Isabella's cold lips, Livia's cupids shoot him with poisoned arrows.

18. The argument is made by Daniel Dodson, "Middleton's Livia," *PQ,* XXVII (1948), 376–381, and accepted without real cavil by Roma Gill in the introduction to her edition, pp. xxiii–xxiv.

19. The reminder is especially frequent in Webster. Flamineo of *The White Devil* so enthusiastically and explicitly directs the sexual reconciliation of his sister Vittoria with her lover Bracciano (IV.ii) as virtually to define the type. The pathological insistence of Ferdinand of *The Duchess of Malfi* upon reserving his sister's sexual activities to his own purposes, and his fevered imaginings when he cannot, are sufficient to warrant including the play in our corpus of incest dramas. *The Devil's Law-case,* also included, contains a peculiar variation on the brother/sister relationship in which Romelio bullies his sister Jolenta into agreeing to act as surrogate mother of the child with whom his mistress the young nun Angiolella is pregnant, thereby creating a wonderfully involved figure of asexually incestuous reproduction. But it is no more involved than the frantic image of Isabella in Shakespeare's *Measure for Measure,* who sees herself forced to give birth to her brother Claudio:

> O you beast!
> O faithless coward! O dishonest wretch!
> Wilt thou be made a man out of my vice?
> Is't not a kind of incest, to take life
> From thine own sister's shame?

(III.i.135–139)

'Tis Pity She's a Whore, reminiscent in both major and minor ways of *Women Beware Women,*[20] greatly intensifies the focus on the incestuous couple. Not only is the incest plot the play's major action, but the incest itself is nuclear, completely witting, and, during the play's rising action, completely reciprocal. Ford stresses the closeness of the sibling relationship at every turn: by Giovanni's cry to the Friar that one womb has created and justified "one soul, one flesh, one love, one heart, one all" (I.i.34); by the pacing of the marvelously constructed second scene in which Annabella's suitors—the hotblooded Grimaldi, the masterful Soranzo, the idiot Bergetto—perform one after another below her balcony and she at last comes down to Giovanni; by the repeated stress during the courtship which follows on the kinship terms *brother* and *sister;*[21] by the lovers' echoed oaths on their common mother's dust. Not only is the blood relationship as close but the incest is as demonstrably witting as Ford can make it:

ANNABELLA
You are my brother Giovanni.
GIOVANNI
You
My sister Annabella; I know this

(I.ii.228–229)

But finally it is the fact and quality of the reciprocity between the lovers on which the play both hangs and turns. Its first act is designed to show us two yearning people hastening toward union. Annabella needs no wooing:

20. The most striking resemblance, often remarked, is that between the trios of the matrimonially hopeful guardian, the simpleminded ward, and the obscenely clever servant. Both plays also include the long undeclared affection of the incestuous partners, matrimonial bargaining over the woman as her lover comments, marriage to mask pregnancy, the final revenge banquet, and the minor facts that both Hippolito and Giovanni are scholars from Bologna, and both plays contain the name Hippolito/Hippolita.

21. From his appearance under Annabella's balcony to the end of the scene (I.ii.126–263), Giovanni is called *brother* a total of nine times, while he calls Annabella *sister* eight times. The usages are highly self-conscious and are made to call attention to themselves by their patterning and repetition not just in the shared oath, but throughout.

> thou hast won
> The field, and never fought; what thou hast urg'd
> My captive heart had long ago resolv'd.
> I blush to tell thee—but I'll tell thee now—
> For every sigh that thou hast spent for me
> I have sigh'd ten; for every tear shed twenty:
>
> (I.ii.240–245)

Their confessions made, their vows exchanged, brother and sister have nothing left to do but what they will.

Given the extraordinary reciprocity of their love, it is dramatically fitting that the plot turn on that very factor of reciprocity. More than Annabella's moral qualms are involved. Ford is the most skillfully subtle architect among Stuart dramatists. The play's crisis results from a linked series of plot developments—Annabella's pregnancy, her marriage to Soranzo, Vasquez's discovery of the identity of her lover—as much as her response to the Friar's terrifying description of hellfire. But her repentance, the Friar's advice of marriage, her attempt to send a letter from her prison, the Friar's warning against attending the banquet, her final frightened sense of her brother's danger, all press toward the same thematic point, the need for escape. By their incest, brother and sister have been locked into an intolerably claustrophobic solipsism that excludes God, the society of men, their father's familial hopes. The pregnancy that breaks their concentration on each other gives Friar Bonaventura an opening to urge Annabella to marriage. It is advice for which he has often been critically castigated. But what the Friar urges is the socially necessary alternative to the sexual monopoly of incest. Annabella must marry, must bestow herself beyond her family, as the first step toward health.

Health does not follow marriage, of course, for Annabella has her brother always with her, even in her body. As a result, the marriage perverts the normal social ties, exchanges, and obligations that should accompany it, so that Annabella taunts Soranzo on his obligation toward the "glorious" father of her child (IV.iii.37) and Giovanni literally exchanges Annabella's heart for Soranzo's in the butchery of the final scene (V.vi.73–75). Despite Friar Bonaventura, the sister cannot, the brother will not, free themselves. Entrapment by the situation itself replaces reciprocity of desire and act. The difference shows in Annabella's death scene (V.v) which, unlike the courtship scene, is no duet. Between her fears at the first of the scene (ll. 5–29) and Giovanni's deadly resolve at its end (ll. 45 ff.) there is, it is true, a brief, touching, almost languorous harmony as brother and sister speculate on last things (ll. 29–41). But Annabella's death itself is Giovanni's: he orchestrates it, paces it, justifies it. Reciprocity is gone, replaced by his madness to possess and master totally.

Though Annabella's histrionic wit nearly equals Giovanni's histrionic extravagance, though Livia's panache as *metteur en scène* produces the most brilliant effects of her play, though Malefort's passion ends in a literal bolt of lightning, it cannot be said that Massinger, Middleton, or Ford plays with incest. Beaumont and Fletcher do play, however, and *A King and No King* provides a useful summary of the plot possibilities of incest precisely because it so consciously exploits all the dichotomies whose uses we have anatomized. Arbaces the young king of Iberia, long abroad warring in Armenia, returns home victorious to be reintroduced to and fall passionately in love with his sister Panthea, who finds him as attractive as he her. Arbaces fights frantically against his passion, first refusing to acknowledge Panthea as his sister, then having her confined under guard, seeking a pander among his officers, recoiling from the pander in horror, confessing his love to Panthea (and she hers to him), resolving with her to suppress their love, exchanging familial hands and kisses which quickly grow hotter than they may. At last driven beyond control, Arbaces is on his way to Panthea's prison to perform the rape and suicide which seem his only outlet when he learns to his exuberant relief that Panthea and he are not sister and brother and that she is the queen rather than he the king. Never did ruler more joyfully unthrone himself: "Come everyone / That takes delight in goodness; help to sing / Loud thanks for me, that I am prov'd no king" (V.iv.351–353).

This incest is almost maximally intense: biological, nuclear, reciprocal, witting, threatened with consummation. But it is also fictional, hedged round with a remarkably complex and adept structure of exposition, counterpoint, and foreshadowing which carries the play through a risky passage to its comedic end of union between the principals. Now the essence of fictional incest is the matter of whose fiction it is, and why. Not Arbaces and Panthea the children, but Gobrius and Arane the parents are the begetters of the confusion, a confusion twenty years in the making. After the death of her husband the old king, Arane the queen mother had wed Gobrius, the honorable lord protector of the kingdom whose task it was to raise the old king's heir Arbaces. Unbeknown to any but the perpetrators, however, Arbaces is not the son of Arane and the old king. He is the son of Gobrius and his first wife, given as an infant to Arane to pass off as her own when, faced with the impotence of her aged husband, she sought an heir to consolidate her position and the royal succession. But the old king when he died left Arane pregnant with Panthea. So Gobrius and Arane have inherited a tangle of their own making. They have raised Arbaces as king because that is what they claimed him to be. Now Arane, bedeviled with ambition for her daughter Panthea, the rightful heir, seeks by plots and poisons to eliminate Arbaces, while Gobrius, who likewise wants the princess to enjoy her own, tries simultaneously to protect the life and interests of his son.

Essential to the play's conduct are two features that work changes on standard incest plots. One involves Arbaces' personality and status, which the authors take great pains to establish. Though by no means pathologically evil or degenerate, Arbaces is a headstrong, explosively volatile man who glories in exercising both his valor and his passions. And as Iberia's king and military commander, he has potentially total power over its court, its army, its citizens, its conquered domains. The combination makes him exciting, often admirable, and always exceedingly dangerous, a person who may be guided only with tact, subtlety, boldness, and a goodly measure of luck. To attempt to unking such a man is to court disaster. Though exaggerated by plot requirements, both the powerful status and the willful, volatile personality are typical of most male perpetrators of witting incest, and the combination is usually tragic. Beaumont and Fletcher exploit this type ironically by making the very heat of Arbaces' nature and his eventual eagerness to embrace a reduction in status the factors that allow the resolution of the dilemma.

The other mutation involves the second pair of lovers, Tigranes the conquered king of Armenia and Spaconia his betrothed. Arbaces has brought his noble enemy home as potential husband for Panthea; Spaconia has followed to protect her interests. We have seen this Rival Friend quadrangle before, as an unwitting incest plot in which the friend falls in love with the king's sweetheart, thereby becoming a rival to the king, but upon the revelation that friend and sweetheart are brother and sister transfers his allegiance to the king's sister. In *A King and No King,* the wrinkle is that the king's sweetheart *is* the king's sister, or seems to be. In attempting to woo the sister, as he was intended to do, Tigranes (who despite himself is smitten) is blocked by the king's sexual interest in her. Beaumont and Fletcher's variation, made possible by the substitution of witting fictional incest for unwitting actual incest, is *not* to shift allegiances at all, but by the usual fifth-act revelation to keep them constant: because they are *not* related, Arbaces and Panthea may continue to love, as Tigranes and Spaconia, under honorable control once more, may do also.

The central tangle of the play is unwound by Gobrius's exploitation of Arbaces' personality, by manipulating Arbaces into wanting Panthea more than he wants his kingdom so that with skill and care he may in the end have both. For this manipulation to work in dramatic, as distinct from merely dynastic, terms, the audience must know that something is going on, if not precisely what. They must see Gobrius as producer and presenter of this drama but must fear with him the unpredictable temper of the king. The clues to Gobrius's purpose and Arbaces' possible responses come thick: Gobrius's cultivation of the brother's and sister's admiration for each other; their accusations that he has deliberately created their passion and his refusal to deny the fact; his discouragement of the marriage with Tigranes; his early, hinting exchange with Arane that shows them allied yet at cross-purposes; Arbaces' temperamental unwillingness to believe that Panthea is his sister and Bessus's sycophantic "She's nothing like you"; Arbaces' arrogance coupled with a filial piety that can pardon his mother's murderous assaults; the play's very title.

To what end, beyond display of the dramaturgical virtuosity of the authors and their creature Gobrius, does this extraordinary complication tend? Renaissance dramatists, we have seen, demonstrate Lévi-Strauss's central thesis about the attraction and the taboo of incest, that "the joys . . . of a world in which one might *keep to oneself,*" in which one might "gain without losing, enjoy without sharing," are finally "eternally denied to social man." [22] The unwitting incest plays of the Cavalier dramatists show the social pleasures of that denial in their

---

22. *The Elementary Structures of Kinship,* p. 497.

most stylized, most painless form. The witting incest plays of Massinger, Middleton, and Ford, even as they celebrate that keeping to oneself, anatomize the tragedy of its social failure. By its manipulation of fact and fiction, *A King and No King* succeeds in having it both ways by turning loss into gain. At the moment that Arbaces and Panthea lose each other as brother and sister, they gain each other as husband and wife. In a sense they participate in both the joy of incest, if one will, and the social health of exogamy. Critics are quick to see (and to damn) the joy, less quick to appreciate the health. But it is important to understand what Gobrius has managed to bring about: an utterly bloodless palace coup, the recognition and reconciliation of children and parents, marriage between the *de jure* and *de facto* possessors of the throne. The argument against incest, we must remember, is the argument for the necessity of marital exchanges that create and cement social relationships. The marriage of Arbaces and Panthea is clearly appropriate; in fact, it is utterly necessary for the well-being of the realm. The authors' integrity as well as brilliance lies in their refusal to dip into the stock accidents of romance to effect that well-being. The awkward conception of Panthea possibly excepted, all the plot elements, both past and present, result from the psychologically consistent actions of the characters. Arane and Gobrius created the problem; it is Gobrius, with precious little help from Arane, who makes the solution. Not pirates, storms, or fortuitous birth tokens, not beneficent gods or improbable disguises, but the needs, fears, deceptions, accommodations, initiatives, and passions of the characters bring about the loud thanks of the play's conclusion. If by virtue of the relationship between Arane and Gobrius the marriage of their children results in a condition of legal incest, that is merely a final unnoticed playfulness to which Beaumont and Fletcher are surely entitled.

This survey suggests that incest is one of the distinctive motifs of the Jacobean and Caroline theater not primarily because it is sensational, but because it gives superbly dramatic realization to an absolute clash between individual urges and social demands in which the moral is pointed not through sermon, but through structure. Granted that incest is portrayed in virtually every variation, and that justifying arguments of every sort—moving, pitiful, self-serving, perverse—abound.

So much for sensation. Granted also that morally normative characters (Friar Bonaventura) and speeches (Livia's to Hippolito) and situations (Young Beaufort's contract for Theocrine's hand) openly argue against it. So much for sermon. But however incest figures in the plays, its moral point is made primarily by its structural point, which is this: since it prevents absolutely the reconciliation of individual and social desires toward which Renaissance drama always moves at last, incest for so long as it exists literally prevents a play from coming to an end. Not, unlike betrayal or revenge or murder or rape, a tool by means of which the dramatist arrives at that reconciliation, incest is more accurately an image of anti-society, a condition in which solipsism is expressed by a perversely social act and lovers use the family to unmake the meaning of family. Whatever the type of incest, however the resolution of the plot, no matter the tone or manner of the play, this Renaissance sense of the absolute irreconcilability of incest to the final shape of the play accounts, I believe, for much of its dramatic attraction. This is why unwitting lovers can be stopped in their tracks and the whole fabric of a play's relationships can be reknit at a word of revelation. This is why the doom that surrounds witting lovers is so palpable and so poignant. At stake is not merely the punishment of evil, but the elimination of impossibility. Incest, to the spectators' titillation, no doubt, but also to their edification, is society's anti-image. The play can come to rest only by breaking that image.

Machiavelli and the Machiavel

MARGARET SCOTT

I N THE 1890s Edward Meyer set about ransacking the British Museum. He had recently made the acquaintance of "Kyd, Marlowe, Greene, Peele, Jonson, Chapman, Marston, Dekker, Middleton, Webster, Massinger, Ford, and other of Shakespere's great contemporaries" and had been struck by "the number of times Machiavelli and Aretino were referred to" and the manner in which what he "then supposed to be the former's political principles were cited and put into practice by the villains of dramatic literature." [1] Meyer, according to his own account, then made a careful study of Machiavelli and, on turning back to the drama, concluded that Kyd, Marlowe, Greene et al. had perverted the maxims of the Florentine statesman "in a manner infinitely unjust" (p.ix). The Machiavel, he decided, could not have sprung directly from "the works of the great politician" (p.ix) but must have his origins in some secondary source. This, in the course of his ransacking, Meyer discovered in the *Contre-Machiavel* of Innocent Gentillet. [2]

1. Edward Meyer, *Machiavelli and the Elizabethan Drama* (Weimar, 1897), p. ix.

2. Innocent Gentillet, *Discours sur les moyens de bien gouverner et maintenir en bonne paix un royaume ou autre principauté: Divisez en trois partis; a savoir, du conseil, de la religion et police que doit tenir un Prince: Contre Nicholas Machiavel Florentin* (Geneva, 1576).

147

148 MARGARET SCOTT

"Scarcely were a few pages perused, when it became perfectly evident that this was the book from which the dramatists drew: a careful study of the same, together with the discovery that an English translation was made by one Simon Patericke in 1577,[3] the year after its appearance in French, has proved Gentillet, beyond a doubt, the source of all the Elizabethan misunderstanding."[4]

Meyer completed his argument for the severance of the Machiavel from Machiavelli by pointing out that while Gentillet's unjust restatement of "the great politician's" axioms and his 639 pages of refutation were available in an English translation from as early as 1577, "the weightiest writings of Machiavelli remained un-Englished till Dacres's version[5] of the 'Discorsi' in 1636 and of the 'Principe' in 1640."[6]

Since the appearance of Meyer's *Machiavelli and the Elizabethan Drama* in 1897, his thesis, supported by the 395 references to Machiavelli that he turned up during his reading of Elizabethan literature, has appeared so impregnable a monument to thoroughgoing Germanic industry that nobody has shown much eagerness to assault it. Even the most temperate and thoughtful of commentators have apparently accepted Meyer's findings as unquestionable. George Bull, for instance, remarks in his introduction to his admirable translation of *The Prince:* "The legend of Machiavelli's depravity was already established by the time the first English translation appeared in 1640."[7] J.A. Mazzeo is sure that "the numerous explicit defamatory references to Machiavelli in Elizabethan drama must have been derived from Gentillet in the original or in translation,"[8] and Eric W. Cochrane, in an acute

3. Innocent Gentillet, *A Discourse upon the Meanes of Wel Governing and Maintaining in Good Peace a Kingdom*, trans. Simon Patericke (London, 1602).
4. Meyer, p. x.
5. *Machiavels Discourses upon the first decade of T. Livius translated out of the Italian; with some marginall animadversions noting and taxing his errors. By E. D.* (London, 1636); *The Prince. Also, the life of Castruccio Castracani of Lucca. And the means Duke Valentine us'd to put to death Vitellozzo Vitelli, Oliverotto of Fermo, Paul and the Duke of Gravina. Translated out of Italian into English, by E. D. With some animadversions noting and taxing his errors* (London, 1640).
6. Meyer, pp. ix–x.
7. Niccolò Machiavelli, *The Prince*, trans. George Bull (Harmondsworth, 1961), p. 9.
8. J. A. Mazzeo, *Renaissance and Seventeenth Century Studies* (London, 1964), p. 118.

and comprehensive survey of two decades of comment on Machiavelli, dismisses the question of Machiavelli among the Elizabethans with: "A few, finally, have continued the study of the fate of Machiavelli among his successors. They have shown that his Elizabethan critics saw him exclusively through the eyes of Gentillet."[9]

In general, then, the question of the existence of any genuine connection between the Machiavel and the teachings of *The Prince* and *The Discourses* has been seen as settled once and for all. Instead, the Machiavel's affinities with the Senecan tyrant[10] and with the Vice of the morality play[11] have been exhaustively explored with the result that emphases on a taste for gore and impassioned rhetoric or for abetting the devil and capering with unholy glee have lent yet further substance to the widely held conviction that the Machiavel represents no more than a travesty of the doctrines of "the father of political science."

Yet that Meyer's little book should have exerted so enduring and profound an influence must appear surprising to anyone who cares to read beyond his preface. As he proceeds, Meyer, while holding to his Gentillet theory with one hand, industriously undercuts it with the other. By the end of the book one feels impelled to inquire whether, after all, the Machiavel might not reflect both some real knowledge of Machiavelli's teaching and some assessment of that teaching not wholly dependent on the Protestant bias and partisan politics of the *Contre-Machiavel*.

Printing of *The Prince* and *The Discourses* was banned in England throughout the sixteenth century, and much play has been made with the suggestion that the dramatists had no opportunity to form any real acquaintance with Machiavelli's writings, that, in the nature of things, they came at *The Prince* and *The Discourses* only through Patericke's

9. Eric W. Cochrane, "Machiavelli 1940–1960," *Journal of Modern History,* XXXIII (1961), 113.

10. Mario Praz, while recognizing that Machiavelli was known to Donne or Ralegh, insists that the stage Machiavel owes more to Seneca and Cinthio than to the author of *The Prince*. See Mario Praz, "Machiavelli and the Elizabethans," *Proceedings of the British Academy,* XIV (March 1928), rpt. in *The Flaming Heart* (New York, 1958).

11. See, for example, Bernard Spivack, *Shakespeare and the Allegory of Evil* (New York, 1958).

1577 translation of Gentillet, until, in 1636 and 1640, the Dacres versions appeared. Yet, as Meyer himself admits, the first edition of Patericke's work appeared only in 1602. It would seem, then, that for twenty-five years Gentillet indoctrinated the dramatists through the medium of an English translation in manuscript, unless, of course, "Shakespeare's great contemporaries" turned to the original French or to a Latin translation made shortly after the *Contre-Machiavel* was first published.

If Elizabethan dramatists were prepared to read French and Latin (and many, of course, were) there seems no reason why they should have read Gentillet more avidly than other more accurate renderings of Machiavelli. There was a French translation of *The Prince,* dedicated to the Earl of Arran in 1553, as well as a series of at least seven Latin translations, which appeared between 1560 and 1622. There were also the editions of the Italian texts of both *The Prince* and *The Discourses* printed by John Wolfe in 1584. [12] These editions, issued in defiance of the censor, without license and under the false imprint "Palermo," were clearly produced at some risk to meet what must have been a considerable demand.

And this demand evoked more than French, Latin, or Italian versions of Machiavelli's more controversial doctrines. Had Meyer continued his ransacking of the British Museum a little longer he might have come upon three separate Elizabethan translations of *The Prince,* contained in five different English manuscripts as well as an English translation of *The Discourses* dated 1599. These were finally brought to light by Napoleone Orsini in the 1930s, along with two further manuscript translations of *The Prince* and two unfinished English versions of *The Discourses.* [13] These manuscripts, according to Irving Ribner, "were evidently widely circulated." [14]

12. See A. Gerber, "All of the Five Fictitious Italian Editions of the Writings of Machiavelli and Three of those of Pietro Aretino, Printed by John Wolfe of London (1584–88)," *MLN,* XXII (1907), 129-135; L. Goldberg, "A Note on John Wolfe, Elizabethan Printer," *Historical Studies: Australia and New Zealand,* VII (1955), 55–61.

13. See Napoleone Orsini, "Machiavelli's *Discourses:* A MSS Translation of 1599," *TLS,* 10 October 1936, p. 820; Napoleone Orsini, "Elizabethan Manuscript Translations of Machiavelli's *Prince,*" *Journal of the Warburg Institute,* I (1937–1938), 166–169; Hardin Craig, ed., *Machiavelli's* Prince: *An Elizabethan Translation* (Chapel Hill, N. C., 1944), pp. v–xxxii.

14. Irving Ribner, "The Significance of Gentillet's *Contre-Machiavel,*" *MLQ,* X (1949), 154.

The painstaking research of Hardin Craig, Ribner, and Orsini has made it very plain that a dramatist like Kyd or Marlowe would have had little difficulty in securing reasonably accurate and readable versions of Machiavelli's original works—less difficulty, perhaps, than was involved in obtaining a French or Latin edition of Gentillet or a manuscript copy of Simon Patericke's 1577 translation.

It is equally plain that the dramatists, having Machiavelli within easy reach, in some instances took him from the shelf. Material such as the Cambridge letters of Gabriel Harvey ("sum good fellowes amongst us begin nowe to be pretty well acquainted with a certayne parlous booke callid . . . Il Principe"),[15] together with the citation and commentary that occur in the prose writings of a number of poets, scholars, and divines, indicates that Machiavelli was widely read, much debated, and quoted at length in literary circles and at the universities. Moreover, the nondramatic works of some practicing playwrights such as Jonson, Chapman, or Greene can sometimes evidence a detailed, firsthand acquaintanceship with Machiavelli's political theory. Although it has done little to dispel the legend of the dramatists' dependence on Gentillet, all this has evoked considerable interest. An impressive amount of research has been conducted into the reactions to Machiavelli exhibited by Elizabethans ranging from Spenser to Donne and from Ralegh to Bacon,[16] and the influence of Machiavelli on Jonson's *Discoveries* has also received some attention.[17] It has by now been made abundantly clear that in Marlowe's Cambridge or the School of Night, in Elizabeth's court or the precincts of Pauls there were numbers of literati, including playwrights, who were very well acquainted indeed with certain parlous books.

In turning to the testimony of the plays one encounters certain difficulties. It is easy enough to point to lines like Barabas's "But Malta

15. Gabriel Harvey, "A Third Letter of Harvey to Spenser," in *The Works of Gabriel Harvey, D.C.L.,* ed. Alexander B. Grosart (London, 1884), I, 138.

16. See, for example, E. A. Greenlaw, "The Influence of Machiavelli on Spenser," *MP,* *VII* (1909), 187ff.; M. C. Bradbrook, *The School of Night: A Study in the Literary Relationships of Sir Walter Raleigh* (Cambridge, Eng., 1936), p. 72; Mario Praz, "Machiavelli and the Elizabethans," pp. 123, 134–140; Vincent Luciani, "Bacon and Machiavelli," *Italica,* XXIV (1947), 26–40.

17. See, for example, C. H. Herford and Percy and Evelyn Simpson, eds., *Ben Jonson* (Oxford, 1925-1952), XI, 248–250, and Daniel C. Boughner, *The Devil's Disciple* (New York, 1968), pp. 138–152.

hates me, and in hating me / My life's in danger" (*The Jew of Malta,* v.ii.29–30)[18] and to discover their origin in chapter 19 of *The Prince:* "when a prince has the goodwill of the people he should not worry about conspiracies, but when the people are hostile and regard him with hatred he should go in fear of everything and everyone."[19] It is equally easy to insist on the similarity between Barabas's scheme for killing all the Turks at a banquet and Oliverotto of Fermo's plot for ridding himself of potential enemies which Machiavelli describes in considerable detail (*Prince,* chap. VIII). Yet here the ground is sometimes treacherous. A play, as against a prose refutation or a political pamphlet, is unlikely to contain extended quotation or blow-by-blow analyses of whole chapters of *The Prince,* and scattered references to avoiding hatred, to lions and foxes, or to breaking oaths like piecrusts might, once the ball had started rolling, be drawn from earlier plays, from the proliferating prose commentary, or, as in Jonson's *Sejanus,* from the Tacitus, Livy, Sallust, or Plutarch upon which Machiavelli himself relied.

The same kind of difficulty arises in attempting to trace a direct connection between the actions and character of Barabas—or Richard III or Iago—and those of any of the political personae from whose strategies Machiavelli reads lessons for his prince.

Yet, for all this, the difficulties are not always of a kind to send one flying back, in Meyer's wake, to Gentillet. Whether a dramatist worked with *The Prince* at his elbow or whether he simply picked up scraps of quotation and opinion by rubbing shoulders with those who did is not, in the end, the central issue. The more important question is whether the playwrights' knowledge of Machiavelli, firsthand or not, was associated with any genuine understanding of Machiavellian theory.

Even those scholars who have rejected the time-honored "Gentillet theory" and who acknowledge that Machiavelli was available and

18. All quotations from Marlowe's plays are from *Complete Plays and Poems,* ed. E. D. Pendry and J. C. Maxwell (London, 1976).

19. Quotations from *The Prince* are from Bull's translation. I have also consulted *Machiavelli: The Chief Works and Others,* trans. Allan Gilbert (Durham, N.C., 1958). In selecting translations I have been guided by the Italian text of L. Arthur Burd in his still unsurpassed *Il Principe di Niccolò Machiavelli.*

even known to Elizabethan dramatists have been reluctant to admit that the Machiavel owes anything of substance to his namesake. Barabas, they insist, still stands at a great distance from Machiavelli's ideal statesman, and does so not because Marlowe had failed to read *The Prince,* but because he lacked the historical perspective that might have enabled him to understand his reading.

Irving Ribner, in his article, "The Significance of Gentillet's *Contre-Machiavel,*" makes it clear that the Machiavel is the product neither of ignorance nor of exclusive dependence on Gentillet. "This," he asserts, "is the undeniable fact which most scholars so far have failed to face; they have sought to explain the 'Machiavel' on the basis of Gentillet's work rather than on that of Machiavelli himself. And of all the factors which helped to build the monstrous legend with which his name was associated, Elizabethan acquaintance with his own works was the most important." So far, perhaps, so good, but Ribner goes on to suggest that the Elizabethans read Machiavelli's works "without the historical perspective that enables us to understand them today," and they "failed also to realise that *The Prince* was an occasional work not meant to apply to conditions other than those of Italy in Machiavelli's day," and that, finally, "The first reason, then, for the growth of the Machiavellian legend lay in the content of the works themselves and in the inability of the Elizabethan mind to see them in their proper perspective."[20]

That there was a legend in some sense can hardly be denied. It was, of course, older than Gentillet,[21] with its origins in the indictment brought against Machiavelli by Ascham, Pole, and a host of Continental adversaries.[22] Whether the principal charge—that of atheism—proceeded from any fundamental misunderstanding of Machiavelli's writings is debatable. What has to be admitted is that allegations of atheism

---

20. Ribner, p. 155.

21. See J. C. Maxwell, "English Anti-Machiavellianism before Gentillet," *N&Q,* N.S.I (1954), 141.

22. See Roger Ascham, *A Report and Discourse . . . of the Affaires and State of Germany,* in *English Works,* ed. W. A. Wright (Cambridge, Eng., 1904), pp. 160, 166–168; Reginald Pole, *Apologia ad Carolum V,* in *Epistolarum Reginaldi Poli* (Brescia, 1744), I, 137–152. For discussion of Machiavelli's Continental critics such as the Dominican, Caterino, or the Portuguese bishop, Osorio, see L. Arthur Burd, ed., *Il Principe di Niccolò Machiavelli* (Oxford, 1891), pp. 45–61.

were followed by assertions of diabolical allegiance.[23] As the devil's henchman, or even the devil incarnate, Machiavelli became associated with every kind of sin. The idea of *The Prince* as a spiritual poison occurs in Pole, and everyone knew that Italians, especially the Borgias, whom Machiavelli admired, were addicted to poisoning each other. Consequently, Machiavelli, who may counsel murder but nowhere enjoins the use of poison, became in legend as fiendish a poisoner as Barabas.[24] He became also "veneriall Machiavel,"[25] in lust second only to Aretino, and a monster of rapacity who made no "scruple of conscience where profit presents itself."[26] And in all this there was, inevitably, little attempt to distinguish between what might be educed from Machiavelli's precepts and what could be justly said of his own practice. He was accused of leading a wicked life and of dying a bad death. "The brocer of this Diabolicall Atheisme is dead, and in his life had never the felicitie hee aymed at: but as he began in craft; lived in feare, and ended in despaire. . . . This murderer of many brethren, had his conscience seared like Caine: this betrayer of him that gave his life for him, inherited the portion of Judas: this Apostata perished as ill as Julian. . . . "[27]

Greene's diatribe is instructive. It spirals into hysterical libeling, with its accusations of mass murder and of perishing in the manner of Julian the Apostate, yet the evidence suggests that behind the parading of scandalous legend lies a full knowledge of Machiavelli's original productions. And that Greene's reading had led him to see Machiavelli as a "brocer of this Diabolicall Atheisme" (and so capable of anything and everything) is not necessarily indicative of faulty perspective or incomprehension.

23. See, for example, William Covell, "Religions Speech to Englands Children," in *Polymanteia or the Meanes Lawful* (Cambridge, Eng., 1595), sig. Bb3^r—Bb3^v. Punning on Machiavelli's name was common. He became "Mach-evill," "Hatch-evil," and, finally, "Old Nick."

24. See Thomas Nashe, *Summers Last Will and Testament,* in *Works of Thomas Nashe,* ed. R. B. McKerrow (London, 1910), III, 277, and *Pierce Penilesse His Supplication to the Divell,* in *Works,* I, 186.

25. Nashe, *Christs Teares Over Jerusalem,* in *Works,* II, 153.

26. Robert Greene, *A Groats-worth of Wit,* ed. G. B. Harrison (Edinburgh, 1966), p. 12.

27. Greene, *Groats-worth,* p. 44.

The figure of the stage Machiavel reflects in rather more complex form the Machiavelli of the prose literature. From the advent of Barabas and Kyd's Lorenzo he is often a compendium of all the vices, a "black Prince of Divels";[28] as such his origins can be traced back beyond either the real Machiavelli or the purveyors of the legend to those Senecan tyrants or to those Vices, rejoicing in evil for evil's sake, whose relationship to the Machiavel is fully recognized. He can be eminently lustful, like the Moors, Aaron and Eleazar, or, like Marlowe's Jew, enormously rapacious. His life is presented as wicked and his death—unless, in the nick of time, he change his spots—as a punishment fitted to his crimes.[29] And yet, under the scandalous accretions, the suggestions of diabolicial allegiance, the sadism and wicked glee, the Machiavel reveals certain fundamental characteristics which seem to proceed not simply from the playwrights' knowledge of the world of *The Prince,* but from an interpretation of that world grounded in something more solid than deficient historical perspective.

Machiavelli sets out, quite deliberately, to do what is new. In chapter XV of *The Prince* he promises "an original set of rules" by which the ruler may govern his conduct. "Many have dreamed up republics and principalities which have never in truth been known to exist," but Machiavelli will deal only with "things as they are in real truth," with "what is actually done," rather than with "what should be done." In the introduction to the first book of *The Discourses* Machiavelli announces that he has "determined to enter upon a path not yet trodden by anyone." He alone, it appears, has discovered that the conduct of men is as unchanging as the motions of the planets, that history reveals a series of recurrent patterns governed by fixed, definable laws, and that actions which produced a given effect in one age will produce it in another. History, then, has become a repository of scientific formulas,

28. The reference is to Eleazar in *Lust's Dominion,* V.iii.166. The play, earlier ascribed to Marlowe, is printed in *The Dramatic Works of Thomas Dekker,* ed. Fredson Bowers (Cambridge, Eng. 1961), vol. IV.

29. Barabas, of course, falls into the cauldron prepared for Calymath. Chettle's Hoffman is killed with the burning crown used to murder his first victim, Otho. More interestingly, Suffolk in *I Henry VI,* having charged Gloucester with treason and engaged in a travesty of justice in arranging his murder, is condemned as a traitor to England by the pirate captain and hauled away to summary execution.

which, once discovered and understood, will yield lessons "in setting up states, in maintaining governments, in ruling kingdoms, in organising armies and managing war, in executing laws among subjects, in expanding an empire."[30]

Machiavelli, then, has no concern with imaginary, idealized states, like those of Dante or Aquinas; taking his stand on observation and experience he repudiates the idealist standpoint of all earlier prince literature.[31] Moreover, in turning to history for lessons in conduct, Machiavelli will set forth no exempla that direct men to eschew the vanities of the world, to scorn Fortune, and to seek the security of spiritual union with the divine. Instead, Machiavelli will elicit from his study of history guidance that will assist men to understand and to control the world in which they live, a world in which the forces which determine events will be seen as primarily political.[32] He will, in fact, then, concern himself with " what should be done," but his criteria of action will be based upon "what is actually done" in the effective pursuit of political power and not upon what might or might not be done in the service of anything less concrete.

This may all seem reasonable enough, but it does lead one to enquire whether, in rejecting the traditional methodologies, Machiavelli did not also reject the body of philosophical, religious, and ethical as-

---

30. Quotations from *The Discourses* are from Gilbert's translation. I have also consulted *The Discourses of Niccolò Machiavelli,* trans. Leslie J. Walker, 2 vols. (London, 1950), and Guido Mazzoni and Mario Casella, eds., *Tutte le opere storiche e letterarie de Niccolò Machiavelli* (Florence, 1929). Some amplification of Machiavelli's view regarding the changeless nature of history can be found in chapter XXXIX of the first book of *The Discourses* ("all cities and all peoples have the same desires and the same traits and . . . they always have had them"), and in chapter VI of *The Prince* (Men, already much alike in all ages, "nearly always follow the tracks made by others and proceed in their affairs by imitation"). In consequence the governments which men establish pass through the same stages. The most detailed account of the state's inevitable development and decline is found in *The Discourses,* I.ii.

31. One of the most illuminating discussions of this aspect of Machiavelli's innovative theory is contained in Felix Gilbert, "The Humanist Concept of the Prince and *The Prince* of Machiavelli," *Journal of Modern History,* II (1939), 449–483.

32. For discussion of the distinction between the incidental realism of medieval historiography and the "conceptual realism" of Machiavelli and Guicciardini, see F. Chabod, *Machiavelli and the Renaissance,* trans. David Moore (London, 1958), pp. 175–180.

sumptions from which the methodologies had derived. Once the idealist vision had vanished, what became of its supramundane origin?

Even Machiavelli's most ardent devotees have been forced to admit that the supramundane does not figure very prominently in *The Prince* and *The Discourses*. Where there has been an attempt to counter the charge of atheism, the usual defense has been to argue that Machiavelli had no wish to undermine Christian religion or morality, but that he saw politics as a special kind of activity, like botany or bricklaying, with its own scientific principles and its own techniques. Beyond the political arena the traditional creed and code remain, apparently, intact.[33] And yet, to see Machiavelli as handing out assorted tips to a prince who must reluctantly put his faith and conscience away on statecraft days will not quite do.

Machiavelli's view of how "things are in real truth," the view on which his rules of political conduct are based, necessarily encompasses more than what is done from one day to the next in the political arena. Machiavelli is concerned with the ability of the ruler or the aspirant to rule, to control events, and hence with far-reaching questions of fundamental causation. He moves beyond analyses of the strategic errors of Servius Tullus or the masterly strokes of Cesare Borgia to adumbrate a vision of a world governed by unchanging laws, which exist independently of the will of a just God, and by Fortune, which, while sometimes amenable to the laws of nature and science, is more often akin to a pagan goddess, independent, capricious, and malign.[34]

And Machiavelli's territory is as broad as it is long. Politics, it seems, includes the establishment of settlements, the levying of taxes, the manipulation of relationships between the nobles and the people, the management of wars, the execution of laws, and the regulation of a ruler's own generosity, compassion, and piety. Machiavelli's prince never ceases to be a political figure; he is, in Burd's phrase, "a force, an embodied idea, almost as impersonal as the state itself";[35] in his deal-

33. See, for example, Cochrane, p. 115, and Chabod, p. 142.

34. In chapter XXV of *The Prince* Fortune is pictured first as a raging torrent which can be tamed by the technical expertise of the builder of dikes and embankments. Soon, however, Machiavelli likens Fortune to a woman, who favors young men and may submit to impetuosity and force. In neither guise has Machiavelli's Fortune any connection with the Dantesque vision of Fortune as an arm of God's providence.

35. Burd, p. 215.

ings he shapes and touches the lives of his subjects at every point. Yet in all this, questions and answers regarding human conduct are to be framed in terms of the political science which Machiavelli may be said to have founded. Nothing as amorphous or irrelevant as Christian faith or ethics is to be allowed to intrude. God, in short, is banished not only from the state but from history and from human experience.

Religion remains simply as grist to the prince's mill. This is brought out clearly in all three books of *The Discourses* and in chapter XVIII of *The Prince.* In chapters XI–XV of the first book of *The Discourses* Machiavelli shows that the Romans realized that religion has its value as a set of fictions through which the ruler may command the belief of the ruled. The example is given of Numa "who pretended he was intimate with a nymph who advised him about what he was going to advise the people." The people, it seems, were impressed and developed a respect for the immortals that "facilitated whatever undertaking the Senate or those great men of Rome planned to carry on."

If Machiavelli was not an atheist at heart, he certainly looks very much like one on paper, so that it is hardly surprising that well before Gentillet appeared upon the scene a Pole should see *The Prince* as showing "the means by which religion, goodness and all the fruits of virtue may be destroyed,"[36] or that later the stage Machiavel should so often reveal himself as God's enemy. Not all Machiavellian villains expound an atheistic creed with the thoroughness of Greene's Selimus, but many echo Marlowe's Machevill's "I count religion but a childish toy" (*Jew of Malta,* Prol. 14), curse heaven in defeat, pour scorn upon conscience and Christian virtue, and celebrate a total allegiance to evil or to their own ambitions. Some, like Sir Doncaster in Munday's *The Death of Robert Earl of Huntingdon*, show their contempt for all things holy in their laconic mockery of piety and the pious or in their zestful persecution of anyone who "saies his prayers, fasts eves, gives alms, does good."[37] But, above all, the Machiavel proclaims his atheism in the adoption of just that cynical stance which Machiavelli assumes in the early chapters of *The Discourses.*

36. Pole, *Apologia,* p. 136.

37. Anthony Munday, *The Death of Robert Earl of Huntingdon,* ed. John C. Meagher (1601; rpt. Oxford, 1967), iii. 325.

"Concerning my author," writes John Levitt in 1599, "it is objected against him, that . . . he would hold religion to be but a mere civil intention to hold the world in reverence and fear." [38] This same objection is embodied in the Machiavellian Selimus, who thinks,

> these religious observations
> Onely bug-beares to keepe the world in feare,
> And make men quietly a yoake to beare,
> So that religion of it selfe a bable
> Was onely found to make us peaceable [39]
>
> (*Selimus,* iii.835–839)

Such sentiments are shared by all those villains who, if less didactic than Selimus, are equally ready for the cynical employment of "politic religion" and who pride themselves on their ability to manipulate their dupes by seeming saints when most they play the devil. [40] It might well be, then, that the creators of these politic hypocrites, like those commentators to whom Levitt makes reference, saw the gist of the early chapters of *The Discourses* in a perspective very much more "proper" than that of Ribner or of all those who, since 1897, have so steadily maintained that the atheistic Machiavel is no more than a gross libel upon the author of *The Prince.*

It might also seem that in allowing Machiavelli's "politic religion" to rear its head in Spain, Malta, or North Africa as well as in Italy, the dramatists reveal a recognition that Machiavelli was concerned to do

38. John Levitt, "The Epistle of the Translator to the Reader," in Napoleone Orsini, *Studii sul Rinascimento italiano in Inghilterra* (Florence, 1937), p. 43.

39. *The Tragical Reign of Selimus,* ed. W. Bang (1594; rpt. London, 1908). Bang remarks "that there is exactly the same evidence for ascribing *Selimus* to Greene, as for ascribing *The Battle of Alcazar* to Peele," p. v.

40. Lorenzo in *Alphonsus, Emperor of Germany* sets two maxims from chapter XVIII of *The Prince* side by side in his advice to Alphonsus: "A prince above all things must seem devout; but there is nothing so dangerous to his state, as to regard his promise as his oath" (I. i.109–111). His advice is heeded by Richard III, with his two bishops (III.vii), and adapted by Barabas who, like so many other Machiavels, will use religion to hide "many mischiefs from suspicion" (I.ii.281).

Quotations from *Alphonsus* are taken from *The Tragedies of George Chapman,* ed. T. M. Parrott, 2 vols. (London, 1910), and those from *Richard III* from Mark Eccles's Signet Classic Shakespeare edition (New York, 1964).

more than commentators such as Ribner have suggested. The very nature of Machiavelli's fundamental convictions makes it impossible that
he should simply "write an occasional work not meant to apply to
conditions other than those of Italy in Machiavelli's day."[41] It was because he believed that he had discovered cyclic patterns in history that
Machiavelli felt himself qualified to suggest remedies for the ills of his
own country in his own time. Writing as a teacher, a polemicist, Machiavelli sets out to persuade first the Medici and after them the world
that what has worked well in the past must necessarily work well in
the present and the future. Precisely because the condition of fif-
teenth-century Italy is not unique Machiavelli can set forth rules or
maxims designed to solve the recurrent political problems of a world
that can never change.[42] This the Elizabethans understood, and it was
their understanding that led them to descant so insistently upon the
growth of Machiavelli's godless influence. There is some irony in the
fact that Ribner, having failed to grasp Machiavelli's own historical
perspective, can go on to accuse the Elizabethans of reading his works
"without the historical perspective that enables us to understand them
today."[43]

Once God had been jettisoned and religion reduced to a tool of policy it seemed to some Elizabethan commentators that no moral imperative remained, that in the "Machiavellian State and Regiment" only naked egoism, unchecked by "scruple, fear, or conscience of hell and
heaven"[44] must direct the conduct of ruler and subject alike.

Whereas medieval prince literature "deduces the prince's political
duties from those principles of natural justice by which the prince
himself was bound and which it was his duty to see applied,"[45] Machiavelli recognizes no *lex aeterna,* no natural justice, and no duty to
anything beyond the political arena. In his world the only law is that

---

41. Ribner, p. 155.

42. Herbert Butterfield is one of the few scholars who have pointed out that Machiavelli saw his own maxims as "permanently applicable and universally valid." See *The
Statecraft of Machiavelli* (1940; rpt. London, 1955), p. 25.

43. Ribner, p. 155.

44. *Treatise of Treasons against Queen Elizabeth and the Crown of England* (1572),
sig.a5ᵛ. The anonymous author of the *Treatise* gives peculiarly clear and forceful expression to the Elizabethan horror of the state in which "vain fame only and fear of lay
lawes" remains to "bridle" men from evil.

45. Gilbert, *The Humanist Concept,* p. 460.

of the lawgiver, who must always "presuppose that all men are evil and that they are going to act according to the wickedness of their spirits whenever they have free scope" *(Discourses,* I.iii). And the law-giver himself, it seems, is not so very different from his subjects. In both *The Prince* and *The Discourses* Machiavelli appeals almost always to the self-interest of the prince. The lawgiver is exhorted to avoid the more foolish and dangerous forms of tyranny simply because history has shown that rulers such as Scipio, Agesilaus, Timoleon, and Dion are "exceedingly praised," while others such as Caesar, Nabis, Pha-laris, and Dionysius are "censured to the utmost." Moreover, "Timo-leon and the others did not have in their native cities less authority than did Dionysius and Phalaris." On the contrary they "had more se-curity" and proved more capable than "wicked" rulers of avoiding as-sassination *(Discourses,* I.x.). Machiavelli, then, addresses his prince as the supreme egoist, who recognizes no power which transcends his own, and who will strive to establish the stable government that Ma-chiavelli hopes to promote only because he is eager for glory, author-ity, and personal safety. And where the prince's desire for power con-flicts with a republic's love of liberty, Machiavelli is prepared to pander to the prince and advise the republic's destruction *(Prince,* chap. V). The lawgiver of *The Prince* and *The Discourses* emerges fi-nally as a dangerous beast in a god-forsaken world of beasts; if he can be harnessed to the state he may, through natural self-interest, haul it to security for a time: but sometimes he must be allowed to have his head.

The Machiavel, like Machiavelli's exemplary lawgiver, is not only godless but totally egocentric. He is rarely prepared to repose much trust in others, whom he commonly regards as fools or knaves, to ad-mire anything but his own abilities, or to serve any cause but his own. Alphonsus tells himself he will trust no man "further than tends unto thy proper good" *(Alphonsus, Emperor of Germany,* I.i.25), preens himself on his superior cunning, and is "zealous indeed of nothing but my good" (I.i.35). Kyd's Lorenzo determines to "trust myselfe, my selfe shall be my friend" *(The Spanish Tragedy,* III.ii.118).[46] Their creed is that of the villain, Fallerio, in *Two Lamentable Tragedies:*

---

46. *The Works of Thomas Kyd,* ed. Frederick S. Boas, 2d ed. (1901; rpt. Oxford, 1955).

> But nature, love and reason tels thee thus,
> Thy selfe must yet be neerest to thy selfe
>
> (sig. C^y)[47]

This is echoed by Richard in his famous "I am myself alone" (*3 Henry VI*, V.vi.83),[48] and by Barabas in his "For so I live, perish may all the world!" (*Jew of Malta*, V.iv.10).

For the Elizabethans, the man who saw the world as godless and who recognized no imperative beyond his own ambition was a danger to all order. He was the inevitable foe of piety and virtue; in the pursuit of his own desires he would murder individuals or even wipe out whole communities; if it suited his purpose, he would pull down kings, stir up revolts, and throw the state into havoc; his destructiveness could even create reverberations in the realm of nature, until, finally, he brought destruction on himself and his soul was consigned to damnation. Robert Greene, for one, sees the spread of Machiavellian doctrine as the harbinger of apocalyptic confusion:

What are his [Machiavelli's] rules but meere confused mockeries, able to extirpate in a small time, the generation of mankinde. For if sic volo, sic jubeo, hold in those that are able to command: and it be lawful Fas et ne fas to doe anything that is beneficiall, only Tyrants should possesse the earth, and they striving to exceed in tyranny, should each to other be the slaughter man; till the mightiest outliving all, one stroke were left for Death, that in one age man's life should end.[49]

In attempting to decide whether in this Greene is "infinitely unjust" to Machiavelli, or whether the Machiavel, who is preeminently destructive, is faithful to Machiavellian precept, one encounters certain new difficulties. There is, as I have attempted to show, ample evidence to support the Elizabethan contentions that the world as Machiavelli presents it is godless and amoral, and that "the brocher of this Diabolicall Atheisme" sets out to teach men to act accordingly. But one can hardly

---

47. Robert Yarrington, *Two Lamentable Tragedies,* ed. John S. Farmer (1601; facsimile rpt. New York, 1970).

48. Shakespeare, *The Third Part of King Henry VI,* ed. Andrew S. Cairncross, Arden edition (London, 1964).

49. Greene, *Groats-worth,* pp. 43-44.

argue that Machiavelli envisages his prince as destructive of true "religion, goodness and all the fruits of virtue" when, in Machiavelli's world, these things have no reality.

Yet, if the Elizabethans were not pointing to a process observable in the world of *The Prince,* they may still be seen as engaging in legitimate speculation upon the effects which Machiavelli's disciples might produce in their own world. Machiavelli's Numas, when they devise new religions and new laws to secure their own power, are presented as merely filling a void or as substituting the fresh and efficacious for the outworn. The Machiavel, however, who in the context of Elizabethan drama seeks to exploit religion for his own ends or to persuade others to accept his authority and his precepts, is necessarily the enemy of true religion, established order, and real virtue. Like Edmund or Iago he is seen as opposing his own egoistical ethic, his own divinities of hell against established and sanctified codes of conduct and belief which are natural for man. Even where the policies of the Machiavel are framed to stifle dissension or to repel invaders, their author is still condemned because he is seeking not to preserve God's order but to establish his own, and his own order is one which must inevitably emerge as tyrannical, spurious, and disruptive. Henry IV, who longs to bring his country to peace and safety, is shown as inevitably frustrated because he has been, and in part still is, Machiavellian. He remains trapped in the web of pretense that he has woven, and doomed to endure the chaos which his attempts to secure his own power have bred. And when he offers his son the tainted wisdom of the usurper who met the throne by "indirect crook'd ways," the policy of the prince who sets the appearance of virtue before the reality, Hal's reply is, in one sense, a rejection of the proffered advice and an appeal to the Christian ideal by which, in Elizabethan drama, Machiavellian policy is commonly judged:

> I shall hereafter, my thrice gracious Lord,
> Be more my self.
>
> (*1 Henry IV,* III.ii.92–93)[50]

---

50. Shakespeare, *The First Part of King Henry IV,* ed. A. R. Humphreys, Arden edition (London, 1960).

This "self" will be the virtuous reality that is at once the rightful heir, the chosen of god, and the pattern of Christian princes, dealing in honor more genuine than Hotspur's and in majesty intimately connected with personal worth in a way which Henry, with his talk of politic masks, can hardly envisage.

There seems no doubt that the Elizabethans were correct in suggesting that the political counsel of Machiavelli was antagonistic to their religion and to their morality, and that the dramatists did nothing to distort Machiavelli's teaching when they showed the Machiavel, let loose in a God-centered world, as the natural enemy of true religion and Christian virtue. If Machiavelli did not set out to destroy these things, he at least proposed a system of belief and conduct in which they no longer mattered. He attacked not by direct onslaught but by the fostering of a seductive rival. If the power of that rival requires any further attestation, one has only to recall how vigorously the father of political science has been defended against the Elizabethan charges and how readily these charges have been ascribed to obscurantism, prejudice, ignorance, and malice.

Marston's Piero, when he vows to "pop out the light of bright religion" (*Antonio's Revenge*, IV.1.267)[51] certainly appears more deliberately mischievous than his Florentine mentor who is content to accept religion's fictions as serviceable social cement. But when Piero engages in other forms of destruction the relationship between the Machiavel and Machiavelli becomes very much plainer.

Murder, as everyone knows, is chief among the Machiavel's more characteristic occupations, and on this subject Machiavelli offers an abundance of advice which many villains follow with attention. In chapter VII of *The Prince* the advisability of eliminating tool villains is stressed; even though they sometimes fail in their purposes, Marlowe's Mortimer, Ragan in *King Leir,* Mendoza, Eleazar, Lorenzo, and others attempt, in this, to emulate the exemplary Cesare Borgia. Then again, Machiavelli emphasises the wisdom of eliminating anyone likely to prove troublesome before any hostile action can occur (*Prince,* chap. VII); in particular he insists upon the need to wipe out the ruling

51. John Marston, *Antonio's Revenge: The Second Part of Antonio and Mellida*, ed. G. K. Hunter, Regents Renaissance Drama Series (1965; rpt. London, 1966).

dynasty when one usurps a throne (*Prince,* chap. IV). [52] In the discussion of the projected murder of the Duke of Gloucester in *2 Henry VI,* Suffolk's advice is thoroughly Machiavellian:

> No; let him die, in that he is a fox,
> By nature prov'd an enemy to the flock,
> Before his chaps be stain'd with crimson blood.
> . . . .
>   for that is good deceit
> Which mates him first that first intends deceit.
>   (III.i.257–259; 264–265) [53]

Similarly, the usurpers Selimus, Muly Mahamet in *The Battle of Alcazar,* and Mortimer recognize the unwisdom of sparing at least their more obvious rivals.

Just as he offers counsel on the killing of individuals, so Machiavelli is prepared to advise on the dismantling of states in order to secure the personal power of a lawgiver. In chapter V of *The Prince* Machiavelli faces the difficulties created by the most extreme form of resentment which a prince is likely to encounter in a mass of subjects. When states newly acquired have been accustomed to living freely under their own laws, "the memory of their ancient liberty does not and cannot let them rest." There is only one remedy. "Whoever becomes the master of a city accustomed to freedom, and does not destroy it, may expect to be destroyed himself." Elsewhere, Machiavelli is prepared to offer advice on the management of successful conspiracies (*Discourses,* III.vi) or on "the many ways the Romans took cities" (II.xxxii), or on how one may "usurp supreme and absolute authority . . . in a free state" (III.viii).

The Machiavel, like his master, is wholly indifferent to a concept of society as bound by what Edwin Muir has called "a sort of piety and

---

52. See also chapter VI of the third book of *The Discourses* in which Machiavelli stresses the folly of failing to exterminate anyone who might avenge a deposed prince, and tells the cautionary tale of some imprudent conspirators of Forli who, having killed their ruler, hesitated to murder his wife and young children. Such infirmity of purpose brought disaster; the conspirators "with lifelong exile . . . paid the penalty of their imprudence."

53. Shakespeare, *The Second Part of King Henry VI,* ed. Andrew S. Cairncross, Arden edition (London, 1957).

human fitness."[54] To an Edmund, as to Machiavelli and to Machiavelli's princes, the state is simply a political unit, held together by force and appetite. The Machiavel, like the aspiring tyrants of *The Prince,* recognizes no moral barrier to the wholesale slaughter of any who oppose him, to rebellion, civil war, or usurpation. Selimus, who follows Machiavelli in seeing the laws of God and man as mere "policie" devised to "keepe the quiet of societie" (ii.346–347), wades to his throne through the blood of subjects and recognizes no impediment to rebellion against his own father. Similarly, Muly Mahamet, early established as "unbelieving" and murderous, falls readily into the role of the traitor who leads his "barbarous rebels" (*Battle of Alcazar,* I.ii.127)[55] against the rightful king. Rebellion leads on inevitably to civil war, a form of chaos which seems to have a bracing effect upon the Machiavel who is more lion than fox. But most Machiavels, though their actions frequently result in open warfare, prefer to proceed by cunning, murder, and a devious sowing of dissension. Eleazar, although he causes civil war in Spain, does not plunge directly into open rebellion, and Gonorill and Ragan attempt to consolidate their power by guile and assassination before launching into battle with Leir's champion, the King of Gallia.

Whatever path may lead him to his goal, the Machiavellian usurper is destructive of that rule of good law which corresponds to the sovereignty of reason in the mind of the individual.[56] Like Selimus, or those evil counselors, Lorenzo and Tresilian, the Machiavellian ruler recognizes no law beyond the will of the lawgiver.[57] In consequence the

54. Edwin Muir, "The Politics of *King Lear,*" in *Essays on Literature and Society* (London, 1949), p. 47.

55. *The Works of George Peele,* ed. A. H. Bullen, 2 vols. (London, 1888).

56. I have in mind particularly the following passage from Thomas Starkey, *A Dialogue between Reginald Pole and Thomas Lupset,* ed. Kathleen M. Burton (London, 1948), p. 59: "good order . . . by good laws stablished . . . by which the whole body, as by reason, is governed and ruled, to the intent that this multitude of people and whole commonalty . . . may with due honour, reverence and love religiously worship God . . . everyone also doing his duty to other with brotherly love, one loving another as members and parts of one body."

57. Lorenzo in *Alphonsus, Emperor of Germany* sums up the gist of much of the counsel contained in *The Prince* when he tells Alphonsus that "To keep an usurped crown, a prince must swear, forswear, poison, murder, and commit all kinds of villainies, provided it be cunningly kept from the eye of the world." Tresilian, "that sly Ma-

"justice" that he administers becomes distorted to serve his own ambition, jealousy, or fear, and the tyrant's impulse replaces the statute designed to sustain the law of reason and of God and to protect the commonweal. "Here's a good world the while!" cries Richard III's scrivener as he stands with the trumped-up indictment of "the good Lord Hastings" in his hand (III.vi).

Such indifference to the commonweal, which is the hallmark of the Machiavellian rebel, usurper, or tyrant, implies on the one hand rejection of a whole order of which just and godly rule is a part, and on the other allegiance to an egocentric code which, in Elizabethan drama, is seen as inevitably anarchic and antisocial. It is this charge of indifference, of readiness to destroy the lives and liberties of subjects in the pursuit of personal ambition, that is repeatedly leveled at the Machiavellian ruler and which often defines him as what he is. In *Edward III* the Black Prince turns on John of France:

> I, that approves thee, tyrant, what thou art:
> No father, king or shepheard of thy realme,
> But one, that teares her entrailes with thy handes,
> And, like a thirstie tyger, suckst her blood . . . [58]
>
> (III.iii.155–161)

In some plays the destruction wrought by the Machiavel is less extensive and its political consequences less overt. Like Iago, he may throw a mind rather than a nation into turmoil, or, like Kyd's Lorenzo, his chiefest crimes may consist in severing bonds of kinship and love rather than in violating any political tie. But however limited his sphere, the chaos that the Machiavel creates is commonly reflected in images of a sterile and disordered universe, one of crooked trees and savage beasts, of darkness, fire, tempest, poison, and disease.

In the earlier plays this universe, though for a time disturbed, commonly recoils upon the cause of its disorder. The Machiavel's divorce

---

chiavel" (*Woodstock*, I.i.63), encourages Richard II in his belief that "Kings' words are laws" (III.i.64) while at the same time seeing himself, in his capacity as Lord Chief Justice, as the ultimate lawgiver: "It shall be law, what I shall say is law" (I.ii.49). Quotations are from *Woodstock: A Moral History*, ed. A. P. Rossiter (London, 1946).

58. *Edward III*, in *Shakespeare's Apocrypha*, ed. C. F. Tucker Brooke (Oxford, 1908).

of *virtù* from virtue, which Machiavelli finds unavoidable, results, then, in the reaffirmation of an order that the Florentine does not recognize and in retribution at the hands of a deity whose power he discounts.

Consequently, the Machiavel is usually less successful than his counterparts of *The Prince* and *The Discourses*. Either he never attains his ambition, like Edmund, or, if he does, he is quickly and effectively assailed by the forces of righteousness and, like Richard III, laid low. Because of this the Machiavel appears more intent upon outright destruction than do either Machiavelli or the actual and putative rulers that he discusses. Whereas Machiavelli is primarily concerned with the reconstruction or establishment of stable power, once any necessary destruction has been carried out, the political Machiavel is rarely, if ever, allowed to proceed to the creative stage. Even where, as in the case of Henry IV, a character with Machiavellian traits manages to establish some measure of effective control, his efforts are doomed. In Elizabethan drama, if not always in Jacobean, crime does not pay; in the world in which the Machiavel moves there is no possibility of erecting stable political structures in isolation from the universal hierarchy which the ambition of the Machiavel inevitably violates.

This may explain in part why the Machiavel has been seen as no more than a caricature of Machiavelli's prince. His destructiveness is emphasized and is presented as impious and wicked; he is unable to supply any justification for the chaos which he creates by going on to establish any form of stable government. Yet this does not change the fact that the precepts upon which the Machiavel's conduct is based are essentially those by which Machiavelli's politicians are guided; the difference is between the judgments, overt or implied, of the literary contexts in which they appear.

The final major charge that is leveled repeatedly against Machiavelli by the Elizabethans is that of instructing men in the formulation of deceitful "policy," in the art of gaining advancement or advantage by ruthless cunning. Warnings abound in nondramatic literature against "Machiavelian artes, as Guile, Perfidie, and other Villanies." [59] In the drama the Machiavel is invariably a clever schemer who dedicates his

59. Simon Patericke, "The Epistle Dedicatorie," in *A Discourse Upon the Meanes of Wel Governing.*

wit to the pressing of his own fortune and to the construction of pit-falls for his victims. Above all, he is a masterly hypocrite who can mask his designs with a convincing display of devotion, piety, or blunt honesty. Once again the charge seems not without foundation and the Machiavel more genuinely Machiavellian than has been allowed.

Machiavelli's conviction that the perfidy of mankind at large makes the imitation of the fox obligatory for anyone who hopes to "come off best" (*Prince,* chap. XVIII) is suitably notorious. Less well-known are the great number of other similar pieces of advice which together im-part to Machiavelli's political teaching "a certain flavour which it would not be unjust to impute to a love of stratagem."[60] One of the more interesting examples occurs in chapter XLIV of the first book of *The Discourses.* Here Machiavelli tells how Valerius and Horatius, rep-resentatives of the Senate, refused to hand over the decemvirs to the people of Rome since the people had made plain their intention of burning the ten alive. Machiavelli comments: "Here it is plain how much folly and how little prudence there is in asking a thing and say-ing first: I wish to do such an evil with it. One should not show one's mind but try to get one's wish just the same, because it is enough to ask a man for his weapons without saying: I wish to kill you with them. For when you have the weapons in your hands you can satisfy your de-sire."

Elsewhere Machiavelli demonstrates that "Men Go from Low to High Fortune More Often Through Fraud than Through Force" and, having dealt with the importance of fraud to aspiring princes, goes on to show that republics, too, must resort to fraud "until they have be-come powerful, and force alone is enough" (*Discourses,* II.xiii). In *The Prince* the ruler is given many lessons in how to render himself secure by judicious trickery. Cesare Borgia shows how, as Nashe puts it, one may "use men for my purpose and then cast them off,"[61] but it is Ce-sare's father, Alexander IV, who is hailed as supreme in the histrionic art of hypocrisy: "There never was a man capable of such convincing asseverations or so ready to swear to the truth of something, who would honour his word less. Nonetheless his deceptions always had

60. Butterfield, p. 98.
61. Thomas Nashe, *Pierce Penilesse,* I, 200.

the result he intended, because he was a past master in the art"
(*Prince,* chap. XVIII).

The fidelity with which the Machiavel follows Machiavelli's advice
in all this hardly requires much demonstration. "Policy" in the sense
of subtle, deceitful cunning based upon a coolly rational and material-
istic assessment of men and situations is the most apparent of the characteristics shared by Machiavelli and the Machiavel. Almost all Machiavels are adept at persuading other characters, including victims and
tool villains, to further ambitions that are concealed from all but the
audience. Many emulate Cesare Borgia's treatment of his catspaw, Re-
mirro de Orco, and cunningly dispose of those they have used once
their usefulness is outworn. Thus Kyd's Lorenzo employs Pedringano
to kill Serberine, and Eleazar arranges the shooting of the friars that he
has employed to establish the illegitimacy of Philip. And in all this
nearly every Machiavel deludes his victims by playing a role or assuming a disguise. Richard III not only will seem a saint when most he
plays the devil, but, as he moves toward the culmination of his
schemes, appears in "rotten armor, marvelous ill-favored" (III.v.),
while Hoffman spends most of his play disguised as his victim, Otho,
and Barabas goes in disguise to poison Ithamore, Bellamira, and Pilia-
Borza.

Often, as in *Woodstock* or *The Spanish Tragedy,* the assumption of
disguise is associated with plays or masques, and where, as in the revenge plays, these entertainments form part of the denouement, they
stand as images in which all the deception of the preceding action is
focused in the moment before masks are stripped away and the truth
revealed. Yet while such disguising can lead in one sense to the enactment of justice and to the kind of revelation that concludes *The Revenger's Tragedy,* it can also make plain the power of the vision of the
Machiavel.

The Machiavel is indifferent to human feeling and is ultimately concerned to manipulate action. His world is one of simplified design,
patterned in accordance with his own materialism and his own appetite. He reduces those about him to types, ascribes to them roles, and
sets them moving in a scenario of his own devising. Yet usually he
finds that his masque of fools ends in a manner that he has not fore-
seen, that he has cast his characters in inappropriate roles by under-

estimating adversaries or tool villains, that he has left loose ends, such as conscience[62] or incriminating letters, dangling in his plot. Such failures of Machiavellian stage management constitute, in effect, a series of practical comments upon the limitations of Machiavelli's political— and "politic"—theory. The three parts of *Henry VI,* for instance, reveal a world where all order is discounted, loyalty sacrificed to ambition, truth and trust set by, and the law of God and man displaced by force and fraud. In such a world no man, including the Machiavel, lives in safety. However politic a Winchester, a Suffolk, or a York may be, he is unable to survive for long in the milieu he has created; inevitably, he becomes the victim of any rival who, for a moment, is a little more fortunate, or a little stronger or more politic than himself. Machiavelli, having held up the career of Cesare Borgia as an example to every aspirant to power, attributes his fall to the malice of Fortune (*Prince,* chap. VII). Shakespeare—and his contemporaries—make it clear that when a Machiavel, like Cesare, has reduced all commerce between men to force and fraud, neither the ferocity of the lion nor the cunning of the fox will protect him against the beasts that surround him on the day that Fortune turns away her face.

And even while Fortune smiles there is, as Machiavelli himself makes clear, danger inherent in his politic techniques. In the chapter on conspiracies in *The Discourses* he speaks of the perils which reside in confiding one's projects to others, while conceding that at times such risks are unavoidable. The dramatists go on to show that the Machiavel, however determined he may be to trust none but himself, however hard he may strive to stop all mouths, cannot, in the nature

---

62. That is, conscience in others, such as the tool villains employed by Fallerio or Hoffman. Your true Machiavel, unless he steps abruptly into another role, never gives way to any conscience of his own. The most that can be said is that, at Bosworth, Richard's suppressed guilt becomes one of the forces marshaled against him and, if Macbeth never becomes fully Machiavellian, his play makes plain the price exacted by the conscience when a man, who is not born a monster, attempts to deny his humanity. "Not all kill and forget, as Machiavelli had once implied. Some kill and remember. That is the ultimate Elizabethan critique of Machiavelli" (George Watson, "Machiavel and Machiavelli," *SR,* LXXXIV [1976], 648). Watson may well be right, but he neglects to distinguish between a Macbeth, who embodies such a critique, and the genuine Machiavel who, in forgetting too much too readily, embodies warnings of a rather different kind.

of things fool all of the people all of the time, or eliminate every kind
of evidence which may one day betray him. As Alphonsus tells Lorenzo:

> that's the hardest point;
> It is not for a prince to execute,
> Physicians and apothecaries must know,
> And servile fear or counsel breaking bribes
> Will from a peasant in an hour extort
> Enough to overthrow a monarchy.
>
> (*Alphonsus, Emperor of Germany*, I.i.165–170)

As I have shown, "the nature of things" in the world of Elizabethan
drama is normally very different from "the nature of things" in the
world of *The Prince* and *The Discourses*. Behind the natural sequence
of cause and effect by which the Machiavel may come to ruin, often
the dramatists reveal the evolution of supernatural purposes whose influence upon his plot and play the Machiavel discounts until too late.

The Elizabethan critique of Machiavellian policy, which emerges
from the dramatic treatment of the Machiavel, is, then, a combination
of "realistic" objections with others which are grounded in moral and
religious conviction. Yet the Elizabethans' refusal to forget morality
and religion when they took up *The Prince* does not, of course, mean
that they misunderstood what they read. It means only that they accepted morality and religion as realities in a way that Machiavelli did
not and that they saw as false premises which he took for granted.

It is true that the Machiavels of the Elizabethan stage are not at all
points similar to Machiavelli's exemplary power-seekers, or always representative of Machiavellian theory. Although the earlier Machiavels
are all in some way interested in winning and exercising power, they
are not, like Machiavelli's Cesare Borgia, mere embodiments of an obsessive desire for political supremacy. They are capable of jealousy and
personal hatred, of pique and a lust for vengeance. Sometimes their
desire for power can take forms other than the simple ambition to win
a crown, so that, like Iago, they may engage in practices from which
no obvious political advantage can accrue. They are, unlike Machiavelli's figures, capable of humor and of self-congratulatory or sadistic
delight.

Yet it is a profound mistake to imagine that the Machiavel is no more than his sensational trappings. The transformation of Machiavelli's characters, who are merely figures in a political diagram, to dramatic characters fleshed out by human traits and the stuff of legend may appear unjust to the author of *The Prince*. But the crucial differences between a Cesare and an Alphonsus are not ones of dramatic or psychological elaboration. The important differences are the product of a process of definition and assessment, of transporting Machiavelli's power-seeker from beyond the Alps to stand against the backdrop of a God-centered world. In that world the emphasis upon the monstrous and diabolic nature of the Machiavel's evil becomes preeminently an inevitable function of judgment. It may be unjust to present Alphonsus as Machiavelli's diligent disciple when he uses poison, but it is not unjust to present Alphonsus, the ambitious, ruthless politician, as damned if one happens to believe in hell.

Together, the Machiavels bear witness to the Elizabethan understanding of Machiavellian theory. Beyond that they constitute part of an attack upon attitudes which were, in the sixteenth century, gaining ground in many areas and receiving impetus from developments as diverse as those in experimental science and those in the capitalist organization of industry. The Elizabethan commentators who attack Machiavelli in polemical debate and the dramatists who assail him through the creation of a particular type of stage villain show an awareness of the imminence of the secular state and of the emergence of the "new men"[63] whose creed Dekker condemns:

> Nature sent man into the world, (alone,)
> Without all company, but to care for one
> (*If this be not a Good Play, the Devil is in It*)[64]

> (IV.i.80–81)

Egocentricity, of course, was not new any more than the unscrupulous tactics which Machiavelli advocates were new. The novelty lay in

63. J. F. Danby has likened Edmund to the "new men" of Elizabethan commerce in *Shakespeare's Doctrine of Nature* (London, 1949).
64. *The Dramatic Works of Thomas Dekker*, III.

the renunciation of the possibility of being anything other than self-absorbed and ruthless and in the energetic advocacy of amoral conduct as the only key to success. It is an awareness of the danger inherent in such advocacy which informs the atheistic and self-dedicated figure of the Machiavel, whose energies are turned to destruction, and whose reason, while seeming to rule each cunning act, remains always in the service of an appetite that devours all compassion and all love save love of self.

Alphonsus and Edmund are the progeny of an apprehension of danger. Later figures, like Webster's Francesco de Medicis, who survives unscathed at the end of *The White Devil,* seem to grow from a despairing conviction that this danger is not to be averted. Yet, today it is fashionable to regard such alarm and despondency as groundless. Machiavelli's abnegation of religion and morality and his advice on how to destroy and deceive no longer evoke much dismay. And any incipient uneasiness can be quelled by claiming that Machiavelli, viewed from a modern "historical perspective," did not mean what he said, or by appealing, yet again, to Gentillet and the *Contre-Machiavel* as pretexts for denying any genuine kinship between "the great politician" and his politic cousin of the Elizabethan stage.

Intrigue Tragedy in Renaissance England and Spain

WALTER COHEN

COMPARISONS BETWEEN English and Spanish drama of the late six-teenth and early seventeenth centuries characteristically evoke the magical names of Shakespeare and Lope de Vega. Each playwright combined extraordinary verbal and stylistic range with a violation of neoclassical norms; each displayed a profound interest in the fate of the nation, manifest not only in the symptomatic mingling of kings and commoners but also in the recurrent recourse to the genre of the national history play itself; each wrote for the commercial public the-aters that emerged in the late sixteenth century and soon focused the-atrical activity on the capital cities of London and Madrid; each thrived under the sway of a partially centralized monarchy. These par-allels might be considerably extended, and they might be, and indeed often have been, generalized to suggest the unique similarities be-tween the Spanish and English theaters in the age of the Renaissance. Yet the resemblances can be overstated, not only because the two countries differed from one another, but also because what they had in common they also shared as well with the rest of Europe.

Such is the case with intrigue tragedy, a genre that came into its own in England between 1609 and 1614 and in Spain between 1622 and

175

1643. In these transitional years, English drama and Spanish drama began to lose their collective uniqueness, a movement coincident with and in part conditioned by changes in the theatrical context and the social and political milieu. It is against this larger background that I hope to explain the origin, nature, and significance of intrigue tragedy.

I

In the early seventeenth century, both England and Spain entered a period of crisis that culminated, during the 1640s, in aristocratic rebellion against the crown, civil war, and, consequently, the virtual destruction of absolutism. These developments constituted less a radical break with the past than an elevation to preeminence of those subversive tendencies that were present all along, beneath the superficial calm of the absolutist state. Profound economic problems lay behind the political eruptions of mid-century. The complex chain of causality differed in the two nations, but in both it led to aristocratic revolt against the state—the defining feature of the general crisis of the seventeenth century.[1]

The early Stuart monarchs inherited from the Tudor line both irreducible feudal premises and profound conflict with a capitalist nation. The commercialization of agriculture, the growth of manufacturing, and the increase of domestic and foreign trade all accelerated after 1600, as England embarked on its great colonialist adventure. So, too, did the corresponding social changes—the rise of the gentry, the merchants, and the common lawyers, and the simultaneous decline of the crown, the peerage, and the clergy.[2] The Stuart monarchy, in the absence of an adequate fiscal base from which to remedy its traditional lack of an integrated nationwide administrative apparatus, a sizable armed forces, and a homogeneous institutionalized religion, generally had recourse to a combination of budget-cutting and extraparliamen-

---

1. Perry Anderson, *Lineages of the Absolutist State* (London, 1974), pp. 53–55.
2. Christopher Hill, *The Century of Revolution, 1603–1714* (New York, 1966), pp. 15–42; and Lawrence Stone, *The Crisis of the Aristocracy, 1558–1641* (Oxford, 1965), pp. 139, 162–164, 269, and *The Causes of the English Revolution, 1529–1642* (New York, 1972), pp. 68, 71–72.

tary fund raising. The latter method also served the more general conservative purpose of strengthening absolutism by stabilizing the social structure, building up the aristocracy, and aligning the crown with the peerage and urban patriciates, while excluding the gentry and newer mercantile interests, centralizing the economy, and restricting the growth of capitalism. [3]

But absolutist dynamism generated an increasingly vocal, organized, and united opposition. Conflict arose from the first year of James's reign and soon ranged over such issues as economic policy, international trade, finance, court extravagance and corruption, diplomacy, religious ritual, and the legal system. The period from 1610 to 1614 represents something of a turning point. The first of these years saw the failure of the Great Contract, a compromise that would have abolished the monarchy's feudal economic prerogatives in return for an annual grant from Parliament of a fixed sum. By then, whatever slim chance there remained for a national church had also disappeared. In both 1610 and 1614, the king dissolved Parliament without receiving the supplies he wanted. And in the later year, the monarchy's disastrous intervention in the economy via the Cokayne Project helped end a decade of prosperity and inaugurate a prolonged depression that lasted until mid-century. When Commons, by then the central institution in the struggle against the crown, met again in the 1620s, it tended to view specific local issues in broader, constitutional terms. Well before 1640, a crown that combined High Church Anglicanism or even Catholicism with prerogative courts, restrictive economic regulation, and arbitrary exercise of power found itself dangerously isolated against a coalition of Puritan ministers, common lawyers, free traders, and, most important of all, the gentry both in Commons and in the country. [4]

In Spain, too, the seventeenth-century monarchs inherited the basic problems from their predecessors, only to exacerbate them. After the turn of the century, imperial overextension in Europe forced the

---

3. Anderson, pp. 138, 140–141; Hill, pp. 29, 47, 52–53, 69–73; and Stone, *Causes,* pp. 62, 86, 117–135, and *Crisis,* pp. 65–128.

4. Stone, *Causes,* pp. 83, 92–95; Hill, pp. 10, 35–37, 49–51, 80, 321 (Appendix D); and Anderson, p. 138.

crown to attempt a belated centralist solution to its problems, with the not surprising result that the aristocracies of the periphery threw off the Castilian yoke. At the same time, the flow of American bullion into the royal treasury began to slow down: the volume during the 1620s was less than half what it had been in the 1590s. The chronic fiscal crisis of the state, unsolved by the widespread sale of offices, is evident in the backruptcies of 1607 and 1627, as well as in the alternating inflation and deflation of the currency—a recurrent pattern throughout the century.[5]

The political turning point for Habsburg absolutism probably came in the two decades following 1618 or 1621, with the revival of imperialism. As late as 1628 Spain could have extricated itself from its European involvements, serious military reverses began only after 1635, and genuine collapse was a phenomenon of the second half of the century. But the logic of the Spanish state was always to sacrifice domestic economics and politics—capitalism and absolutism—to imperial needs. The onset of the Thirty Years' War in 1618 therefore evoked a predictably aggressive response in Madrid. The opening of Philip IV's reign in 1621, coincident with the expiration of the Dutch peace treaty, then determined the course of the monarchy. Under the new *privado,* or favorite, the Count-Duke of Olivares, Philip IV's government, like that of Charles I in England, pursued a more active program than had its predecessor. On the one hand, Olivares's grandiose European strategy led inexorably to conflict with France's refurbished military apparatus and hence to the defeat of Spain.[6] On the other, the *privado* realized that the success of his foreign policy depended on the absolutist integration of the Habsburg empire, and especially of the two main peripheral regions of the peninsula, Portugal and the Crown of Aragon. But his attempt to implement this program failed disastrously in the 1640s, as a series of regional rebellions came close to dis-

    5. J. H. Elliott, *Imperial Spain, 1469–1716* (New York, 1964), pp. 175, 297–299, 320–321; Antonio Domínguez Ortiz, *The Golden Age of Spain, 1516–1659,* trans. James Casey (London, 1971), pp. 144–145; Jaime Vicens Vives, *An Economic History of Spain,* collab. Jorge Nadal Oller, trans. Frances M. López-Morillas (Princeton, N.J., 1969), pp. 446–450, 463; Fernand Braudel, *The Mediterranean and the Mediterranean World in the Age of Philip II,* trans. Siân Reynolds (London, 1973), II, 755–756; and Anderson, pp. 76–77.

    6. Elliott, pp. 330, 375; Domínguez Ortiz, pp. 90–97; and Anderson, pp. 78–79.

membering not only Spain's European empire, but its territorial homeland as well. [7]

Increasingly, as the century progressed, all open ideological roads led backward into the past. As in politics, 1620 represents a point of demarcation, after which reformism gave way to escapism. Feudal separatism on the periphery triggered off in the center not a capitalist revolution, as in England, but just more feudal separatism. For those unwilling to abandon monarchical consolidation for aristocratic particularism, the options were even narrower. In the words of Pierre Vilar, "around 1600, on its own soil in Castile, *feudalism entered upon its death struggle without there being anything to replace it.*" [8]

II

The consequences for the stage were relatively straightforward. During the first half of the seventeenth century, absolutist centralization, combined with deepening social conflict, gradually led to the decline of the public theater. Despite some striking chronological coincidences between England and Spain, the pace of theatrical events differed in the two countries. A tentative periodization might stress the following analogies: England 1597–1608 and Spain 1598–1621, England 1609–1614 and Spain 1622–1643, England 1615–1619 and Spain 1644–1650, and England 1620–1642 and Spain 1651–1700.

As noted earlier, our primary concern is with the second of these subperiods, 1609–1614 in England and 1622–1643 in Spain. These were the last ages of major public theater in each country. Although it is customary to date the decline of the London public stage from this era, by 1609 it was the private, children's companies that were in trouble. [9] The real threat to the public theaters came from within, specifi-

7. Elliott, pp. 339–373; Domínguez Ortiz, pp. 98–111; Vicens Vives, pp. 465–466; and Anderson, pp. 80–82.

8. Pierre Vilar, "The Age of Don Quixote," *New Left Review,* no. 68 (July-August 1971), pp. 59–71, esp. pp. 60, 67–68. The quotation appears on p. 66.

9. Leo G. Salingar, Gerald Harrison, and Bruce Cochrane, "Les Comédiens et leur public en Angleterre de 1520 à 1640," in *Dramaturgie et société: Rapports entre l'oeuvre théâtrale, son interprétation et son public aux xvie et xviie siècles,* ed. Jean Jacquot, with Elie Konigson and Marcel Oddon (Paris, 1968), II, 556, and E. K. Chambers, *The Elizabethan Stage* (Oxford, 1923), II, 7, 22–23, 54–55, 60–61, 67.

cally in the form of the decision of the King's Men in 1608 to spend their winter season at the private theater known as Blackfriars. The long-run theatrical significance of the children's companies, in other words, was to reveal to the professional actors a means of raising their profits by concentrating primarily on an upper-class clientele.

After Shakespeare's death, Blackfriars was the main theater of the King's Men, and by the 1630s they seem to have spent almost two-thirds of the year at it, with the summer reserved for the Globe. Average daily receipts at this time were more than twice as high at the indoor as at the outdoor playhouse, and the discrepancy in prestige was comparably great.[10] This may not have been the case between 1609 and 1614, however. Certainly, the Globe was still considered London's leading theater. And even if the King's Men and their theaters are excluded as atypical, the position of the public theaters during this period appears quite strong. Both the number of professional companies and the number of active public theaters in London increased.[11] There seems little doubt, moreover, that the total audience at the public playhouses continued to grow throughout the first fifteen years of the seventeenth century.[12] Finally, the public-theater plays themselves scarcely reveal signs of decline. Dekker was active until 1611 or 1612 at the Fortune and the Red Bull, and Heywood continued writing through 1612 for the latter theater. In the same year, the Red Bull was also the site for the initial performance of Webster's *White Devil*. Middleton's *Chaste Maid in Cheapside* probably opened at the Swan in 1613, and Jonson's *Bartholomew Fair* inaugurated the Hope in 1614. In a manner partly reminiscent of Shakespeare's final plays, these works do not entirely belong to the popular dramatic tradition. But they are strong evidence that through 1614 the public theaters continued to produce some of the most distinguished plays on the English stage. In short, the period from 1609 to 1614 was that unique transitional moment when the public and private theaters were of almost

10. Gerald Eades Bentley, *The Jacobean and Caroline Stage* (Oxford, 1941–1968), I, 3, 23–24; VI, 12–17, 192–194.

11. Chambers, II, 236–240, 242–243, 246–247, 404, 413–414, 464–469; and Bentley, I, 158–160; VI, 124, 130–131, 134, 200–201, 206–207.

12. Bentley, VI, 219; Chambers, II, 189, 371, 465; and Alfred Harbage, *Shakespeare's Audience* (New York, 1941), p. 33, and *Shakespeare and the Rival Traditions* (New York, 1952), pp. 24, 45, 124 n. 56.

equal importance, before the latter achieved the dominant position in English drama they have never subsequently relinquished.

The overall pattern was much the same in Madrid from 1622 to 1643. It has been necessary to counter the tendency in English scholarship to pronounce a premature death for the public theater. Owing to the recent, and justified, revaluation of Calderón and his school, it is equally essential to stress the early symptoms of decline in Spain not of the stage in general, but of the public stage in particular. The first two decades in the reign of Philip IV saw an extension and intensification of the centralizing trends of the early seventeenth century. The machine play, meanwhile, began to pose a still more serious challenge to the traditional *comedia*. The opening in 1633 of Buen Retiro, the new royal palace, provided another impetus to stage pageantry, and in subsequent years the physical reproduction of the *corral* at court inevitably entailed a loss of spontaneity and authenticity. What is often claimed of the *comedia* in the public theater was undoubtedly true of the court play, whether open to a popular audience or not: it was a conscious instrument of royal propaganda. [13]

Crown patronage of the drama also had the effect of turning players and playwrights from the *corrales* to the court. Beginning in the 1630s, spectacle plays in particular earned them far more than they could hope to receive in the public theater. Calderón began writing as much for the palace theaters as for the *corrales* from about 1635 on, and he was hardly alone in this respect. Finally, the tastes of a more aristocratic audience than attended the public theaters partly account for the elevation of style and tone in the *comedia* after 1620, even though most plays, whatever their premiere, ultimately found their way to the *corrrales*.

After this ambiguous era, in which the open-air, commercial stages of London and Madrid continued to thrive despite the encroachments of more aristocratic drama, there came a period of collapse from

13. Hugo Albert Rennert, *The Spanish Stage in the Time of Lope de Vega* (New York, 1909), pp. 233–237; Ruth Lee Kennedy, *Studies in Tirso, I: The Dramatist and His Competitors, 1620–26,* North Carolina Studies in the Romance Languages and Literatures, Essays, no. 3 (Chapel Hill, N.C., 1974), pp. 65, 194–195; N. D. Shergold, *A History of the Spanish Stage from Medieval Times until the End of the Seventeenth Century* (Oxford, 1967), pp. 275, 278, 284, 293, 295, 300, 329, 549; and Charles V. Aubrun, *La comedia espanōla (1600–1680),* trans. Julio Lago Alonso (Madrid, 1968), p. 81.

which the public theaters never fully recovered. We need only follow these developments in England where, between 1615 and 1619, there was a crisis of overexpansion, exacerbated by the overall slump of the British economy. [14] The consequences were predictable. The number of professional companies fell from five to four, the number of active public theaters from five to three. Most of the leading playwrights abandoned the stage, and it is in this period that one can first detect a decline in the quality of the drama performed in the public theater. [15] By the beginning of the recovery of 1620, the public theater was in clear decline and had lost the lead to the private playhouses and the court. This was particularly true after 1629, with the opening of still another private theater, the Salisbury Court, and the much increased involvement of Charles and Henrietta Maria's court with the stage. While the public theater seems to have undergone a weakening that was more qualitative than quantitative, the private stages catered to an increasingly aristocratic, even courtly, coterie. The plays designed for these theaters were far superior to those at the Caroline public playhouses and often scarcely inferior to the private-theater drama composed earlier in the century. [16] Finally, it must be noted that these changes occurred not, as most critics have argued, because the audience abandoned the actors, but because the actors abandoned their audience. But their decision was merely consistent with the growing divisions in all areas of English life.

III

Intrigue tragedy is one of the characteristic dramatic responses to this social and theatrical conjuncture. Its defining features are a loss of a national perspective combined with a sense of the problematic na-

14. Andrew Gurr, *The Shakespearean Stage, 1574–1642* (Cambridge, Eng., 1970), p. 142; Hill, pp. 317–318 (Appendix C); and Salingar, Harrison, and Cochrane, pp. 550, 555–558.

15. Bentley, I, 158–164, 177, 201; III, 243, IV, 556, 609–610, 754, 857; and VI, 208–209.

16. Salingar, Harrison, and Cochrane, p. 560; Bentley, I, 47 n. 3; and VI, 32–36, 146–149, 166, 194, 238–247.

ture of moral action. Compared to Shakespeare's tragedies of the previous decade, the British plays reveal a narrowing of range and a deeper pessimism. Though the constriction was not so extreme in Spain, the break was if anything sharper, involving as it did the elevation of tragedy to generic preeminence for the first time since the 1580s. In both countries, the new form dramatizes not so much the failure of the nobility to adapt to political change as the irrelevance of politics altogether. As history relinquishes its dynamic significance, the dominant temporal perception is of decay, entrapment, or stasis. In the absence of alternative modes of coherence, the characters and their deeds acquire a kind of opacity that defies clear judgment [17] and that consequently has resulted, as we shall see, in substantial interpretive controversy over a number of plays.

It may prove more illuminating than reductive to establish an internal subclassification of a major form, in this instance positing three main kinds of intrigue tragedy—heroic, satiric, and romantic—according to the relative influence of prior drama. Thus the satiric strain is stronger in England, the heroic and romantic in Spain. On the London stage, it is possible to discern a chronological progression from heroic to satiric to romantic that corresponds to the reduction of scope mentioned above and that usually constitutes a defensive reaction to rising social opposition and growing isolation. This is not the case in Spain, but within each type the tragedies of the 1630s generally present a darker vision than those of the previous decade. The peninsular theater dramatizes a class disoriented not, as in England, by a threat to its hegemony, but by a loss of self-confidence, by an awareness of an inability to function effectively or to prevent collapse.

Heroic intrigue, though sharing many of the assumptions of prior national drama, portrays the values that underlay traditional aristocratic power in such a way as to drain them of political significance. Chapman's *Bussy D'Ambois* (1604) and *The Revenge of Bussy D'Ambois* (1610), composed for the private theaters, focus from the start on the court, rather than the nation. As different as the two works are, the

17. For a roughly similar description, see Jean Alexander, "Parallel Tendencies in English and Spanish Tragedy in the Renaissance," in *Studies in Comparative Literature,* ed. Waldo F. McNeir (Baton Rouge, La., 1962), pp. 84–101.

protagonists, both of whom display only the most casual and intermittent interest in politics, are victims of state power at court: the heroic temper is ineffective and, more often than not, irrelevant. The earlier and more complex play dramatizes the gap between Bussy's assertion of virtue, freedom, and natural law, on the one hand, and the sordid, increasingly private conduct that defines him as a neofeudal aristocrat out of place at an absolutist court, on the other. *The Revenge of Bussy* culminates in the main character's suicide, which is justified as Stoic individualism and constitutes a conscious withdrawal that condemns the monarchy. In both plays, then, the protagonist's ideology serves a classic rationalizing function. Whatever Chapman's awareness of this process may have been, in both plays a reactionary perspective, typically indebted in part to bourgeois values, produces a simultaneously critical and positive vision that, while damning the present, looks to both past and future. [18]

Philip Massinger's *Unnatural Combat* (1624–1625) re-creates the contradictory outlook particularly of *Bussy D'Ambois,* perhaps because it is probably a late public-theater play composed by a primarily private-theater dramatist not entirely comfortable with the task. [19] Its hybrid nature is a consequence of this temporal, institutional, and authorial conjuncture. Frequently criticized for structural disunity, [20] the play begins as a heroic drama, but increasingly turns into an intrigue tragedy. Similarly, although Theocrine, the protagonist's daughter, is as innocent and virtuous as the young female victims of Shakespearean tragedy, she is raped and, it seems, "deform'd" before she dies. [21] The bluff Captain Belgarde also is at home in the public theater, where he was apparently meant to appeal to patriotic enthusiasm and lower-class pride. [22] Bursting in on an aristocratic state dinner, he rebukes the Governour for not granting him his back pay:

18. For similar descriptions, but symptomatically opposed evaluations of the plays, see Leonard Goldstein, "George Chapman and the Decadence in Early Seventeenth-Century Drama," *Science and Society,* XXVII (1963), 23–48, and J. W. Lever, *The Tragedy of State* (London, 1971), pp. 37–58.

19. For attribution to the Globe, see Bentley, IV, 824.

20. E.g., by T. S. Eliot, *Selected Essays* (New York, 1950), p. 187.

21. *The Unnatural Combat,* in *The Plays and Poems of Philip Massinger,* ed. Philip Edwards and Colin Gibson (Oxford, 1976), vol. II, V.ii.190. Subsequent references are noted in the text.

22. Edwards and Gibson, II, 183–184.

> and yet remember
> Tis we that bring you in the meanes of feasts,
> Banquets, and revels, which when you possesse,
> With barbarous ingratitude you deny us
> To be made sharers in the harvest, which
> Our sweat and industrie reap'd, and sow'd for you.
> The silks you weare, we with our bloud spin for you.
>
> (III. iii.84–90)

This extraordinary passage is the ideological key to the play. It is, of course, an expression of popular assertiveness and in particular an insistence on the reality and fundamental significance of surplus extraction, viewed from the perspective of the exploited class. The imagery suggests that Massinger has in mind the position of the peasant in the feudal mode of production. As the context reveals, however, Belgarde is really talking about the booty won for the ruling class by the common sailors. In the zero-sum game of feudal economics, the quickest path to accumulation is not technological innovation but outright expropriation. Although the metaphor of the harvest is in one sense mystified, in another it accurately reveals the dramatist's precapitalist premises.

For, despite the attack on the court here and elsewhere from a popular point of view, *The Unnatural Combat* is resolutely aristocratic in outlook. It largely lacks the critical perspective of Chapman's works or, for that matter, of almost all the other Jacobean intrigue tragedies, public or private, that we will be considering. It is not only a matter of the passing jibes at wealthy city merchants, remarks that seem to be unnaturalized immigrants from Massinger's satiric comedy. It is mainly the fate of Belgarde himself. The Governour and his aides generously respond to the pleas of the Captain, who learns as a result, and to his chagrin, what we have already been told in the previous scene: that to be a poor servant is preferable to being a wealthy lord. Belgarde likewise discovers that it is advisable to know one's place. At the end of the play, he is given an appropriate soldier's reward—not money, but responsibility for a fort.

Massinger's ambivalence is also evident in the portrayal of his protagonist. Essential knowledge about Malefort is withheld until almost the end of the play. We are always being surprised by the revelation of another of his former crimes, a method that is totally alien to earlier technique in the tragedies of the public theater. More damaging, in the first scene the Governour refers to him as "Our late great Admirall," praising "his faire actions, / Loyall, and true demeanour" (I.i.203, 208–209). Only much later, however, does the same man reveal his true, far more negative, opinion (III.ii.34–39). Thus we are never sure what purpose our ignorance, and that of the other characters, is meant to serve. Is Massinger incompetent, opportunistic, or original? Whatever the answer, the play suggests the dilemma of tragedy in the public theater after 1620.

The Spanish heroic tragedy, precisely because neither its competence nor its integrity is in doubt, raises theoretical issues of interpretation even more clearly. The anonymous *La Estrella de Sevilla* (1623–1624) and Calderón's *El médico de su honra* (1635) consider the painful consequences of applying the traditional and rigid standards of the feudal code of honor to complex social relations. In *La Estrella de Sevilla* the code is unquestioned. Indeed, unless the audience accepts it as a premise, the play becomes literally incomprehensible. The second, and related, assumption on which the plot is based is the inviolability of the monarch, rooted in the medieval notion of the king's two bodies. The tragedy is generated by the lecherous and murderous conduct of the young ruler, abetted by his amoral *privado*. If these two characters are modeled on Philip IV and Olivares, respectively, the uncommonly harsh portrayal of the king in particular acquires an additional critical edge.[23] In any case, the consistently honorable response of the Sevillians is exemplary in intent and effect. The erring monarch is educated against his will and virtually forced to take public responsibility for his crimes. Insofar as his moral conversion is permanent, the honor code, though here confined to a private affair, has demonstrated its ultimate efficacy in a manner that has potential political relevance. Just as important, however, the play reveals the costs of honor when the crown fails to act according to its principles: two people are murdered, and two others have their lives ruined.

Midway through Act II, Busto tells his sister Estrella of his fear that she had engaged in dishonorable conduct the night before when the king sneaked into their house to visit her. Here is a significant moment in the exchange:

23. For the identifications, see Kennedy, pp. 53–54, 340–341.

BUSTO
Esta noche fué epiciclo
del Sol; que en entrando en ella
se trocó de Estrella el signo.
ESTRELLA
Las llanezas del honor
no con astrólogo estilo
se han de decir: habla claro,
y deja en sus zonas cinco
el Sol. [24]

Estrella's stylistic critique seems to be to the point, but then we recall that the entire play is about "las llanezas del honor" and that both before and after this scene the noble characters, Estrella included, consistently employ precisely the rhetorical elaboration that she here reproves. Elevated conduct apparently requires elevated diction, from which there can be only brief escape. So it is with the conduct itself. At the end of the play, Estrella and Sancho's culminating feat of honor—mutual rejection, despite mutual love—elicits this sequence of comments from the *privado,* the *gracioso* (or clown), and the king:

DON ARIAS
!Brava constancia!
CLARINDO
Más me parece locura. [*Aparte*]
REY
Toda esta gente me espanta.
(III.xviii, p. 221)

Clarindo and the king speak for at least part of the audience, evoking the absurdity and the terror of the extravagant behavior that has dominated the action. But these qualifications do not suggest a positive alternative: in the end there is no ethically defensible choice but the code of honor, with its attendant tragic price.

El médico de su honra presents a more extreme version of the same dilemma. *La Estrella de Sevilla* concerns the violation of the code at the apex of the feudal pyramid—a serious matter. In Calderón's play,

24. *La Estrella de Sevilla,* in *Peribáñez y el Comendador de Ocaña; La Estrella de Sevilla,* by Lope de Vega (Madrid, 1938), II.ix, p. 165. The subsequent reference is noted in the text.

however, the problem is the code itself, which leads a husband to murder his innocent and beloved wife, only to be rewarded for his pains
by the king. For whom is the plot problematic, however, for Calderón
or for us? Nineteenth-century scholars, assuming that the playwright
approved of his protagonist's conduct, were understandably appalled.
Only in the last thirty years have critics consistently argued that Calderón was attacking the honor code, at least in this its most extreme
form.[25]

It seems fair to conclude that a critical polarization of this sort could
arise only because the bases of Calderón's own judgment are unclear.
In the greatest peasant plays—Lope de Vega's *Peribáñez* (1604–1614)
and *Fuenteovejuna* (probably 1612–1614), and Calderón's *El alcalde
de Zalamea* (1630–1644)—or in *La Estrella de Sevilla,* once the audience understands the principle of honor, it experiences no difficulty in
appropriately allocating its sympathies to the various characters.
Here, the same understanding produces no such result. Although Calderón's exact intention may thus be irretrievable, this very obscurity
can be explained. Wife-murder over a point of sexual honor was more
common in the Middle Ages than in the seventeenth century, when it
was almost always condemned and usually punished quite severely.[26]
Calderón's return to the sources of Spanish national character is accompanied by a fourteenth-century setting, in the reign of Pedro I of
Castile, known to history as both *el Cruel* and *el Justiciero.* It is this
duality that is built into the code of honor in *El médico de su honra.*
But cruelty is not the mere excess of justice: it is equally inherent in the
code. The play reveals that Spain cannot have it both ways. *El médico
de su honra* is a critique from within, launched by a great dramatist
against the only ideology available. Calderón's play simultaneously affirms and decries the essence of aristocratic culture. It is at once a
moving and horrific sign of the impasse of Spanish society.

In both countries, then, the ideological ambivalence that accompanies the potent critique of the present is traceable to the dramatists' reactionary perspectives. By and large, this is also the case in those in-

25. A relatively moderate statement of the currently dominant position is C. A. Jones,
Introd. to his edition of *El médico de su honra* (Oxford, 1961), pp. ix–xxv.

26. Melveena McKendrick, *Woman and Society in the Spanish Drama of the Golden
Age: A Study of the "mujer varonil"* (London, 1974), pp. 35–39.

trigue tragedies indebted to satire, with its ironic view of lust, greed, and social conflict. The seemingly irresolvable critical disputes that many such plays have inspired may be understood, though of course not adjudicated, from this point of view. The tragedies of Marston, Tourneur, Webster, and Middleton are satiric intrigues. Marston, Middleton, and to a lesser extent Webster composed satiric comedies, and Middleton's *Women Beware Women* (1621) almost seems like his *Chaste Maid in Cheapside* (1613) rewritten with a generic surprise at the end. [27] That this wholesale appropriation of social satire, to the exclusion of politics, risked undermining the recipient form altogether is suggested by Middleton's recourse to an unsatisfying melodramatic finale for the later play, in order to give the illusion of tragic doom to decidedly untragic characters and events. Something of the same might also be said, though with reservations, of the leading tragedies by all four dramatists. The similarities should not be overstated, however. The extremism of Middleton may be a sign of both his atypicality and the special properties of satiric intrigue tragedy. The detached, morally rigorous, and consistent perspective of *Women Beware Women* and *The Changeling* (1622, with the comic subplot by William Rowley) probably derives from Middleton's adherence to the parliamentary Puritan cause, a decidedly progressive, rather than reactionary, position.[28] Webster, moreover, does not seem unquestionably backward-looking either. Precisely because of the predominant negativity produced by satire, playwrights of opposing outlooks could employ the same form—just as opposition to Stuart policy at least temporarily united groups and classes that had little else in common. This generic linkage had an institutional basis as well. Like satiric comedy, satiric intrigue tragedy, though owing much to the private theater, was usually most successful when it had some contact with the public stage. Middleton again constitutes the major exception, but the form generally seems to have reached its apogee in the transitional era from 1609 or a little earlier to 1614.

27. T. B. Tomlinson, *A Study of Elizabethan and Jacobean Tragedy* (Cambridge, Eng., 1964), p. 158.

28. The ending of *Women Beware Women*: Robert Ornstein, *The Moral Vision of Jacobean Tragedy* (Madison, Wis., 1960), p. 179; Middleton and the Puritans: Margot Heinemann, *Puritanism and Theatre: Thomas Middleton and Opposition Drama under the Early Stuarts* (Cambridge, Eng., 1980), esp. p. 173.

In Spanish intrigue tragedy, the nearest approach to a satiric vision occurs in Tirso's ultimately unclassifiable *El burlador de Sevilla* (probably 1616–1620) and Lope's *El castigo sin venganza* (1631). The final title of Tirso's play conceals a double meaning: "de Sevilla" can refer to Don Juan's hometown, but it can also designate the victim of his "burlas."[29] In the latter sense, it points to a function of the protagonist that links him to important characters in the English tragedies. Like Webster's malcontents, for example, "el burlador" combines witty insouciance with an at times murderous immorality in such a way as to reveal the sordid reality lurking just beneath the surface of society. More generally, Tirso treats Don Juan's activities, as well as the sexual immorality and social climbing of many of the other characters, with an ironic, but scarcely tragic, detachment that may recall Middleton's technique in *Women Beware Women*.[30] Although in his concluding damnation Don Juan becomes something of a lightning rod for the sins of society, the play does not leave us with a sense that moral order has been fully restored, despite the best efforts of a good king.[31]

El castigo sin venganza is even darker in tone. Like the English tragedies, it ultimately draws on Italian sources and re-creates an Italian setting centered on the sexual corruption of the court.[32] Lope condemns his unpleasant protagonists to a claustrophobic world of passion from which they can find no escape. The sense of entrapment is in turn compounded by a pattern of self-deception. But though deeply ironic, the play is not satiric. The characters are developed with unusual psychological depth, and hence with some sympathy, and the whole is pervaded by a tragic sense. Guilty at once of incest and adultery, the doomed young lovers are aware of their wrongdoing and its inevitable consequence, but can do nothing about it.

29. Henry W. Sullivan, *Tirso de Molina and the Drama of the Counter Reformation* (Amsterdam, 1976), pp. 152–153.

30. Raymond R. MacCurdy, Introd. to *"El burlador de Sevilla y convidado de piedra" and "La prudencia en la mujer,"* by Tirso de Molina (New York, 1965), p. 19. The reference to *El burlador de Sevilla* below is to this edition and is noted in the text.

31. Edward M. Wilson and Duncan Moir, *The Golden Age: Drama 1492–1700,* vol. III of *A Literary History of Spain,* gen. ed. R. O. Jones (London, 1971), p. 90.

32. Amado Alonso, "Lope de Vega y sus fuentes," in *El teatro de Lope de Vega: Artículos y estudios,* ed. José Francisco Gatti (Buenos Aires, 1962), pp. 200–212, discusses Lope's reworking of his sources here.

In both countries, the satiric tragedies were also influenced by earlier efforts in the Italian Senecan revenge tradition. For the English playwrights, the seminal works were Kyd's *Spanish Tragedy* (1587) and, later on, Shakespeare's *Hamlet* (1601). The fullest anticipation of the characteristic Jacobean combination of satire and revenge, however, is probably to be found in *The Jew of Malta* (1589).[33] But sixteenth-century Elizabethan revenge tragedy, despite its significant popular dimension, did not completely succeed in striking roots in British soil. The final nationalization of Seneca was carried out partly by Shakespeare, of course, but also by Marston and the author of *The Revenger's Tragedy,* who accomplished this end, paradoxically enough, by setting their tales in Italy.[34] The increasing replacement of a personal by a social perspective in seventeenth-century tragedy did not usually allow for detailed scrutiny of the psychology and morality of the avenger in the manner of Kyd and Shakespeare. But revenge motifs and at times even characteristic revenge structures continued to appear, in the drama of Chapman, Webster, Middleton, and others.

Particularly in the satiric intrigues, the revenge tradition gave a specificity to social criticism by centering it on the well-established Renaissance opposition of court and country. A Senecan concern with the tyranny of the former soon gave way to a primarily social, rather than political, attack. What is repeatedly portrayed is the treacherous surrender of the feudal aristocracy, supposed guardian of medieval morality, to the forces of capitalism. As in Shakespeare's late tragedies, the absolutist state is betrayed from within—an important, if not wholly accurate, perception. But it is somewhat misleading to speak of the state at all in these plays. As the social status of the protagonists becomes increasingly incidental to their deeds, the scene shifts at least in part to the country or the city, where gentry and merchants, respectively, take the leading roles: *Women Beware Women* and Tourneur's *Atheist's Tragedy* (1609) exemplify the trend. But this democratization reflects not an ideological allegiance to capitalism, but a grim rec-

33. The most extended treatment of the subject remains Fredson Bowers, *Elizabethan Revenge Tragedy 1587–1642,* rev. ed. (Gloucester, Mass., 1959).

34. G. K. Hunter, "English Folly and Italian Vice: The Moral Landscape of John Marston," in *Jacobean Theatre,* ed. John Russell Brown and Bernard Harris, Stratford-upon-Avon Studies, no. 1 (London, 1960), pp. 91–106.

ognition of its presence. The metaphysical optimism of Tourneur's play is thus balanced by a social pessimism. Moreover, the change in social setting entails a diminution of scope: the lives of members of the capitalist classes were not yet able to typify the fate of the nation.

Usually, however, the country retains its standard connotation as the innocent antithesis of the court. *Bussy D'Ambois* opens with its main character in a green world and proceeds to assess the impact of the court on a natural man. *The Revenge of Bussy* and Marston's *Antonio's Revenge* (1600) conclude with Stoical retreats from court to monastery, the efficacy of which, however, is called into question, at least in Marston's play. In Webster's *Duchess of Malfi* (1614), even a flight from court to country cannot protect private, family experience, based on interclass marriage (III.v.18–21). *The Revenger's Tragedy* (1606), by Tourneur or Middleton, is perhaps the most interesting case. Vendice is a country gentleman come to cleanse a court whose corruption he instead succumbs to. Speaking for the gentry, he complains of the court's impoverishment of the land. His morally dubious, but ultimately successful, testing of his family thus generates a fundamental contrast between the lust and greed of the court and the chastity and poverty of the country. Given the class background of Vendice and his family, and the dynamic, if unequal, relationship established between the two social poles of the action, the reactionary ideological assumptions of *The Revenger's Tragedy*, ironically, contribute to the historically progressive formation of precisely the gentry-dominated country party that was later to overthrow the monarchy.

In Spain, of course, the revenge tradition was far weaker. But *El burlador de Sevilla* is partly indebted to Juan de la Cueva's Senecan tragicomedy, *El infamador* (1581),[35] and in the concluding act the references to "venganza" become increasingly insistent and ominous (e.g., III.2260–2267). For this very reason, the play reveals a symptomatic incongruity between human and divine justice. The benevolent monarch remains consistently in the dark about Don Juan's true conduct, busying himself with futile efforts to marry the powerful aristocrat off and thus, he hopes, maintain social stability. Only after the actual execution of divine vengeance does he call for the protagonist's death.

---

35. MacCurdy, pp. 14–15.

All of this is orthodox enough theologically, but it inevitably raises doubts about even the best of human institutions. Conversely, the difficulty most critics have had in finding in Don Juan's deeds sufficient cause for his damnation raises questions about divine justice. In general, the vitality of "el burlador" and the at once alarmingly and attractively anarchical challenge he represents to human and metaphysical order perhaps inadvertently transform a superficially didactic work into a tragedy that is both personal and social, one that moves, moreover, on two related but different planes.[36]

The title of *El castigo sin venganza* reveals a similar concern, although in this instance the morality of revenge is given a deeply ironic treatment. The Duke sees his concluding murder of his wife and son as "el castigo sin venganza." But his own considerable responsibility for their sins, his near-lifelong commission of the very same ones, and the covert and underhanded method by which he executes his sentence produce the opposite result, vengeance without punishment or, it may be added, justice. To preserve social appearances, to give the illusion of "el castigo sin venganza," the Duke's son "is punished for a crime he did not commit in revenge for a crime which he did." From the perspective of divine justice, however, the resolution of the plot does produce "el castigo sin venganza," not only for the Duke's wife and son, but also for the Duke himself, who must live on with the knowledge of having been responsible for the deaths of the two people about whom he most cared and thus of having deprived himself in addition of a much-desired heir to the throne.[37] In the intractable dilemma of the belatedly reformed Duke, in the slippery, often antithetical relationship between human and divine justice, in the discrepancy between intention and consequence, Lope's drama offers a critique of the state that seems to reflect as well the country's growing inability to control its own destiny.

Both Spanish plays, then, investigate the ironic interplay of revenge and justice far more deeply than do the comparable English tragedies, where the very notion of justice dispensed at court is all but unimaginable. Complementarily, the contrast between country and court does

---

36. *Ibid.,* pp. 19–21

37. R. D. F. Pring-Mill, Introd. to *Lope de Vega (Five Plays),* trans. Jill Booty (New York, 1961), pp. xxxi–xxxv. The quoted passage appears on p. xxxiii.

not figure prominently in *El burlador de Sevilla* and *El castigo sin venganza*. In a way, Tirso's play effaces the distinction. Don Juan sexually deceives four women—first an aristocrat, then a peasant, then another aristocrat, and finally another peasant. The pattern seems more iterative than developmental. Although the two classes are not conflated, Tirso's main purpose is to emphasize the range both of Don Juan's subversiveness and of society's failings. To do so, however, it was necessary to take seriously not just the honor of the nobility, but that of the peasantry as well. The flawed conduct of the latter class could not acquire its full force unless it was seen as a deviation from that class's own ideals. Tirso's prior experience with peasant drama probably served him well. Finally, the concentration on court intrigue in *El castigo sin venganza* precludes extended concern with the country, but here, too, the antithesis is denied. The illicit passion between Federico and Casandra has its origins not in the back rooms of the palace, but in a pastoral *locus amoenus*. By 1631, it would seem both pastoral and peasantry had lost their redemptive powers, at least for Tirso and Lope.

The distance between these two plays and the comparable English works may be suggested by saying that where the Spanish characters are defective, the British ones are repellent. This is so because the satiric intrigue tragedy had a different historical function in each country. In England, its effect was mainly destructive; despite an anticapitalist outlook that even today retains a contemporary appeal, it fundamentally served to remove the remaining ideological justifications of absolutism, to clear away the detritus, as it were, of a disintegrating social system, so that another might be constructed in its place. The mission of the Spanish tragedies was in a sense more modest. With fundamental change out of the question, they could only draw attention to the crisis confronted by their nation and clarify its nature. Theirs is a more normal world, governed more firmly by traditional morality, than the one portrayed in the English plays. Hence, on the one hand, Tirso and Lope do not approach the cynicism or nihilism of the Jacobean satiric tragedians but, on the other, they are also largely denied the moments of not-quite-conscious re-creation that we have observed in Chapman and *The Revenger's Tragedy*, and that is also present in the latter part of *The Duchess of Malfi*.

Even sharper contrasts emerge from a review of romantic intrigue tragedy. In a sense, however, the comparison is inappropriate. Although the relevant plays in both countries fall mainly in the 1620s and 1630s, it will be recalled that this was in effect an earlier historical and theatrical period in Spain than in England. There is accordingly a qualitative difference between the pathetic tragedies composed for the private stage in London and the love tragedies designed for the *corrales* of Madrid.

Pathetic tragedy is an extreme version of English intrigue tragedy, recapitulating and intensifying selected features of the form. In its pure state, pathetic tragedy has no other purpose than to elicit a pitying response from its audience. Although incompatible with ideas and out of touch with serious moral and political issues, it skillfully plays with them so that they will heighten the emotional effect without acquiring any significance in the process. Beaumont and Fletcher's *Maid's Tragedy* (1610) is both the founder and most perfect representative of the form. [38] The heyday of pathetic tragedy did not come until the Caroline era, however: Ford's *Broken Heart* (1629) and Shirley's *Traitor* (1631) are leading examples. The dominant moods of such plays include aristocratic quiescence, withdrawal, indifference to life, and attraction to death.

Slightly to one side stand two other works by Ford, *'Tis Pity She's a Whore* (1632) and *Perkin Warbeck* (1633). The former, like *Women Beware Women,* sets its scene among the merchant patriciate, a class whose sordid social life provides a contrast and impediment to the protagonists' idealistic, incestuous, and doomed love. The latter is still more unusual. An English history play, it conscientiously investigates national issues, particularly through the character of Henry VII. But the protagonist of the piece is not Henry but the titular figure, a fraudulent pretender whose persistent self-delusion finally becomes a tribute to his nobility. Politically defined and damned by his lower-class following, and easily defeated by Henry, he nonetheless triumphs in the private sphere, where the pattern of devotion he engenders, cen-

---

38. A corroborating description may be found in John F. Danby, *Poets on Fortune's Hill: Studies in Sidney, Shakespeare, Beaumont and Fletcher* (1952; rpt. Port Washington, N.Y., 1966), pp. 152–183.

tered on his loyal wife, evokes Ford's characteristic heroic pity. Shakespearean tragedy, despite its repeated depiction of aristocratic failure, almost always leaves open a path to the future, if not for the protagonist then at least for his society. This is hardly so in intrigue tragedy, where the conclusion of the play signifies the end of history, the closing off of opportunities. But as *Perkin Warbeck* shows, in pathetic tragedy not merely the future has been lost: for the protagonist, for several of the supporting characters, and at least in part for the author himself, the past has disappeared as well.

Pathetic tragedy is also the form in which women came into their own. The feminization of tragedy is discernible in Shakespeare's final efforts with the genre, is given special impetus by *The Maid's Tragedy*, and is unmistakable in Webster and Middleton. There is thus no absolute distinction to be made in this respect among the various kinds of intrigue tragedy or even of tragedy in general. Behind the growing prominence of women lay a broader emerging concern with the sex's social position. To this extent, intrigue tragedy helped extend the range of the genre, and its frequent depiction of the oppression of women may be considered a humane and progressive perception. At the same time, such an orientation was inseparable from the abandonment of politics and a consequent reduction of scope. But women became uniquely functional even in intrigue tragedy only with the full exploitation of the helpless victimization and sentimental appeal that are characteristic of pathetic tragedy.

With these contradictory implications in mind, it may be possible to evaluate the ongoing concern with the decadence of Jacobean and Caroline tragedy. The charge is often extended back to Marston and sweepingly made to include virtually all of his successors. Here, we may limit the investigation to the more restricted compass where the case is strongest, to the plays of the pathetic tragedians. Although Caroline tragedy at times displays a hostility to both the court and the bourgeoisie, it lacks the aggressive destructiveness that is one of the most distinctive and distinguished qualities of the generally earlier satiric intrigue tragedies. It is aimed not at another class, but at its own, the nobility. Pathetic tragedy enables us to imagine how a class feels when it senses that it no longer has a social function, that history has passed it by. The substitution of nobility of sentiment for a larger coherence of meaning that is no longer available is not an expression of universal truth, but an act of accommodation by a class that has lost its hegemony. Ironically, however, in this fashion pathetic tragedy unwittingly serves the progressive purpose of reconciling one sector of the aristocracy to its own supersession. The special prominence it accords to women likewise undermines the ostensible intention of the form. Even female characters of the highest social birth rarely have available to them the ordinary power and freedom of their class: their sex systematically reduces their status. The women of pathetic tragedy thus mark an initial break with a class-based conception of tragedy. In these ways, then, the form contradictorily retains not just a historical and theoretical interest, but a human plausibility and social significance as well.

Spanish love tragedies such as Lope's *El caballero de Olmedo* (1620?) and Luis Vélez de Guevara's *Reinar después de morir* (by 1644) share with pathetic tragedy, and especially with Ford's plays, a sense of fated defeat, of doom combined with a preoccupation with private life scarcely obscured by a superficial interest in affairs of state. But these two works, and especially Lope's, are really much closer in spirit to *Romeo and Juliet* (1595) and Lope's own *El marqués de Mantua* (1596), and thus to a tradition of tragedy with deep affinities to romantic comedy: *El caballero de Olmedo* has even been faulted for the excessively comic tone of its first two acts.[39] To the extent that either drama is not understood in these terms, both its emotional force and its ideological significance are lost. The relatively recent tendency to view Lope's play as a tragedy of moral failing and deserved retribution seems to have given way to a far more defensible and traditional insistence on the innocence of the protagonist in a just and divinely ordered, but nonetheless inscrutable, universe.[40] Inés de Castro, the heroine of *Reinar después de morir,* has remained free of any comparable suspicions of misconduct, but the play may seem at least as concerned to attack *Realpolitik* as it is to celebrate love. In fact, the political issue is suppressed. Only the king even feels a conflict between

39. See Wilson and Moir, p. 67, who reject the charge.
40. The claim that the hero is justly punished is made by A. A. Parker, "The Approach to the Spanish Drama of the Golden Age," *TDR*, IV (1959), 46–48. The counterposition is argued by Willard F. King, Introd. to her edition and translation of *The Knight of Olmedo (El caballero de Olmedo),* by Lope de Vega (Lincoln, Neb., 1972), pp. xi–xxvii.

private morality and reasons of state. His son and heir, who is also Inés's lover, must not, or else the purity of his love would be compromised. In general, moreover, national problems cannot be too strongly developed; otherwise, the audience would share the king's dilemma. Vélez makes certain that we respond exclusively to the lovers' predicament, however.

What assumptions underlie the dramatization of a tragic destiny? Like much other Renaissance drama, both plays appropriate bourgeois values to serve aristocratic ends. Here, the crucial borrowing is marriage for love, with all its attendant idealism. In the name of this principle, *Reinar después de morir* rejects the class-conscious condescension of Inés's more nobly born rival. Vélez would appear to be on more traditional aristocratic terrain in his attack on the king and his *privados,* and in his antithetical praise of the country. Yet the pattern is complicated by linking the country to domesticity and family life. Finally, as in *El caballero de Olmedo,* the central love relationship is expressed in courtly, Petrarchan terms.

The feudal dimension of Lope's play is much less ambiguous and the tragic irony of its crisis correspondingly more social in resonance. The chivalric valor that brings Don Alonso fame also leads him to his death. Although he is frightened by a supernatural warning in the form of a popular refrain, his feudal code forces him to press on. A matchless swordsman like Bussy D'Ambois, he, too, is murdered by gunshot, military symbol of the supersession of medieval aristocratic warfare.[41] The repetition of the portentous refrain earlier in the play develops a feudal perspective in another way as well, by producing a double vision. On the one hand, most of the time the audience is emotionally involved in the sequence of events unfolding before it in the present; on the other, the refrain invites it to distance itself from the action, to view with at least historical detachment a tragedy set in the romantic, glamorous, but irrecoverably past early fifteenth century. In this way, *El caballero de Olmedo* simultaneously celebrates feudalism and intuits its inevitable demise, conceiving of the latter as part of a divine plan whose meaning remains hidden from seventeenth-century Spaniards. In common with *Reinar después de morir,* its dominant mood is one of loss, although the later tragedy, its title notwithstanding, does not

41. Stone, *Crisis,* p. 243.

offer even enigmatic metaphysical consolation. Finally, despite the far more peripheral role of politics in Lope's play than in Vélez's, *El caballero de Olmedo* reveals a surer grasp of historical process, and one, it may be added, that is not really equaled in pathetic tragedy, even by *Perkin Warbeck.*

IV

Golden Age drama is often denied the status of tragedy, although recent decades have seen something of a reversal of this attitude.[42] Certainly there was less tragedy than in England, largely, it would seem, because the relative absence of a conflict between modes of production reduced the ideological space for the genre. On the other hand, if Shakespeare is excluded from consideration, it is possible to argue seriously that during the seventeenth century the *corrales* of Madrid surpassed the London theaters, public and private, not only in serious drama in general—which could include heroic, peasant, and religious plays—but in the narrower field of tragedy as well.

The comparison between England and Spain may also serve a simultaneously broader and narrower purpose. Throughout Western Europe during the sixteenth and seventeenth centuries, intrigue tragedy's characteristic combination of depoliticization and moral uncertainty represented a response to a crisis in the state. The predominance of a relatively unsuccessful form of intrigue tragedy in most of sixteenth-century Italy ultimately testifies to the absence of an indigenous absolutism, to the lack of a political organization that could be the object of serious dramatic reflection.[43] In France, the movement from Cor-

42. Defenses of Spanish tragedy include Edwin S. Morby, "Some Observations on 'Tragedia' and 'Tragicomedia' in Lope," *Hispanic Review,* XI (1943), 185–209; Parker, "Towards a Definition of Calderonian Tragedy," *Bulletin of Hispanic Studies,* xxxix (1962), 227–237; and A. Irvine Watson, "*El pintor de su deshonra* and the Neo-Aristotelian Theory of Tragedy," in *Critical Essays on the Theatre of Calderón,* ed. Bruce W. Wardropper (New York, 1965), pp. 203–223.

43. Hunter, "Italian Tragicomedy on the English Stage," *RenD,* N. S. VI (1973), 130–131, suggests that Italilan tragedy failed to interest the Elizabethans because its protagonists, however exalted, are involved with personal passions that lack political and social resonance.

neille's heroic drama to Racine's tragedies of private experience, pessimism, and moral relativism can be connected to the changing relations
between nobility and monarchy, and in particular to the latter's defini-
tive suppression of the Fronde and with it of centuries of aristocratic
political independence.[44] Similarly, the late-seventeenth-century pathetic tragedies of Dryden, Lee, Otway, and their successors, following hard upon more than a decade of heroic drama, constitute a belated, disillusioned realization that the Restoration of the monarchy in
1660, with the attendant return of the Cavaliers, did not involve a true
restoration of an absolutist state or a neofeudal nobility.[45] In all three
instances, the audience for intrigue tragedy was dominated culturally,
if not always numerically, by the crown and aristocracy. Unlike the
tragedies of Shakespeare or the peasant plays of Lope de Vega, then,
English and Spanish intrigue tragedy of the early seventeenth century
belonged to a broadly international generic movement. The triumph
of the form in London and Madrid accordingly signaled the end of the
unique theatrical development that served as our point of departure.

44. See especially Lucien Goldmann, *The Hidden God: A Study of Tragic Vision in
the "Pensées" of Pascal and the Tragedies of Racine,* trans. Philip Thody (London;
1964), pp. 103–141.

45. Laura Brown, *English Dramatic Form, 1660–1760: An Essay in Generic History*
(New Haven, Conn., 1981), chap. 3.

Notes on Contributors

LOIS E. BUELER, an Associate Professor of English at California State University, Chico, is at work on a book-length study of the tested-woman plot in English Renaissance drama. Recent articles include "The Rhetoric of Change in *The Changeling*," *ELR*, 14, no. 1 (Spring 1984), 95–113, and "The Failure of Sophistry in Donne's Elegy VII," to be published in the Winter 1985 issue of *Studies in English Literature*.

WALTER COHEN is Assistant Professor of Comparative Literature at Cornell University. He has published articles primarily on English and Spanish Renaissance drama and has recently completed a book entitled *Drama of a Nation: Public Theater in Renaissance England and Spain* (Ithaca, N.Y., 1985).

RONALD HUEBERT, who teaches Renaissance and modern drama at Dalhousie University, is the author of *John Ford: Baroque English Dramatist* (1977) and the editor of Shirley's *The Lady of Pleasure*, forthcoming in the Revels series. Readers who dislike his article on Johnson will probably despise "Tobacco and Boys and Marlowe," in *The Sewanee Review*, XCII (1984).

THOMAS HYDE is Associate Professor of English at Yale and has published a paper on Spenser in *English Literary Renaissance*. His book on the poetic theology of love will be published this year by the University of Delaware Press. He is working on a book about Renaissance mythography.

MARY BETH ROSE is Director of the Center for Renaissance Studies at the Newberry Library. She is currently completing a study of love and sexuality in Renaissance and Restoration drama and is working on English women writers of the sixteenth and seventeenth centuries.

MARGARET SCOTT is a Lecturer in English at the University of Tasmania. She is working on a book on Machiavellian villains.

WILLIAM W. E. SLIGHTS is Professor of English at the University of Saskatchewan. His work on genre theory has appeared in a series of articles on lyric poetry, romantic novels, Shakespearean pastoral, revenge tragedy, the prose paradox, the literary letter, satiric comedy, and *genera mixta*. He is now working on a book on Ben Jonson's experiments with genre.